TRANSACTIONS OF THE PARISIAN SANHEDRIM,

Or
Acts of the Assembly
of
Israelitish Deputies
of
France and Italy

BROWN CLASSICS IN JUDAICA

Editorial Board

Jacob Neusner
Chairman

TRANSACTIONS

OF THE

PARISIAN SANHEDRIM,

OR

ACTS OF THE ASSEMBLY

OF

𝕴𝖘𝖗𝖆𝖊𝖑𝖎𝖙𝖎𝖘𝖍 𝕯𝖊𝖕𝖚𝖙𝖎𝖊𝖘 𝖔𝖋 𝕱𝖗𝖆𝖓𝖈𝖊 𝖆𝖓𝖉 𝕴𝖙𝖆𝖑𝖞,

CONVOKED AT PARIS BY AN IMPERIAL AND ROYAL DECREE,
DATED MAY 30, 1806.

TRANSLATED FROM THE ORIGINAL PUBLISHED BY
M. DIOGENE TAMA,
WITH A PREFACE AND ILLUSTRATIVE NOTES
BY F. D. KIRWAN, Esq.

UNIVERSITY
PRESS OF
AMERICA

LANHAM • NEW YORK • LONDON

Series Introduction, Introduction

Copyright © 1985 by

University Press of America,® Inc.

4720 Boston Way
Lanham, MD 20706

3 Henrietta Way
London WC2E 8LU England

All rights reserved

Printed in the United States of America

Originally published by Charles Taylor,
London, England, in 1807.

Library of Congress Cataloging in Publication Data

Assemblée des Israélites de France et du royaume
    d'Italie (1806-1807 : Paris, France)
    Transactions of the Parisian Sanhedrim, or, Acts of
the Assembly of Israelitish Deputies of France and
Italy, convoked at Paris by an Imperial and Royal
Decree, dated May 30, 1806.

    (Brown classics in Judaica)
    Translation of: Collection des actes de l'Assemblée
des Israélites de France et du royaume d'Italie.
    Reprint. Originally published: London : C. Taylor,
1807. With new introd.
    Bibliography: p.
    Includes index.
    1. Jews—France. 2. Jews —Italy. 3. Judaism and
state. I. Sanhédrin (1807 : Paris, France) II. Title.
III. Title: Acts of the Assembly of Israelitish
Deputies of France and Italy. IV. Series.
DS135.F82A85   1985   944'.004924   85-15824
ISBN 0-8191-4488-6 (pbk. : alk. paper)

BROWN CLASSICS IN JUDAICA

Classics of scholarly exposition of important problems and themes in Judaism gain renewed life in the series at hand. The criterion for selection for reprint explains the purpose of the editors. We seek to place into the hands of a new generation the enduring intellectual achievements of an earlier time in our own century and in the one before. The issues of Judaism and the life of the Jewish people, analyzed in a rigorous and responsible way, retain perennial relevance. For what being a Jew meant in times past derived from the on-going imperatives of Judaism, on the one side, and the condition of eternal Israel, the Jewish people, on the other. The editors therefore maintain that scholars speaking to a broad audience in one age continue to address the lasting realities of ages to come. For scholars to begin with ask not what is current but what is true, not what presses today but what is urgent everyday, for all times.

The records of the past teach diverse lessons. The one we wish to impart is how first-rate minds confront the record of the past as an on-going encounter with an enduring condition and an on-going human reality. So we promise that the books of this series exemplified in this one, will speak to today's readers as much as it did to the ones who first received the works we now reprint. The series highlights modes of address we find exemplary. When scholars speak,

v

they demand a hearing because they ask the tough questions and trouble to discover rigorous answers to them. Scholars are not always right. Time alone will sort things out. But scholars always take responsibility for knowing the requirements of truth and attempting in good faith to meet them. They do not make things up as they go along and declare new truth morning by morning.

This series proposes to renew the life of classics of Judaic learning because the editors deem an important task the ongoing renewal of sustained learning in the realm of Judaic discourse. So this book is in this series because it shows, in one way or in another, how, when it comes to the study of Judaism and of the life of the Jewish people, we think people should carry on the labor of learning.

Jacob Neusner

In behalf of the board of editors

INTRODUCTION TO THE BROWN CLASSICS IN JUDAICA SERIES EDITION

The Transactions of the Paris Sanhedrin is one of the preeminent historical sources for understanding West European Jewry's central experience in the modern era, its struggle for civic and political emancipation. The work contains the proceedings of assemblies Napoleon convened in Paris in 1806-07: the questions Napoleon's commissioners presented to the Assembly of Notables; the Assembly's deliberations over those questions; the answers the Assembly formulated; and the further assembly, the Sanhedrin, called to give the answers religious sanction. The work also contains the legislation which resulted from the assemblies, as well as extensive selections from the debate waged over emancipation in the fifteen years preceeding the assemblies.

Because the Sanhedrin both determined the nature of emancipation in France and influenced its course throughout Western Europe, the *Transactions of the Paris Sanhedrin* offers the reader a firsthand account of one of Jewish emancipation's most formative moments.

The *Transactions of the Paris Sanhedrin* reveals the key supposition of the emancipation process: rights were predicated upon regeneration. Napoleon convened the Assembly of Jewish Notables in 1806 to redress the balance between the Jews' rights and their regeneration. He thought the revolutionary government's grant of rights in 1790-91 had been an act of "unwise generosity."[1] While the revolutionaries had assumed that rights would engender regeneration, Napoleon was convinced that the Jews remained unregenerate. He thought their continued concentration in usury and their alleged dualist ethic,

---

[1]Quoted in Simon Schwarzfuchs, *Napoleon, the Jews and the Sanhedrin* (London, 1979) 47.

which set different standards of treatment for Jews and non-Jews, made them unfit for citizenship. He intended the assemblies to be a means to introduce discriminatory legislation which would rectify the imbalance. Although an undeniable antipathy colored Napoleon's view of the Jews, that antipathy did not determine his actions. His decision to correct the revolution's act of "unwise generosity" belonged to his overall political program. Napoleon attempted to discard the revolution's abuses in order to reconcile its democratic heritage with despotic state centralism. In his eyes the Jews' citizenship was among the most flagrant of those abuses.

Napoleon's commissioners presented the laymen and rabbis who comprised the Assembly of Notables with twelve questions designed to ascertain whether Judaism in principle precluded the regeneration necessary for the Jews' complying with France's laws and its civic morality. Do Jews allow bigamy, divorce and intermarriage? Do Jews consider Frenchmen as brethren and will Jews

obey the laws of France? What powers do the
Rabbis have, who appoints them, and are their
powers sanctioned by law or custom? Can Jews
practice all professions and is usury permitted
equally towards Jews and non-Jews? An ominous
threat accompanied the questions. "The wish of
his Majesty is that you should be Frenchmen; it
remains with you to accept of the proffered title,
without forgetting that, to prove unworthy of it,
would be renouncing it altogether."[2]

This threat did not succeed in compromising
the deputies' integrity. The deputies were convinced that Judaism did not preclude regeneration. They discussed the questions with remarkable candor and managed to formulate answers
virtually all of them could accept. Such wide-
spread agreement represented a considerable
achievement not only because of the coercion to
which the Assembly was subjected, but also because of the Assembly's diversity. The deputies

---

[2]See below, 132.

were divided by the character of their religious belief, the nature of their religious practice, language (French, German, Italian) and community background (Ashkenazi, Sephardi). Yet neither a traditional Ashkenazi Rabbi like David Sintzheim (1745-1812), the guiding light for all issues touching on rabbinic law, nor a Sephardi enlightener like Abraham Furtado (1756-1817), the President of the Assembly, felt that they had compromised themselves. Sintzheim in particular corresponded with other rabbinic authorities in Europe throughout the proceedings and justifiably believed that he had remained faithful to *Halakha*.

While not violating *Halakha,* the Assembly's answers showed that the required regeneration did entail a fundamental recasting of Judaism's relationship to the nation state and civil society. Judaism was secularized, being reconstituted as just a religion, with its sole legitimate concern the narrowly defined religious life of the Jews. In the political realm secularization meant that the Jews had to recognize the uncontested authority of the state. Throughout their deliberations the deputies professed their undivided loyalty to the Emperor and to France. Napoleon emphasized the state's and his own political supremacy in designating the Assembly called to give religious sanction to the Assembly of Notables' answers the "Sanhedrin." He arrogated to himself the messianic presentiments that were attached to the renewal of a religious institution that had governed the Jews' affairs in Palestine fourteen centuries earlier. The Emperor usurped for himself the function of the Davidic messiah: he wanted the Jews to "find Jerusalem in France."[3]

Secularization in civil society required the Jews to recognize the essential equality of their French compatriots. This meant seeing Christians as "sons of Noah" (*Bnei Noach*) who conform to universal

---

[3]*Napoleon's Correspondance* 32 vols. (Paris, 1858-70) 13: 126.

standards of morality and consequently deserve
just treatment, rather than as idolaters who do
not. Secularization also implied recognition of the
supremacy of civil law: the validity of civil law
could not be disputed on the basis of *Halakha*.
The rabbis could refuse to give religious sanction
to a mixed marriage, but they had to recognize
that the marriage was legally binding.

The Assembly's answers and the Sanhedrin's
ratification of them satisfied not only their
authors' consciences but also Napoleon. A regenerated Judaism had been achieved, the
ominous threat averted. Napoleon's commissioners consequently proposed an institutional
framework to sustain this new Judaism. Judaism
was reorganized as a centralized "consistory"
following the model of the French churches.
Relying on the Catholic dea of a clerical hierarchy, the consistory made Judaism a rabbi-
centered religion. The Rabbi was to teach Jewish
doctrine in accordance with the decisions of the
Sanhedrin. Yet he and the consistory had another

range of duties as well. The consistory and the Rabbi were also functionaries of the state, responsible for the Jews' military service and occupations. The consistorial system subjected them to the same domineering centralized supervision and control as the other institutions of French society. Napoleon's goal of despotic state centralism had been achieved.

Napoleon had convened the Assembly in search of a pretext for discrimination. During the final sessions of the Assembly his commissioners pushed through a motion requesting that the government adopt measures to insure that the Jews' regeneration be achieved. Using the legal fiction of the motion, Napoleon's government issued the so-called "Infamous Decrees" on March 17, 1808, which regulated the Jews' economic activities and residential rights for a period of ten years.

Despite the Infamous Decrees, the Assembly and the Sanhedrin provided French Jewry with a useable ideology which guided the Jews in their historic attempt to become an integral part of the

French nation-state. The ideas of uncompromising loyalty to the state, the supremacy of civil over religious law, and the redefinition of Judaism as a religion alone become the Jews' credo as they pressed their claim to participate in all areas of French civil and political life. The *Transactions of the Paris Sanhedrin* is thus a classic document of the West European Jewish experience in the modern era.

David Sorkin
Brown University
Providence, Rhode Island

PREFACE.

THE novelty of a Jewish assembly deliberating on the national interests of a people which has so long ceased to be numbered among nations, induces us to offer an account of its proceedings to the English public. The French-Jewish editor, M. Diogene Tama, in an advertisement prefixed to his collection, expatiates with wonderful complacency on the immense utility of his publication. Without being quite so sanguine in our expectations, we cannot help expressing our conviction that it will prove highly gratifying to that curiosity which has been excited by the first mention of the meeting of such an assembly.

The ultimate views which Bonaparte may have on the Jewish nation are, to this day, involved in obscurity; while the supposed advantages he so pompously conferred on them may reasonably be called in question. This will warrant our attempting to elucidate them, as far as his dark purposes can admit of investigation.

The conduct of the former government of France toward sits Jewish subjects happily united tolerance and even encouragement with circumspection: indeed their state was, in many instances, preferable to that of the Protestants; they were secured in the enjoyment of their property; their religious ceremonies were acknowledged by law, (which, till the reign of Louis XVI. was not the case in respect to the Protestants,) and those who proved really useful citizens received letters of naturalization.

Some local badges of their former slavery still existed in several of the provinces; but, as early as the year 1785, government had in contemplation to remove them; and it is rather singular that this very M. Furtado, who appears so conspicuously as President of the present assembly, should have been called to Paris, with several other Jews, by M. de Malesherbes, Minister of Louis XVI. to give the necessary information on the subject.

It is more than probable that Bonaparte, in this instance, as indeed in most others, has taken up the plan of the ancient French government, giving it, at the same time, that theatrical form which is so peculiar to his conceptions, and *happily* fixing the meeting of the assembly at a time when it was the less necessary. For the decree of the National Assembly, which had assimilated the Jews to the rest of the nation, and which was then in full force, apparently left nothing to be done for men who were considered as French citizens to all intents and purposes. The usurious practices of the Israelites of some departments of France were only a plausible pretext, for it is well known, that the Jews were not the only people in France who followed that nefarious traffic: the total want of laws to repress it, the universal laxity of morals, and the uncertainty of every kind of speculation, had made it almost general among monied men, and five per cent. per month has been not unfrequently exacted by Christians lenders, even with the security of landed property.

A motive more likely to have influenced the rapacious French government on this occasion is the *douceur* of thirty millions of livres which had been required from the Jews as the price of the honour conferred upon them; and it probably was with a view to frighten them into a compliance with this demand, that several French writers have been *allowed* seemingly to differ in opinion from their government, and even to propose the annulling of the act which granted to the Jews all the privileges of French citizens, such as they are.

Yet, making every allowance for the stage tricks which the crafty agents of a despot usually employ to cover the rapacity of their master, and for that innate instinct of despotism which impels the French ruler to extend his sway even over conscience, there are, in the Questions proposed to the assembly, and in the measures adopted, several features which it is difficult to reconcile with the avowed object in view, and which seem to convey more than is intended to meet the eye.

The questions, indeed, are mostly of a nugatory nature, and such as might have been easily answered without any recourse to a Jewish assembly: others are evidently captious; and it is not without a motive, although not a very obvious one, that such a stress has been laid on the obligation of defending the country, and on the organization of the Rabbinical body.

When we consider that the Jewish population of France and of Italy is not calculated, by the deputies themselves, at more than one hundred thousand souls, (a small number indeed when compared with the population of those countries) we are at a loss to see what great advantages could immediately result to Bonaparte from the Jews embracing zealously the profession of arms. We well know that his gigantic plans of ambition rest on the laws of the conscription; but the Jews are already liable to them; they can hardly escape their excessive rigour; and even the whole of the Jewish youth, of the requisite age, would, in point of number, make but a contemptible reinforcement to the immense armies of France.

These exhortations to embrace the profession of arms, so zealously repeated by the leading members of the French Jews, are, besides, always coupled with strong recommendations to follow mechanical trades and husbandry; in short, those professions without which *a nation cannot exist by itself*, but which are not more particularly useful than any others to a small given number of people, who consider *as their country* an empire in which these professions abound.

We find these same recommendations strongly inforced in the answer of M. Furtado to the commercial Jews of Frankfort, who hardly can have a choice of employment. " We have," says he, " too " many merchants and bankers among us, and too " few artificers and husbandmen, and, above all, too " few soldiers:" but if their *countrymen* thoroughly fill these branches of employment, what necessity is there for having husbandmen, artificers and soldiers *of their own?*

The Jewish deputies say that Bonaparte conceived the idea of their *regeneration*, or their *political redemption*, in the land of Egypt, and on the *banks of the Jordan.* This we doubt not; and though we are almost ashamed to hazard the extravagant supposition, we feel a conviction that his gigantic mind entertains the idea of re-establishing them in Palestine, and that this forms a part of his plan

respecting Egypt, which he is well known never
to have abandoned.

No one will contend that this idea is too wild
for his conception ; it is, on the contrary, perfectly
consonant with his love for extraordinary, dazzling
enterprises; he acts in this even with more than
his usual foresight, by attempting to prepare
the Jews for the new situation he intends for them.
It is with this view that he encourages them to
follow those professions which are necessary for
men forming a distinct nation in a land of their
own; for certainly, a body wholly composed of
merchants and traders could never exist as such.
He attempted, in a like manner, to introduce the
arts of civilization among the Copts and the Arabs
of Egypt, and with the same views. *Idque apud
imperitos humanitas vocabatur, cum pars servitutis
esset. Tacit.*

These measures, we know, are represented as
the means of uniting the Jews more thoroughly
with their fellow-citizens, and of checking their
supposed propensity to usury.

We have already said that the reproach of usury

b

was only the pretence made use of to call them
together; remedies for an evil so general now
among the French, and of such a magnitude,
are not to be found in exhortations to a few individuals, who, in their rapacious pursuits, are regardless even of the precepts of their sacred law.
The other alledged motive is equally fallacious.
For why recommend the same measures to Jews of
foreign countries? It is well known, besides, that
men are more closely united in a state o society
by their mutual wants than by the similitude of
their occupations; and, in short, the Regulations
forced upon the Israelites prove that the intention
of Bonaparte was to separate them more than ever
from the rest of Frenchmen.

This will be evident on a mere perusal of them.
It will be seen that the Israelites have separate
elective assemblies, separate contributions, and a
separate police, exercised by their own Rabbies,
who are to inforce military service among them,
keep an exact account of their numbers, and even
interfere in their private concerns. In this, they
are indeed under the hand of government, but

they are totally secluded from the mass of the people. Their actual strength, their several occupations, will be known accurately ; they may be ready at a moment's warning.

These Regulations have another remarkable feature, common to all the recent politico-religious conceptions of the French government. The Rabbies are by them set as spies over the Jews, like the ministers of the Roman Catholic religion over the rest of Frenchmen. Nor does this part of the plan stop here ; by means of the close union existing between the several Jewish communities scattered over Europe, the French ruler hopes to extend the system far and wide. Already deputies of all the Synagogues have been invited to Paris, to assist at the GREAT SANHEDRIM. An uniformity of doctrine will connect them more closely with those among the French Jews who are devoted to Bonaparte. What other advantages had he in view in framing the too famous *Concordat* with the Pope of Rome?

This part of the plan is far from being incompatible with the further views we have alluded to;

b 2

it will even prepare and insure, in some measure, their success; and, should they be frustrated after all, will secure advantages sufficient to lessen the disappointment. Let it be remarked here, that, while the French ruler is so anxious to extend his influence in foreign countries by means of the Israelites, he has taken care, by the eleventh and twenty-sixth articles of his Regulations, to prevent a retaliation from foreign powers. Indeed these clauses destroy completely the idea entertained at first, by many, that he had in contemplation to intice the Jews indiscriminately to settle in France; and we here repeat it, his motives for calling that assembly were his love of money, his fondness of theatrical pomp, his plans on the east, and his extensive system of espionage.

It could not be reasonably expected that, under Bonaparte, an assembly of any kind should enjoy a great share of liberty in their deliberations. Indeed, little care was taken, in this instance, to disguise the exertions of power; the answers and the measures were evidently agreed between the Imperial Commissioners and a few of the leading

members, and read afterwards to the assembly
pro forma; the power attributed to the President,
devoted to the court, his naming the members of
every committee, his dissolving the meeting at
pleasure, hardly left the shadow of deliberating
forms, while the casual opposition some of the
propositions experienced was removed by means
WE should deem unwarrantable in any meeting.

From the speeches of the deputies, it will be
seen that the Jewish assembly could boast of as
great talents as could probably have been expected from any other *French* assembly of the same
number of men, taken indiscriminately in any
class, and this fully justifies our assertion, that,
under the old government, the Jews enjoyed a
sufficient share of liberty to encourage the display of their natural abilities, and that, with
equal protection, and liberty of conscience, is
perhaps the full extent of the advantages which
non-conformists can expect from a regular government.

But while we pay a just tribute to their talents,
we must deplore the way in which they have been

shamefully abused, in many instances. Few of
them, indeed, have raised their voices against the
tyrannical Regulations, which have been imposed
upon them; some of their answers it is true, are
highly satisfactory, and, among them, those concerning usury; but, in many other cases, they have
manifested a culpable readiness to accede to or
even to anticipate whatever might suit the views
of their government, without much regard to the
precepts of their law. But for the strong opposition of the Rabbies, the assembly would, as far as
its authority could have gone, sanctioned the
marriages of Jews with Christians, nay, in the
tumultuous debate which took place on the occasion, a member broadly declared that marriage
had nothing of a divine institution, and that the
first precept was *increase and multiply*. Nor is
this the only instance in which we remark, with
sorrow, that the contagious infidelity of France
had crept in among the Israelites. In the festival of
the 15th of August, the cyphers of *Napoleon* and
of *Josephine* were profanely blended with the un-
utterable name of Jehovah, and the Imperial Eagle
was placed over the Sacred Ark. This we under-

stand has given much offence, and with very just
reason, we think, to the most respectable men
of that community in these kingdoms.

The answer to the sixth question, by which the
French Jews acknowledge France as their country,
without any restriction whatever, is a still more
heinous dereliction of the tenets of the Mosaic law;
for they give up, by it, the hope of the expected
Messiah, and of the everlasting possession of the
promised land of Canaan, which they deem a part
of the sacred covenant between God and his chosen
people.

While we thus inculpate the Jewish deputies,
it cannot be expected that we shall lay too great a
stress on the fulsome and frequently impious flattery which characterises all their productions.
Perhaps we even ought to make some apology for
having so faithfully translated them, could we
think it possible that any rational man should
adopt or suspect us of entertaining sentiments
which the Jews themselves, most probably, only
feigned to suit their own purposes.

But flattery is the opiate of the guilty conscience; it sooths the pangs of remorse; and great

criminals cannot be approached without it, like the golden branch of the Sybil, it softens the fierceness of those infernal divinities, and is the only safeguard left to mortals who appear before them.

It would be unjust, therefore, to expect from the Jews more stoic firmness than the Roman poet, the republican Lucan, himself possessed, who, after describing, with his usual energy, the scenes of blood through which the Romans waded to arrive at the *blessings* of an imperial government, says, even to NERO—

Quod si non aliam venturo fata Neroni
Invenere viam, magnoque aeterna parantur
Regna Deis, cœlumque suo servire Tonanti
Non nisi sævorum potuit post bella gigantum :
Jam nihil, O Superi, querimur; scelera ipsa, nefasque
Hac mercede placent . . . .
. . . .
Multum Roma tamen debet civilibus armis,
Quod tibi res acta est . . . .
. . . . tibi numine ab omni,
Cedetur : jurisque tui natura relinquet,
Quis deus esse velis, ubi regnum ponere mundi.

We understand that this passage is omitted in French translations, and we know that it is not to be found in that of Marmontel.

TRANSACTIONS

OF THE

PARISIAN SANHEDRIM.

═══════════

*Collection of Writings and Acts, relating to the for-
mer Condition of Individuals professing the Hebrew Religion in France.*

PREVIOUS even to the memorable epoch of
the convocation of *Les Etats Généraux*, opinion,
in what concerns us, had experienced changes conducive to public weal.

Reason had reassumed her rights over prejudice, which, to justify oppression, had, for a long
time, represented us as unworthy of having a
country.

In centuries of error and of injustice, degrading statutes pointed at our fathers as objects of
public contempt. All were made to share in the
punishment deserved only by traitors, who, like
those of Judea, had, by their calumnies, brought
destruction on their virtuous and benevolent brethren.

But when, at last, more liberal ideas had produced sentiments of universal justice, we were no longer beheld with contempt, we groaned no longer under the iron hand of oppression.

France gave the example of liberality: it was the general wish among us to adopt her as our country; and petitions consonant to those wishes were eagerly laid by us before the ancient government.

In these attempts we were thwarted by prejudice.

Many, however, of tried loyalty, among us, having proved by their meritorious conduct that they were entitled to public esteem, received from the sovereign letters of naturalization. They purchased landed property in France; educated their children to honorable professions; proved themselves worthy of that first favour; and their conduct, silencing the clamours of prejudice, accustomed Frenchmen to behold us with that good will, which man in every country owes to his fellow creatures.

From hence, the *cahiers*, (1) prepared in 1789, proposed to give those professing our religion the means of becoming more useful to the state, by opening for us the way to preferment.

As early as the first of October of the same

(1) These *cahiers* were written instructions given by the electors in the several towns and provinces of France to the deputies they sent to *les Etats Généraux*.

year, a member of *les Etats Généraux,* obtained from that assembly a vote that, on a future day, it should, in a sitting held on purpose, *take into its consideration the condition of the Jews in France.*

And this member, I must observe, was a clergyman, a dignitary of the second rank.

The sitting thus granted was delayed by matters of general interest. But on the one hand, a special decree, of the 24th of December, granted to all non-catholics the right of being elected members of the assembly, and opened for them the way to all employments, civil and military,

And on the other, the decree of the 28th of January, 1790, acknowledged, as active citizens, all those among us who, previous to the year 1789, had obtained letters of naturalization.

As this decree is the first step towards our adoption, I shall give it at full length.

Decree of the 28th of January, 1790, sanctioned the same month,

" *All the Jews, known in France, under the name*
" *of Portuguese, Spanish, and Avignonese Jews, shall*
" *continue to enjoy the same rights they have hitherto*
" *enjoyed, and which have been granted to them*
" *by letters patent.*

" In consequence thereof, they shall enjoy the
" rights of active citizens, if they possess the other

(4)

" requisite qualifications, as enumerated in the
" decrees of the national assembly."

Still however prejudice led into error. A general
ferment served too well the evil intention of a few
unjust men.

The decree of the 16th of April, 1790, sanctioned on the 18th, shews the kind protection of which
we stood in need, and which was considered as
justly due to us.

" The National Assembly again places the Jews
" of Alsace, and of the other provinces of the king-
" dom, under the special protection of the law;
" forbids any one from disturbing their peace, or
" otherwise injuring them; directs all municipal offi-
" cers and national guards to exert their authority for
" the protection of their persons and property."

There still remained a ground of prejudice
against us. In some parts of the country, people
could hardly bring themselves to look upon us as
worthy of the advantages granted by the law,
because we were still liable to *personal* taxes.

We were freed from this burthen by a special
decree of the 20th of July, 1790, sanctioned the
7th of August following.

" The National Assembly, considering that the
" public protection is due to all the inhabitants of
" the kingdom, indiscriminately, without any other

" *condition but that of discharging their share of the*
" *general contributions;*

" *Having heard the report of its committee of*
" *demesnes,*

" *Has decreed and decrees, that the annual tribute*
" *of* 20,000 *livres, paid by the Jews of Metz and of*
" *the Messin country, under the denomination of*
" *duty of* habitation, protection *and* toleration, *is*
" *suppressed and abolished, without any indemnity to*
" *the present owner of and contractor for the said tri-*
" *bute.*

" *Decrees also, that all tributes of similar nature,*
" *under whatever denomination they may be, which*
" *are, any where else, levied on the Jews, shall likewise*
" *be suppressed and abolished, without any indem-*
" *nity from those hitherto liable to them, whether such*
" *tributes are paid to the public treasury, or towns,*
" *corporations or individuals: reserving, nevertheless,*
" *to decide on a future day, on such indemnities as*
" *may be due by the nation to the government con-*
" *tractors who may be aggrieved, the same being*
" *certified by the directors of the departments in which*
" *such tributes are raised; and for this end the titles*
" *and writings of the owners and contractors, shall be*
" *produced in the course of the present year.*

" *Decrees, lastly, that no arrears of the aforesaid*
" *tributes can be demanded, and that all lawsuits to*
" *recover the same shall be totally stopped.*"

These various resolutions were the forerunners

of that which has placed the Jews in the full enjoyment of all civil and political rights.

The rule had been laid down in the decree of the 28th of January, 1790. There only remained to do away the limitation, by which the advantages it granted were confined to those Jews who had obtained letters patent, to the exclusion of those who had not this kind of privileges.

A general resolution was wanting to fix with certainty our rank in society. It was decreed that the taking of the civic oath would enable us all, without distinction, to participate in the advantages granted by the decree of the 28th of January, 1790.

This was the design of the adjournment adopted in the sittings of the 1st of September, 1789.

This was the design of the restriction contained in the decree of the 24th of December following.

This was again the design of the exceptions arising from that of the 28th of January, 1790.

By its dispositions the well-known decree of the 27th of September, 1791, sanctioned on the 13th of November following, has referred to January, 1790, the epoch from which we date the full enjoyment of our present condition. And indeed, this consequence sprung from the very constitution itself, which was then in full activity.

" *The National Assembly, considering that the*

" *conditions requisite to be a French citizen, and to be-*
" *come an active citizen, are fixed by the constitution,*
" *and that every man who, being duly qualified, takes*
" *the civic oath, and engages to fulfil all the duties pre-*
" *scribed by the constitution, has a right to all the ad-*
" *vantages it insures;*———

" *Annuls all adjournments, restrictions, and excep-*
" *tions, contained in the preceeding decrees, affecting*
" *individuals of the Jewish persuasion, who shall take*
" *the civic oath, which shall be considered as a renun-*
" *ciation of all privileges granted in their favour.*"

All the Jews residing in France hastened to take the oath which constituted them citizens, and which, from its nature, is a solemn pledge given by them of their submission to the laws and of their obedience to the ruling powers.

According to their principles of morality, an oath, naturally binding for a man of probity, is further strengthened by their religious maxims.

The God of their fathers, called to witness of their engagements, has forbidden all manner of infringement.

They have been, they are unshaken in the performance of all their duties as citizens, without a single exception, in the whole of their political or civil conduct.

Of this they are conscious: they have stood the test; they will not swerve from their fidelity to the country.

In the year 9, they were deemed worthy of receiving a proof of national regard. French agents obtained for them an exemption from the tributes levied on them in the country of Mentz.

In the year 10, the then government gave them leave to establish regulations founded on justice, by which the debts of their ancient communities have been discharged.

It is then true that motives of gratitude have daily added new strength to those engagements by which we are become French citizens; and as, from this, we should be the more guilty, were it possible that we could be wanting in due submission to those measures which are at last to make us completely worthy of the honour conferred upon us by our adoption; so the world cannot be surprised at the eager joy which we have manifested on receiving the decrees dictated by the benevolence of our sovereign, to complete the great work of our regeneration.

Already we were acquainted with his heroic virtues; already our hearts, filled with veneration, had indulged in the most flattering hopes; we saw in the CONQUEROR of the WORLD, in the MODEL of SOVEREIGNS, the support of our political and civil existence, the man whom our children should bless as the author of their felicity.

At the grand epocha of his elevation, our temples have resounded with joyful exultations; our pray-

, the effusions of guileless hearts, have been
poured before the Eternal, with that exquisite
feeling which is produced by the prospect of future
happiness.

Hymns sung with solemnity, preceeded and followed by fervent prayers, have crowned those days
of happiness and festivity.

In that too, we have vied in loyalty with all
classes of citizens.

In that too, our religious ceremonies have confirmed our engagement of concurring, by every
means in our power, in whatever may tend to promote that degree of illustrious celebrity and prosperity which the exalted views of our august EM-
PEROR are preparing for the French empire.

In the productions to which the exemplary zeal
of our brethren gave birth, we must mention with
distinction the hymn composed by M. Meubel
Kargeau, translated into French by M. Michel
Berr.

I should have given it a place in my collection,
but that the principles, the respectful sentiments,
and the wishes it contains, are to be found in writings which come more specifically within the plan
of my work.

I must record here, what should be known in
all our families, that at the very epoch of that famous decree, which, in September, 1791, gave every

c

one of us a country, many among us, in congra-
tulating their brethren on the greatness of the boon,
addressed to them instructions on the full extent
of their duties, and proved the necessity of altering,
in our habits and in our manners, whatever might
tend to perpetuate prepossessions and prejudices
which had kept us till then in a state of forlorn
misery.

I must give at full length the famous letter which
M. Berr-Isaac-Berr, manufacturer at Nancy, father
of M. Michel Berr, addressed to all his brethren at
the close of the year 1791.

Those among us who are acquainted with it will
be gratified by this opportunity of again perusing
it; those who have not yet seen it will gratefully
receive the instructions of enlightened men, whose
knowledge and judgement have constituted them
our supports and directors.

They will be convinced that our religious maxims, agreeing with every rule of morals and of civilization, elevate us to that rank and those rights
which a generous nation has conferred on us.

Our teachers, our children, will therein see those
principles which will concur in the great work of
our happiness.

Letter of M. Berr-Isaac-Berr *to his Brethren, in* 1791, *on the Rights of active Citizens being grant-ed to the Jews.*

" Gentlemen and dear brethren,
" At length the day is arrived when the veil, by
" which, parted from our fellow-citizens, we were
" kept in a state of humiliation, is rent ; at length
" we recover those rights which have been taken
" from us more than eighteen centuries ago. How
" much are we at this moment indebted to the cle-
" mency of the God of our forefathers !
" We are now, thanks to the Supreme Being,
" and to the sovereignty of the nation, not only
" Men and Citizens, but we are Frenchmen!——
" What a happy change thou hast worked in us,
" merciful God! So late as the 27th of September
" last, we were the only inhabitants of this vast
" empire who seemed doomed to remain for ever
" in bondage and abasement; and on the follow-
" ing day, on the 28th, a day for ever sacred among
" us, thou inspirest the immortal legislators of
" France. They pronounce, and more than sixty
" thousand unfortunate beings, mourning over their
" sad fate, are awakened to a sense of their happi-
" ness by the liveliest emotions of the purest joy.
" Let it be acknowledged, dearest brethren, that

c 2

" we have not deserved this wonderful change by
" our repentance, or by the reformation of our
" manners: we can attribute it to nothing but to
" the everlasting goodness of God: He never for-
" sook us entirely; but, finding that we were not
" yet worthy of seeing the accomplishment of his
" promises of a perfect and lasting redemption, he
" has not, however, thought proper still to aggra-
" vate our sufferings: and surely our chains had
" become the more galling from the contemplation
" of the rights of man, so sublimely held forth to
" public view. Therefore, our God, who reads
" the heart of man, seeing that all our resignation
" would have proved unequal to the task, and that
" supernatural strength was wanting to enable us
" to support these new torments, has thought of
" applying the remedy; He has chosen the gene-
" rous French nation to reinstate us in our rights,
" and to operate our regeneration, as, in other
" times, he had chosen Antiochus, Pompey, and
" others, to humiliate and enslave us. How glori-
" ous it is for that nation, who have, in so short a
" time, made so many people happy! And surely,
" if Frenchmen are become so themselves, by the
" additional rights and the additional liberty they
" have just acquired, how much the more are we,
" in particular, gainers by the change! and what
" bounds can there be to our gratitude for the hap-

" py event! From being vile slaves, mere *serfs*, a
" species of men merely tolerated and suffered in
" the empire, liable to heavy and arbitrary taxes,
" we are, of a sudden, become the children of the
" country, to bear its common charges, and share in
" its common rights.

" What orator could presume to express to the
" nation and to it's king, all the extent of our
" gratitude, and of our unalterable submission?
" But neither the king nor the representatives of the
" nation seek for praises or acknowledgments; their
" only wish is to behold people happy. In that
" they expect and they will find their reward.
" Let us then, dear brethren, let us conform to their
" wishes; let us examine with attention what re-
" mains to be done, on our part, to become truly
" happy, and how we may be able to shew, in some
" measure, our grateful sense for all the favours
" heaped upon us. On this subject, gentlemen
" and dear brethren, give me leave to submit to
" your judgment the result of some reflections,
" which our change of condition has suggested to
" me.

" The name of active citizen, which we have just
" obtained, is, without a doubt, the most precious
" title a man can possess in a free empire ; but this
" title alone is not sufficient; we should possess also
" the necessary qualifications to fulfil the duties

(14)

" annexed to it: we know ourselves how very de-
" ficient we are in that respect; we have been in a
" manner compelled to abandon the pursuit of all
" moral and physical sciences, of all sciences, in
" short, which tend to the improvement of the
" mind, in order to give ourselves up entirely to
" commerce, to be enabled to gather as much
" money as would insure protection, and satisfy
" the rapacity of our persecutors: in justice to
" truth we must say, however, that these many
" years our hardships have been greatly alleviated
" in France, and particularly in Lorraine, since
" the reign of Stanislaus the benevolent, and that
" we never experienced from our rulers and magis-
" trates but marks of good will and protection;
" yet we always felt the inutility of mental acquire-
" ments, from the impossibility in which we saw
" ourselves of ever making any use of them. We
" must then, dear brethren, strongly bear this
" truth in our minds, that till such a time as we
" work a change in our manners, in our habits, in
" short, in our whole education, we cannot expect
" to be placed by the esteem of our fellow citizens
" in any of those situations in which we can give
" signal proofs of that glowing patriotism so long
" cherished in our bosoms. God forbid that I should
" mean any thing derogatory to our professed re-
" ligion, or to our established form of worship: far

" from me the idea of proposing any innovation
" in them. I should consider as monsters those
" among us, who, from the prospect of some ad-
" vantages they might expect from the new con-
" stitution, would presume to alter the dogmas of
" their religion. If, during our tribulations, we
" have derived some consolation from our strict
" adherence to our religion, how much more are we
" bound to remain firmly attached to it now, when
" we are reaping the fruits of our perseverance and
" of our attachment to our religious worship,
" when we behold that of all ancient nations
" we are the only one who has been able to with-
" stand the heavy tides of misfortune, succeeding
" each other for centuries! And now, expressedly
" chosen by the French constitution, should we, at
" the first dawn of liberty, prove refractory to our
" laws, after having remained faithful to them
" during eighteen centuries of persecution? No; I
" shall not believe any of my brethren capable
" of this. I shall not therefore address you on this
" head, not doubting but we all perfectly agree
" on the fundamental point. But I cannot too
" often repeat to you how absolutely necessary it is
" for us to divest ourselves entirely of that narrow
" spirit, of *Corporation* and *Congregation*, in all
" civil and political matters, not immediately con-
" nected with our spiritual laws; in these things

" we must absolutely appear simply as indivi-
" duals, as Frenchmen, guided only by a true
" patriotism and by the general good of the nation;
" to know how to risk our lives and for unes for the
" defence of the country, to make ourselves useful
" to our fellow citizens, to deserve their esteem and
" their friendship, to join our efforts to theirs in
" maintaining public tranquility, on which that of
" individuals depends; such ought to be the princi-
" pal aim of our daily employment; and as we
" are not yet able to fulfil those noble functions our-
" selves, we must turn our minds to the means
" necessary to be acquired, and, above all, in our
" attention on our children, and procure for them
" all the necessary instructions. Let us do for the
" present what is within our power; let us take the
" civic oath of being faithful to the nation, to the
" law and to the king. This oath contains only the
" sentiments we have always professed. We have
" never been accused of being breakers of the
" law, or of having rebelled even against those
" who domineered over us; we have always respected
" and obeyed even those by whom we were ill-treat-
" ed: we shall then, upon much stronger grounds,
" remain faithful to laws which reinstate us in our
" rights, and place us, on the same footing with all
" Frenchmen, leaving us at the same time, at full
" liberty to profess our religion, and to follow our

" mode of worship. This oath, I say, which, on our
" side, is nothing but a renunciation of those pre-
" tended privileges and immunities which we en-
" joyed, cannot, under any point of view, wound
" the conscience of the most orthodox and the most
" scrupulous of our brethren; our privileges and
" our immunities were only relative to our state of
" slavery. We had the privilege of forming a dis-
" tinct body of people and a separate community;
" but this carried with it the exclusion from all
" other corporations, and the submission to parti-
" cular taxes, much above our means and our
" resources, and arbitrarily imposed. If a member
" of that community was accused of any misde-
" meanor whatever, the reproaches and the humilia-
" tion fell on the whole; we were exempt from
" militia and from public works, but it was be-
" cause we were deemed unworthy of it; and to
" palliate the injustice of such proceedings, we were
" exempted, on condition of paying in money three
" times the value of such services, &c. It is certain-
" ly no hard matter to give up such privileges.

" By the taking of this oath, which will be con-
" sidered as a renunciation to all privileges and im-
" munities heretofore introduced in our favour, we
" shall enjoy the rights and qualities of active citi-
" zens, provided always we have the other necessary
" qualifications. You see then, dear brethren, that

D

" there cannot be a shadow of difficulty or of scru-
" ple about taking this oath, by means of which
" we shall be *constitutionally* acknowledged as
" French Jews.

" This oath once taken, let us exert ourselves to
" fulfil the duties within our reach, but let us avoid
" *grasping* at our rights; let us not rush headlong
" against the opinions of some of our fellow citizens
" who, rendered callous by prejudice, will reject the
" idea of Jews being fellow men, fellow creatures.
" Let it be sufficient for us, at present, to have ac-
" quired the invaluable right of assisting at all as-
" semblies of French citizens; but let us not attend
" them, till we have acquired knowledge sufficient
" to make ourselves useful members; till we know
" how to discuss and to defend the interests of the
" country; in short, till our most bitter enemies are
" convinced, and acknowledge the gross miscon-
" ceptions they had entertained of us.

" If we cannot ourselves enjoy all the sweets of
" the new constitution, for it is a hard matter to
" change habits and manners indulged in for thirty
" or forty years, we shall at least see the first blos-
" soms of the thriving plant gathered by our chil-
" dren; we may even expect that indulgence from
" our generous fellow citizens, should not our own
" regeneration proceed as rapidly as we ourselves
" could wish. Our education has been defective

" in many points of view. Already the famous Rab-
" bi Hartwik Vessely, of Berlin, has rendered us an
" eminent service, by publishing several works in
" Hebrew on this subject.   One of his productions,
" entitled *Salutary Instructions addressed to the*
" *Jewish Communities of the Empire,* has been trans-
" lated into French, in the year 1782.   It details
" the causes of our present ignorance, and the
" means by which we may deserve once more the ap-
" pellation of the learned and intelligent nation,
" which God himself gave us.   I shall not repeat
" here what you find in these useful publications;
" but I entreat you, dear brethren, to follow this
" author in his meditations; and you will easily re-
" mark that our fate, and the fate of our posterity,
" depends solely on the change we shall effect in
" our mode of education.

    "The first of our parental cares must be, no doubt,
" to see that our children, in preference to all
" things, learn the holy Bible in the very language
" in which it was penned by the divine hand, and
" transmitted to us by Moses our lawgiver; let them,
" then, know perfectly the Hebrew language, which
" notwithstanding its penury, is the key of all other
" languages, and must be, for us in particular, the
" first object of our studies.   But to this day do
" we really understand it? Have we masters able
" to explain it to us, and to give us its true mean-

" ing in a faithful translation? Before we posses-
" ed a real treasure in *the translation of the Bible*
" *in German by Mendelshon*, our children learnt
" Hebrew from masters who explained it in a dialect
" which neither the tutor nor the pupil could un-
" derstand. Each master had his method of trans-
" lating and his manner of speaking, according to
" the country he came from; hardly could we have
" met three children, having learnt from three
" different masters, who would have explained in
" the same manner, in the same language, or with
" the same pronunciation the clearest passage of
" the holy writings.

" Even now that we possess the sublime translation
" of Mendelshon, we have but very few teachers who
" are truly masters of the two languages into which
" the Bible is written and translated. We see now and
" then some scholars from Berlin, who come to this
" country, but they are too few and too expensive to
" allow many of us to avail themselves of their in-
" structions. It is however indispensable that,
" while we are getting our children instructed the
" principles of their religion in the original language,
" we should procure for them an explanation in the
" ordinary language, which they hear and speak
" from their infancy.

" It appears to me that were it possible to get our
" children taught the holy Bible by a French ver-

" sion, instead of a German one, provided such a ver_
" sion should be as faithful as that of the immor-
" tal Mendelshon, a great and material advantage
" would result from the change : they would have
" only two languages to learn at the same time,
" Hebrew and French; whereas now they are obliged
" to learn three at the same time, Hebrew, German,
" and French. Accordingly, this last, which ought
" to be their mother tongue, since they are reared
" with and among Frenchmen, has always been the
" language in which they have made the least pro-
" ficiency, and which very often they scarcely un-
" derstand. It is only when compelled by necessity
" to speak to and to be understood by their neigh-
" bours that they begin to blunder some inarticulate
" words; from hence proceeds this other inconve-
" niency, that those among us who have felt early
" enough the usefulness of the French language,
" and have acquired the habit of speaking it with
" facility, cannot, however, get rid of a German or
" other foreign accents. Their phrases, too, are
" generally incorrect I even must say myself, that
" while I am thus addressing you in French, I feel
" my want of experience and of proficiency in that
" language, which I have however chosen in pre-
" ference, to prove to you, that Jews may commune
" together and confer with one another in that lan-
" guage, on all topics even on religious matters, and

" that it is entirely in our power to avoid encumber-
" ing the minds of our youth with the useless study
" of foreign languages. Have we not the example
" of the Jews of Asia, the most devout and the most
" scrupulous of our brethren, who read and write on-
" ly Hebrew and the language of their country?
" Why should we continue to bear the name of Ger-
" man or Polish Jews, while we are happily French
" Jews?

" I am well aware, dear brethren, that this pro-
" position cannot be adopted until we have a
" great part of our holy writings faithfully trans-
" lated into French; but till such a time as men
" are found among us equal to that great task, let
" us not neglect the means which may be con-
" ducive to the unfolding of the necessary talents.
" I would, then, propose to you, dear brethren, to
" establish a public school for us, on a plan similar
" to that of Berlin, and of several other places in
" the empire; we shall appoint professors of
" Hebrew, whom we must, it is true, procure from
" great distances; and we shall likewise appoint
" French teachers. I have no doubt but our chil-
" dren will make a rapid progress in both the
" languages thus taught them; they will become
" at the same time the supports of our religion and
" of the French constitution; and, after going
" through the several classes, they will return to

" us with a deep sense of the holiness of our re-
" ligion, whose dogmas they will here learn from
" the true principles, and may prove at the same
" time good Jews and good French citizens. After
" the first essay, we may add to the school pro-
" fessorships of all Arts and Sciences, that our
" children may see glorious careers open before
" them, and may choose, according to their incli-
" nation, that kind of pursuit in which the esteem
" of their fellow citizens, and an honest mainte-
" nance, will be the reward of their exertions.
" We shall then no longer be exclusively addicted
" to that mercantile and trafficking spirit, which,
" till now, has been almost the only one by which
" we have been actuated.

" Moreover, dear brethren, when we have ful-
" filled our first duty towards our children; when
" once they are thoroughly initiated in the prin-
" ciples and spirit of our religion, we may, with-
" out apprehension of danger, avail ourselves of
" the resources offered to us by our generous
" countrymen, by sending them to share the ad-
" vantages of national education in the public
" schools; certainly they will not be thwarted in
" their religious opinions; and once easy on that
" score, they soon will become beloved among
" their comrades, by sharing their emulation and
" their wishes of deserving the approbation of

" their superiors. By means of that union in
" schools, our children, like those of our fellow-
" citizens, will remark from their tender youth that
" neither opinions, nor difference of religion, are
" a bar to fraternal love; and that every one na-
" turally embracing and following the religion of
" his fathers, all may, in fulfilling their religious
" duties, fulfil also those of citizenship; from that,
" all aversion, all hatred, all antipathy between
" them will be done away. In proportion as they
" increase in years, those ties of friendship and of
" fraternity will be drawn closer, in whatever is
" of social and political nature, not contrary to the
" dogmas of religion. They will have learned
" that, on leaving the school, some have been with
" their parents to church, others to chapel, others to
" the synagogue, to worship, in different modes
" and with different dogmas, the true living
" God, the sole Creator of the Universe.

" Let us establish charitable houses of in-
" dustry, in which the children of poor people and
" those who are not born to a higher rank, shall
" learn all the trades and mechanical occupations
" necessary to society. Let us form among us
" carpenters, smiths, tailors, &c. And if we can
" succeed to have a man in each profession, able to
" work as a master, he will soon form appren-
" tices; and gradually we shall see Jewish work-

" men who will strive to deserve esteem by earn-
" ing honourably their livelihood. Thus shall we
" banish sloth and indolence, occasioned by the
" idleness of our youth.

" You will here observe to me, with some truth,
" dear brethren, that it is much easier to propose
" these plans than to carry them into execution,
" and that these proposed establishments would
" require funds probably to a large amount. But
" you will not believe, I trust, that this considera-
" tion has escaped me; and indeed I had already
" found the means of meeting all necessary ex-
" pences, when I determined to impart to you my
" ideas on the subject. Undoubtedly we must
" have fixed and regular revenues before we can
" think of undertaking any of the establishments
" I have proposed. But what Jew is there in
" tolerable circumstances who will not be ready
" to make some sacrifices? Who will refuse to be
" subject even to personal privations, in order
" to contribute something to the general happiness
" of his brethren, and thus give, as far as lays in
" him, a pledge of our gratitude for the fraternal
" act of our fellow-citizens?

" When we were forming a separate community
" in the *ci-devant* province of Lorraine, we had
" excessive charges to support, besides a sum of be-
" tween fifteen and sixteen thousand livres, which

E

" we were bound collectively and individually to
" pay either to the king, or as a tax on industry;
" or for wages of the *Parliament*, &c. We had
" besides, individually, to pay arbitrary taxes in
" the places of our residence, for the quartering
" of soldiers, for the poor, the parish, the public
" works, public wells, &c.; and again, besides the
" charges peculiar to us, the syndics (*wardens*)
" elected by our former community were by it au-
" thorised, with the approbation of government, to
" form lists of contribution, and to tax individuals,
" members of that community, according to their
" means and abilities. Now this community is dis-
" solved; and, thanks to those who were at the
" head of its administration for more than fifty
" years in succession, the receipts and the general
" expences balance each other, without its being
" encumbered with considerable arrears, or loaded
" with any debt whatever. We shall pay in future
" our equal share of national taxes, like the rest of
" assessed people in France, and in the same pro-
" portions: we shall, in a manner, pay only what
" we have consented to pay by the vote of our re-
" presentatives, who are equally those of all French-
" men. In that case, dear brethren, let us make
" one single effort; let us shew ourselves capable
" of foregoing present advantages, to make our-
" selves worthy of greater ones at a future period.

(27)

" not very distant. Let us voluntarily deprive
" ourselves of a part of the benefits conferred upon
" us by the new constitution, in order to enable us
" to offer to the country, in the persons of our chil-
" dren, worthier objects of her favours than we
" ourselves are. Let us form communities, such as
" we had in Lorraine, and invite those Jews to join
" us, who, by the new division of the kingdom in-
" to eighty-three departments, are now, like us,
" inhabitants of that of La Meurthe. Let us
" unanimously and voluntarily consent to support,
" for ten years longer, a charge equal to that we
" were heretofore obliged to pay. Let us employ
" that sum, by which we formerly purchased tole-
" rance and protection, in forming men worthy of
" that liberty they have just obtained. Once sure
" of a fixed and regular income, nothing can pre-
" vent us from forming those establishments ne-
" cessary for the education of our children.

" We shall continue to maintain the Rabbi
" elected by our *ci-devant* community, who will
" fulfil the functions of Grand Rabbi in whatever
" relates to our religious customs and ceremonies.
" Wherever the number of Jewish inhabitants is
" sufficiently numerous, we shall establish parti-
" cular Rabbis, or *vicars*, who shall be named by
" us likewise, shall be approved by the Grand Rab-
" bi, and placed under his inspection. Wherever

E 2

" a vicar shall be appointed, he will have his par-
" ticular district, in which he will be bound to
" discharge his religious and civil functions, inas-
" much as these last are connected with our reli-
" gion. All children of the Jews of the depart-
" ment, and of those who will have voluntarily
" consented to contribute, according to their
" means, to the general fund, shall be admitted in
" the establishments for education, and in the
" houses of industry, instruction, arts, and trade.
" We may easily fix the mode of collecting the ne-
" cessary contributions, and of accounting for the
" produce, by placing at the head of the adminis-
" tration men in whom we can confide. By means
" of this general contribution we shall likewise
" relieve and prevent the wants of our aged and
" infirm poor, who are unable to earn their daily
" bread. It is exclusively to this class that we
" must direct our attention and extend our cares:
" but we must go farther; and when we meet with
" men able to work unblushingly asking for alms,
" let us strive to refuse them; let them experience
" the harshness of a humiliating refusal, however
" repugnant to our charity and to our feelings.
" By this means we shall put a stop to idleness,
" which too often prefers the bread of charity to
" that of labour. If we have been reproached at
" one time with want of industry, indolence, and

" aversion to labour, let us now avoid such re-
" proaches, which might be unjust formerly, but
" which we should now deserve. Let us exert all
" our influence to accustom our poor, who, till
" now, have been fed by our alms, to prefer the
" gains of labour, even at the sweat of their brows.
" In thus imparting to you my humble ideas on
" our present situation, I am, dear brethren, fulfil-
" ling a duty the most congenial to my feelings.
" My thoughts, as you may see, are presented to
" you in a crude state: it is by your attention and
" by your meditations, should you deem them wor-
" thy of them, that they are to be matured and
" quickened into action. Whatever success may
" attend them, I hope, at least, that you shall do
" justice to the fraternal sentiments, which, un-
" mixed with any other motives, have urged me
" to exhort and press you, dear brethren, not to
" lose one moment in taking our situation into
" your consideration.
" I have the honour to be most fraternally,
" Gentlemen and dear brethren,
" Your most obedient
" And very humble servant,
(Signed)   " BERR-ISAAC-BERR."

Every one must feel that this letter deserves to
be preserved, and to be handed down to posterity.

It will be a lasting monument of the good sense of the Israelites acquainted with their duties, and enlightened as to their true interests. It will prove that, at the very epoch when the rights of citizens have been conferred on individuals, till then pining unregarded in an abyss of misfortune, those among them who were able to make them acquainted with all the advantages of their new condition, have been eager to instruct them; and it is certainly obvious that these men, well apprized of the habits, the misfortunes, and, if you will have it so, the weaknesses of their brethren, were before-hand certain of the success of their observations, since they chose to give them so great a publicity.

It would be an absurd thing to suppose that M. Berr-Isaac-Berr was writing in 1791, for the very purpose of anticipating the contrast between the future conduct of the Jews and his sentiments, and was thus preparing, beforehand, against his brethren a mass of proofs to convince them of want of submission and of a breach of the oath they were about to take.

It is impossible not to own that he published this letter because, like all men well informed of the principles of their religion, he was firmly and sincerely persuaded that his brethren would not turn a deaf ear to the voice of the country, and

to that of honour, but would eagerly fulfil all the
duties of their new condition.

We see therefore, a praise-worthy zeal in this
conduct of M. Berr-Isaac-Berr, and in that of the
other Israelites, who, like him, have enlightened
their brethren at the epoch of the decree of September, 1791.

On the other hand, the publication of this letter proves, that there was then a well-grounded
hope and a moral certainty, that all the Israelites
would loyally exert themselves to deserve the favour conferred on them by that law, in fulfilling
all the conditions which did not militate against
their religious principles.

And all this has been confirmed by their conduct since 1791.

In general, the Jews become Frenchmen have
fulfilled their new duties; this is notorious: all
have been faithful to the laws of *regenerated* France;
all have done their duty as national guards; all
have vied with Frenchmen in zeal for the defence
of the country. Many have vested their fortunes
in landed property, others in commercial establishments; some have acquired celebrity in sciences; some, too, have acquired honour in the
fields of glory; and these last are certainly entitled to some praise for their constancy in overcom-
ing the disheartening obstacles thrown in their
way by illiberal prejudices.

The errors of some Jews (2) have aggravated the misfortunes of their fellow-citizens; but the justice of the laws has put a stop to the evil; and, what is still better, the source of the mischief is on the point of being closed by decisions and regulations, for which we shall be indebted to the great thoughts of our august Emperor.

I own it; thus far the habits of some of our brethren have afforded pretences to censure; and indeed there were not wanting men to take hold of the subject, in order to make it the theme of their declamations against us all indiscriminately.

In February, 1806, means were sought to plunge us again into misfortune. M. de Bonald, more advantageously known by other publications, made this the subject of his observations, and I must give an account of them in this collection.

I have pledged myself to disguise nothing, and I shall adhere to my engagements. It is necessary that our brethren, that our children, should be ac-

(2) This is a hint at the enormous usury practised by the Jews, who have been known to take five and six per cent. per month upon bills of landholders, the payment of which was the more secure, as, by the present French laws, landed property is liable to those debts, and a man's estate may be sold there for the most trivial debt of that nature, with less formality and delay than would be necessary to foreclose a mortgage in this country. The evil had risen to such a height, that an imperial decree had suspended actions for debt in departments where Jews chiefly reside. We shall see more on this subject in the course of this work.

quainted with whatever has passed. It is our duty to strengthen our political situation by all the means which can possibly prevent dangerous in-fringements. We must never forget all the pains we have experienced before we could be admitted citizens of a great state; we must frequently look back; we must transmit to our children all that has been published by our enemies, boasting of their zeal, with a view to plunge us again into a state of slavery inimical to prosperity. Our chil-dren, like ourselves, will then appreciate more justly the advantages of our new condition, and all the extent of the duty imposed on them, to shew themselves worthy of it. By this they will shew our sincere gratitude for the benefits which are our pride, and at the same time they will put a stop to those prejudices, which, grounded on the errors of some of us, have uniformly gi-ven birth to declamations against us all, highly detrimental, till now, to our dearest interests.

I am then to give an account of M. de Bonald's observations; but I must first notice a publication of a M. Poujol, entitled, *Some Observations con-cerning the Jews in general, and particularly those of Alsace.*

The general wish has been that I should give the priority to this work of M. Poujol; and I am the more induced to do it, as he has gone farther than any of our enemies. Indeed he has been so far led astray by error, that he has proposed *to deprive us, at least for a time, of the rights of citizenship!* He proposes, consequently, the revocation of the decree of 1791, and would, by an act of the legislature, throw us again in the forlorn state from whence we have been extricated by the first National Assembly, deferring, says he, to restore to us the rank of citizens till such time as the measures he proposes will have made us more deserving of it.

This is plainly proposing the question, Whether the public power should not go back to the decree of 1791, to rescind and annul it?

It is then perfectly right that I should first examine a question which, by attacking that decree, undermines the very basis of our new condition.

This inquiry will further the views of M. Poujol, if, as he has said in his preface, he wishes sincerely that *his ideas should be matured in the contest of a sound discussion.*

Certainly this expression itself is not sufficiently *matured*; however, I understand it. M. Poujol begins the discussion. He courts inquiry, to appear just and impartial; he cannot, therefore, take it amiss, if his ideas are submitted to a close investigation. The task of *maturing* them rested with him; no one but himself can judge or appreciate his meaning but by his expressions: and since I see myself called upon to publish a critical examination, I wish, in my turn, that M. Poujol may read it with the intention of benefitting by the solutions I give of his questions, and which I trust will be found satisfactory.

In a critical discussion, an adversary must expect no favour.

I cannot pass over even the epigraph M. Poujol has affixed to his publication.

It is a strange inconsistency to introduce the idea of all manner of crimes in the title-page of a publication, held out as impartial, and whose pretended aim is to bring about, with more certainty, the happiness of those who are the objects of it.

In this the heart of M. Poujol is not to blame, if, as he says in his preface, he had no injuries of his friends to avenge.

But, what name are we to give to that kind of wit, which, affecting a treacherous indulgence, ushers in his protestations by announcing that the subject he is going to treat will offer the picture of all the crimes which have ever disgraced mankind?

If the inquirer cannot impeach the rectitude of M. Poujol's intentions, he may justly reproach him with a great error of judgment.

Again, was he more judicious in the time chosen to publish his Observations? after the decree of
May 30, 1806, (3) and during the sittings of the assembly it had called together? and at such a moment M. Poujol writes to inquire *what are the fittest
ways to reform the manners and the habits of the Jews,
and to induce them to adopt those of the nation to
which they belong?*

These questions were already decided; the
necessary resolutions were adopted; and this
is proved by the imperial decree of the 30th of
May itself, and by the benevolent declarations
contained in its preamble.

*We had an express declaration that their errors,
or if you will have it so, their faults, sprung from the
degrading state to which they had been too long reduced.*

Another declaration, equally express, states, that
it is not the sovereign's intention *to maintain
and to renew this order of things.*

It is then very evident, that M. Poujol has proposed an useless inquiry. It is evident that his
publication is the produce of error, if not of hatred.

(3) An assembly had been called together to assist by its observations
in the choice of the means which might be successfully employed to induce the Jews to follow *useful professions*, and to replace, by *an honest industry*, those *shameful resources* to which they had too long resorted.

Why open a discussion on matters already settled by a solemn imperial decree?

M. Poujol has been unwittingly hurried by his wish of indulging in unavailing declamations.

This of itself would be a sufficient reason to reject his pamphlet among those publications which are the offspring of error or passion, which do not even deserve the attention of the wise or the honest man.

But there are, besides, special motives which have actuated M. Poujol, and these I must notice.

Mark the drift and meaning of his publication; he proposes to take from us, *at least for some time*, the benefits resulting from the decree of 1791.

And this he proposes because, as he says in the course of his Observations, we must be made to be what we ought to be, before we can be considered as citizens.

But, first. Why that daring censure on the imperial decree of the 30th of May, 1806?

What, our august Emperor, constituted the guardian of the French constitution, has declared that *it is not his intention to maintain or to renew the degrading state to which we have been too long reduced!*

And M. Poujol wants to bring us back to it, simply by annulling the decree of 1791!

In opposition to those benevolent and protecting

intentions, to which we are indebted for the decree of the 30th of May, 1806, M. Poujol proposes an act pregnant with confusion and destruction, such as the blind policy of former centuries too often produced.

If such an idea does not tell against his heart, if it is not the proof of most malignant hatred, it affords, at least, an instance of want of judgment, which borders on insanity.

Indeed this idea of M. Poujol is so vicious in every point of view that it cannot fail of meeting with universal reprobation.

In writing these Observations, M. Poujol had forgot then the assertion he makes in his preface.

He says there, *that the facts and observations he is going to preface can and must be applicable to the German Jews only, and not to the Portuguese Jews, who form a different sect.*

How has it happened, then, that the measures he proposes should be levelled indiscriminately at all the Jews who are become French citizens? M. Poujol has thus given an instance of inconsistency; his warmth or his hatred have carried him beyond the bounds he himself had fixed.

Why did he announce that his Observations were applicable to *German Jews* only, if his intention was to attack all those who have been made French citizens?

Or, if he really intended to stand forth against the German Jews only, why pass over the exception he had made himself in favour of the Portuguese Jews?

I should ask also, why M. Poujol, in acknowledging that he should except the Portuguese, has forgot the Avignonese Jews?

He must know, or assuredly he can learn, that when the first National Assembly took into its consideration the situation of the Jews in France, its decrees expressly mentioned *Portuguese, Spanish, and Avignonese Jews, the Jews of Alsace, and of the other provinces* (4). He may learn, that this assembly having made no distinction, all the Jews residing in France, from whatever country they came, enjoy the rights of French citizens.

Why then except the Portuguese Jews only, from a measure apparently levelled against the German Jews only?

And lastly, Why, according to M. Poujol's ideas, why, I say, include in a kind of general ostracism even those among the Portuguese, Spanish, Avignonese, or German Jews, who, previous to the year 1789, had obtained letters of naturalization? had acquired landed property or commercial establishments, which they securely enjoyed, and had a right to enjoy as French citizens?

(4) Decrees of the 28th of January, and 16th of April, 1790.

For it is notorious, that, besides the Jews of Bourdeaux and of Metz, who had collectively obtained that privilege by letters patent, many individuals had obtained letters of naturalization. M. Poujol may also rest assured, and it is easy to prove, that Avignonese Jews had also been naturalized as Frenchmen, and on the strength of that they had acquired landed property, which was indeed almost their whole fortune.

What would become of them? How should they rank in society, they or their descendants, if, according to M. Poujol's ideas, all Jews should lose their rights of naturalization?

The decree of the 2d of January, which declares that they shall enjoy *the rights of active citizens*, should then be annulled likewise.

And this would produce a fresh degree of confusion.

We must be astonished, from every circumstance, that M. Poujol, who has proved himself an able writer, should not have perceived that his plan and his ideas are in open contradiction with all the principles of public order and of private interest.

How could it have escaped him, that the resolutions of the imperial decree of the 30th of May, 1806, without altering the laws of 1790 and 1791, contains all the rules of our future conduct, and all the means which an enlightened benevolence could suggest to conciliate all clashing interests, and to make all the Israelites, even those who were guilty of the faults laid to their charge, worthy of their new condition.

Instead of a distinction, which a partial measure would have rendered necessary, in order to except those Jews residing in France who have proved worthy of the benefits of the law, the decree of the 30th of May grounds its wise resolutions on the general basis fixed in 1791; and this is certainly a grand and glorious thought of a protecting genius.

Again.---Instead of proposing inquisitorial measures, by which every Israelite residing in France would have been, in a manner, brought to account for his conduct, government has included them all in its thoughts, has selected the good to bring back the weak to their duty, and to create, with salutary foresight, the means of preventing future evils.

M. Poujol has misconceived every thing; the pen should have dropped from his hand, or, better still, he should not have taken it up, since he declares that he has been struck by the sublime wisdom of the measures prescribed by the imperial decree of the 30th of May, 1806.

M. Poujol ought to have perceived also that the kind of measures prescribed in this decree, indicated that the views of His Imperial Majesty were

G

directed towards the attainment of advantages which will be an eternal source of glory and of prosperity for the whole empire.

Is it by rigorous measures that moral improvements are to be effected? That men debarred from civil rights by ancient prejudices are to be restored to society? That they are to be rendered subservient to the interests of arts and of commerce for which they are so eminently qualified by their industry and by their economy?

And why make use of compulsion, when reason and persuasion may, with more certainty and more glory, produce all the wished for advantages?

What then must be the present thoughts of M. Poujol? now that this first examination of his publication must have exposed its glaring errors even to himself? especially now, that our august Emperor has announced, by a recent resolution, that this benevolence calls on all Israelites scattered on the face of the globe, to pave the way for institutions conceived in his sublime wisdom?

The measures proposed by M. Poujol would have prevented any good effects; they would have rendered success impossible. A great Emperor, by his justice, by his wisdom, and by the sublimity of his views, has created means which will be crowned with such successes as to astonish the world.

The great work will be accomplished. France will become the common country of all Israelites, capable of fulfilling all the moral duties of man. A combination of knowledge will produce incalculable advantages; their blessings, ascending to the God of their fathers, will be the solemn pledges of their gratitude.

And when we should give ourselves up entirely to the contemplation of those exalted ideas, M. Poujol presumes to mislead the judgment of his readers, by saying that His Imperial Majesty has conceived the idea of *doing what the greatest sovereigns had vainly attempted to do in former centuries.*

It is not proved that the idea of giving the Jews all the rights of citizens useful to society, has ever been entertained.

Oppressive means have always been unjustly resorted to and renewed against them ; they have always been punished with excessive severity, perhaps for crimes almost justifiable by the injustice to which they have been subjected.

And was it even true, that other sovereigns had ever entertained the idea of giving the Jews an acknowledged rank in the state, still it is beyond a doubt that excessive prejudices have been productive of great evil, by constantly preventing so generous an idea from being carried into execution.

Still, in this point of view, the whole merit is to be solely attributed to the measures of the decree of the 30th of May, and of that now preparing, which will combine whatever instruction and the love of duty can suggest, to assuage, on the one hand, the religious apprehensions of the Israelites, and to conquer, on the other, those prejudices which have too long raised enemies against them.

M. Poujol has filled three chapters of his publication with common place subjects often treated before, and now unwittingly or maliciously reproduced. One is an *exposition of facts, explanatory of the laws concerning the Jews;* the other, *a view of the measures adopted against them in several countries, and particularly in France and in Alsace;* the third is a faithful account of *the manners and present habits of the Jews in general, and particularly of the Jews of Alsace.* Every thing that could be said on this head will be found in the *Moniteur* of the 25th of July, 1806: M. Poujol knew it, since he notices it in his preface.

Why then bring back to our minds the recollection of subjects which, to the wise and impartial man, present only scenes of misfortune?

The remembrance of these things was perfectly fresh; they were recorded in our histories; and, more than once, even in courts of justice, zealous advocates have been heard attempting to overpower the Jews against whom they were retained by the recital of all the imputations laid to the charge of their fathers.

But must the past errors, or, as they are called, the past crimes of some, be for ever the pretence or the ground of the oppression and misfortune of all?

In 1790 and 1791 every thing relating to us was perfectly known. In the very report which was read at the tribune of the first National Assembly, the committee intrusted with the inquiry disguised nothing, neither of the facts recorded in history, nor of the numerous consequences which writers have thought themselves warranted to draw from them.

But this inquiry put a stop to all opposition: it was acknowledged that, by giving the Jews a country and the rights of citizens, it would be laying the basis of their future happiness, and of all those advantages which might be expected from their residence in France.

And since, to sum up all, our august Emperor had formed the same opinion, why seek for pretexts of hatred and prejudice which an enlightened benevolence has determined to bury in oblivion? Would the Israelites be allowed to avail themselves now of the loyalty, of the fidelity, of the stupendous works of their fathers, previous to those

epochas where commenced that long train of misfortunes which are now cited against them?

This, however, would be engaging in the contro-
versy with equal weapons.

But it is agreed, and it is consonant to sound
reason, that no men whatever are to be governed
according to the prejudices which may result from
the conduct, the virtues, or the crimes of their ancestors.

Whenever men can be useful, can serve a country, and increase its means of prosperity, they
have a right to the benevolence of their fellow
men; they may expect from their wisdom all the
encouragements necessary to produce the good
they are capable of effecting.

And what influence can those results have on the
exposition which composes the fourth chapter of
M. Poujol's Observations: *What is the use which
the Jews have made since 1791 of the protection
granted to them by the laws, and of the rights of citizens which it has conferred on them?*

According to right, the faults or the misdemea-
nours of some Israelites cannot be imputable to all.

By the same rule, if some of them have been
guilty of actions which the decree of the 30th
of May, 1806, denominates *shameful resources*, how
many others have shewn talents and virtues which

have rendered them celebrated, and adorned the age they live in?

Among them may be enumerated enlightened administrators; among them may be enumerated men glowing with zeal, which they have proved by their services in the French armies; among them may be enumerated merchants highly valued in their community, and in all commercial towns.

According to the views of government, measures prepared with wisdom and foresight, writings which will disseminate instruction, will prevent the return of the talked of evils.

And most certainly it is wiser to forgive a few misguided men, than to seek in their faults a pretence to punish those who have always fulfilled their duties.

That is by far the surer way to obtain those advantages which may be expected from the great views of a sovereign, who in this, as in every thing else, will be held as a model to future centuries.

M. Poujol has been guilty of a very strange error when he affirms, in his Observations, that *no measures can be taken to correct the manners and the habits of the Jews, without taking from them the rights of citizens.*

To make any class of men better, why should it be necessary to go back to the social contract, to rescind and annul it as far as it concerns them, and to begin by throwing them back in a forlorn state of political nullity?

Can the country find no other means to bring her children back to habits of virtue, that she should resort to the violent measures of exclusion and ostracism against those she wants to improve?

Again, how will M. Poujol reconcile his ideas with the basis laid by the constitutions of the empire, and especially that of the year 8? Are the faults, the usuries, of those Israelites who have neglected their duties, among those evils which carry with them the forfeiture or even the suspension of the rights of French citizens?

M. Poujol will not presume to say so; he must be convinced, then, that the measure he proposes would go beyond the limits fixed by the fourth and fifth articles of the constitution of the year 8: and that the act, which should thus deprive of their rights even those Israelites who have acted wrong, would be in itself an unconstitutional measure.

And what character would it assume towards those whom he acknowledges to be free from the blame he imputes to others?

M. Poujol must wonder himself at having ever conceived the horrid idea of inflicting so terrible a punishment on citizens whom he pronounces blameless.

What assurance, too, to insinuate that it is impossible to mend the morals of the Jews, or to make use *of measures not general*, against them *without depriving them of the rights of citizens!*

Indeed M. Poujol himself has taken care to prove his own error; for he says, a few pages lower down, *that the first National Assembly, in giving the Jews their liberty, seemed disposed to adopt towards them measures calculated to reform their manners and their habits.*

Taking this wish and this resolution for granted, it follows that even then the granting of the rights of citizens was not considered as an obstacle to salutary reforms.

How could M. Poujol form a different idea?

How could he take upon himself to publish an error now demonstrated more clearly than ever by the decree of the 30th of May, 1806, and by the succeeding acts?

It is acknowledged, it is settled, that the benevolence of government will bring back misled citizens to the observance of their duties, in which they will find their greatest happiness.

It is a kind of madness in a man to raise his voice in opposition, and vainly to censure the acts of the first National Assembly, and those of a sovereign who, faithful to his coronation-oath, maintains the bases fixed by our constitutional acts, and

H

magnanimously fulfils his duties by giving strength and efficacy to their dispositions.

But, on the other hand, let us see what are, according to M. Poujol, the obstacles to our reformation, which might result from the rights of citizens?

The Jews require, he says, particular *measures which are inconsistent with the title, the quality, and the prerogatives of citizens.*

Then he adds, *legislative measures are general; no particular ones can be adopted against this or that class of citizens.*

It is necessary then to exclude the Jews from the rights of citizens, in order to submit them to particular regulations, to a kind of inquisitorial police, and to more severe penalties.

Mere sophism, which most certainly proceeds from blindness, from hatred, or from the fancies of a delirious imagination.

What else is this new principle, which goes to prevent, in civil legislation, all recourse to measures required by the paramount consideration of public welfare?

In the first ages of the ancient monarchy, were not the Roman laws adopted in France, while several tribes which had obtained leave to settle in the country continued to follow their own.

In the centuries which followed, down to 1790, did we not remark in the civil code, special laws

between the lords and their vassals, and others
which made unlawful for some classes of citizens
what they allowed to others?

Are not instances of laws affecting only some
particular individuals to be found even in the present civil code?

There is, then, neither contradiction nor inconsistency when the civil law annexes to its dispositions of general interest particular exceptions
which the situation of individuals renders necessary.

Will M. Poujol, speaking as a rash reformer,
pretend that no Frenchman should be bound by
laws not general, without being previously degraded by the forfeiture of his rights of citizen?

He presumes to say that the French government
will do a great deal for the Jews by giving back
to those who may appear to deserve it those rights
which he wishes to see taken from them.

But has he calculated the extent of the calamities which would befal even those he acknowledges
as blameless from the harsh measure he proposes
against all?

Indeed M. Poujol is much to be pitied, if he does
not consider himself bound to renounce publicly
the errors and the injustices he has so plentifully
introduced in his publication.

It is certainly the duty of government to see that

justice is done to debtors who complain of u ury and extortion.

But it is equally certain that courts of justice can pronounce only according to the rules laid down by the laws.

Why then propose, in this publication, to annul written agreements freely entered into by the contracting parties?

Why bring to our recollection the ruinous epochs of the suppression and abolition of debts---measures, which to prevent the success of some partial injustices, aimed a deadly blow to all rights of property, always entitled to the protection of the law?

M. Poujol has proposed a more useful idea, an idea more consonant to the magnanimous views of government, when he has observed that a kind of special jury might with propriety settle all differences between debtors and creditors.

But why did he propose the unconstitutional measure of forming a jury of deputies, who, in the legislative body, represent the departments by which they have been returned?

Legislators can, in no case, receive from the sovereign the commission of distributing justice, as it is one of his prerogatives.

Other men, worthy of his confidence, will then be called upon, to form a special jury, whose equitable verdict will terminate suits which have already lasted too long.

The appeal proposed by M. Poujol is the last of his errors.

A trial by jury does not admit of this mode of proceeding. Our laws have wisely ordered that, in the ordinary course of justice, each suit should bear the test of two judgments.

But trials by special jury are, from their very nature, excepted from this rule. Decisions essentially grounded on the knowledge of facts, and dictated by an impartial view to general interest, admit of no revisions; they may be useful in ordinary cases, where all the rules of actions have been previously laid down by the law, but in special cases they would supersede all motives arising from circumstantial evidence, to make room for general opinions, less applicable to them, and defeating the true purposes of essential justice.

M. Poujol has not said, what, however, is very true, that his special jury would have all the characteristic of a special commission, named by the sovereign to distribute justice in his name.

But at all times and in every circumstance, the unlimited power of putting a stop to law proceedings has justified all the measures taken to fulfil that intention of the sovereign.

Thus special criminal courts have been instituted for forgery and for crimes daily renewed by a set of desperate and hardened ruffians (5).

Thus, to put a stop to the depredations committed in our forests, the court *des eaux et forêts*, (6) has been empowered to pass judgment whenever the accused has been taken in the fact, or when one of the rangers should become an accomplice for the purpose of turning evidence.

In the case before us, debtors, receiving from their sovereign a solemn pledge of his protection, will see with pleasure their interests placed in the hands of men deemed worthy of his confidence.

In this case too, the Jews, who are creditors, will see in the jury who are to decide on their demands, judges invested with a special authority, similar to that which their first lawgiver, in his wisdom, gave to those among their fathers, whom he appointed to stand at the gates of cities, to settle all differences with justice and promptitude.

(5) We believe this alludes to the famous *chauffeurs*, a gang which had ramifications over the whole country, and accomplices in men high in office: they were guilty of the most enormous atrocities, and got their name from their practice of exposing their victims to a raging fire after having rubbed them with grease, in order to make them discover where their money or other property was hid.

(6) A special tribunal, which takes cognizance of trespasses in forests, in rivers, &c.

I would also remark, if it come to my point, that the Emperor Theodosius, wishing to do strict justice to the Jews, thought that the best way was to give them particular judges, especially bound to decide according to the maxims of social interest, always paramount to every other consideration (7).

If this memorable example justifies the idea of forming a special tribunal to pronounce definitively on the merits of judgments, whose execution has been suspended by the decree of the 30th of May, it evinces at the same time the monstrous thought of giving a power of this kind to legislators actually in the exercise of their functions.

But I have said a great deal, and I have certainly dwelt long enough on M. Poujol's publication.

Let us leave him to calculate and anticipate, in his own way, the measures our august Emperor will adopt, to effect the grand regeneration he has in view.

Let us leave him in the full enjoyment of his researches, on the several useful alterations which may be effected in the rules of conduct which the Israelites have received from their doctors, without at the same time encroaching on their religious principles.

But let M. Poujol be persuaded, that, after all, success will crown whatever salutary reforms His

(7.) Theodosian Code, vol. viii. p. 227.

Imperial and Royal Majesty shall, in his wisdom, think fit to effectuate.

Let him know, that in the fifteenth century, Abarbanel, one of he most esteemed writers among the Israelitish doctors, was known by a very learned dissertation on the Bible ; and that, in this production, to which he owes, in great measure, his celebrity, he establishes a judicious distinction between things essentially connected with religious dogmas, and those which have reference only to points of civil morals, which last are always susceptible of changes and modifications, according to the civil and political state of those whose happiness they have in view.

Let us once more tell M. Poujol, and all those who, like him, are liable to unjust prejudices, that the true principles laid down by Abarbanel had been already proclaimed in the twelfth century by Maimonides, one of the greatest Rabbies that the Israelites ever had. It has been said of him, that his philosophical views excited, at first, a violent indignation among all those Hebrews who had thought, till then, that every article of the law of their fathers bore the stamp of a dogma, and, of course, that every attempt to alter them was sacrilegious. But the temperate philosophy of Maimonides soon became a source of light and instruction. There remained but few Israelites who were not convinced by his arguments; and those whom prejudice kept longer in error, were at last persuaded by the observations and proofs which the talents of Abarbanel presented in a point of view the best calculated to ensure conviction.

This first dawn of a new day had certainly been observed, when in 1783, the Academy of Metz proposed to examine *if means could be found to make the Jews happier and more useful to France?*

It was also acknowledged then, that, even without waiting for a change in their political state, it was possible to give them a milder system of morals, and habits more consonant to the interests of those nations by whom they were received and tolerated.

The question occasioned deep researches and profound reasoning; the prize was adjudged to one of those men, who, by their talents and their sublime views, have given the grand impulse to French regeneration. M. Gregoire, now a senator, proved at the same time, that neither the religion of the Jews, nor their mode of worship, were obstacles to their being made better men, and that their system of morality, brought back to its genuine principles, would make them happier and more useful.

In 1790 and 1791, men zealous for the public welfare re-produced these truths already acknowledged. No one has forgot the speeches of the

I

Gregoires, the Lally Tolendals, the Bergasses, the Desezes; their cheering assertions sprung from a consciousness of the advantages which a mild philosophy would produce, and all hearts were opened to those sentiments of benevolence, to which we were at last indebted for the salutary decree which gave us a country.

It was with wonder that in February, 1806, we saw M. de Bonald betray a weakness in blaming what had passed, and a want of candour by reproducing ancient charges which hatred had heaped against us.

His observations found a place in the *Mercure*, and there M. de Bonald wondered at the sentiments we had inspired. He went so far as to blame what had been done in 1783, and to condemn the favour we had received from the first National Assembly. The better to prejudice people's minds against the possibility of our ever becoming better, he wanted to persuade that no one had ever entertained the idea of effecting such a purpose. *The object in view*, says he, *was much rather to improve the political condition of the Jews, than to change their natural state, or to make the individuals themselves better.*

But how could it ever happen that M. de Bonald should publish such declamations, whose

manifest errors cannot but betray in him a great
want of the principles of justice?

He has, first, been guilty of an erroneous pre-
tention, by attempting to mislead the public as to
the object and the true state of the question proposed in 1783 by the Academy of Metz.

The question did not go to examine into the political condition of the Jews; the Academy pointed
out, as the only object of the researches, the means
of giving them a milder system of morality, and
habits more congenial to those of all Frenchmen.
And if, in the various means proposed, and in the
proofs adduced to support them, it has been said
that the Jews, once raised to the rank of citizens,
would be the better disposed to receive benevolent
instructions, this idea was, shortly after, sanctioned by the legislative decree of September, 1791.

M. de Bonald, in the second place, has been guilty of presumption in attempting to attack the decree which raised us to the rank of French citizens.

Doubts and opposition might have appeared
useful when the question was first proposed for discussion by the Academy at Metz.

The examination once closed, and its results,
whatever they might have been, once sanctioned by
the decree of 1791, it was the duty of M. De Bonald, in common with all his fellow-citizens, to ac-

knowledge that a superior wisdom had already placed us in a way of being more happy and more useful; and also that we had been judged by it capable of proving worthy of so great a favour.

In the third place, M. de Bonald has been guilty of the grossest calumnies in his assertions against us.

As late as the year 1767, the answer to the unjust pretentions of the body of Merchants, who wished to see us excluded from the privileges granted, at that epocha, to that class of men, had fully demonstrated, by a number of proofs, that neither our religion, nor our mode of worship, could furnish grounds to perpetuate the abject state of degradation, which was the immediate cause of the ill-conduct alleged against some of us.

The inhiretance which our lawgiver had expected us to retain, essentially constituted us a nation of husbandmen. By our dispersion we were reduced to whatever moveable property we could save from the wreck, and of course, compelled by necessity, to have recourse to commerce as the only means left to maintain our existence; and in these pursuits we reaped the greatest advantages from our economy, which insured and furthered the progress of our industry. From our experience in trade the greatest success was expected; it then became the duty of government to increase the range of our activity, as it was an inducement to grant us every facility in our commercial pursuits.

And all this was to be found in the expositions presented in 1783 to the Academy of Metz.

All this was strengthened by the authority of the benevolent decree of 1791, and by the most incontrovertible demonstrations, which have convinced every mind capable of forming a sound judgment, that our belief and our dogmas do not militate against any improvement in morals or in civilization which may be deemed necessary to make us citizens worthy of the country, and to injure that success which must contribute to its prosperity.

M. Moses Peinado, of Bourdeaux, published an answer to M. de Bonald's philippic; it was strong in proofs, and has met with no reply.

In short M. de Bonald might have been convinced by proofs of another kind before he attempted to write.

These proofs were to be found, in great number, in the observations which M. Gregoire, senator, had just published; and in documents of 1800 and 1801; by which it appeared, that the progress of instruction had already produced among the Israelites the spontaneous resolution of drawing a line, first, in the book of their law, between those institutions which relate to their belief, and those

which simply inforce rules of conduct suitable to
their then politcal situation; and secondly, in the
works of their doctors, between those interpretations connected with dogmas and the mode of
worship, to which they will always bow with faith
and submission, and those which, guided by sound
reason, have carefully selected such articles in the
book of the law and in the writings of the doctors,
as are susceptible of the alterations which a change
in the political and civil situation always renders
requisite.

In 1800 a society of Dutch Jews had published
their resolution to acknowledge only the pure and
genuine law of Moses, and to reject all those institutions which, till then, had been called *Talmudic
laws.*

This society had numerous followers. In 1801
a plan was proposed to assemble at Luneville a general congress of the representatives of all the Jews
scattered in the different countries of Europe.

The object of this assembly was known; the
strength and the authority of the proofs already
adduced left no doubt but, by general resolution,
the prejudices and practices of a baneful fanaticism should be entirely laid aside, to make room,
in whatever was not connected with dogmas and
modes of worship, for institutions calculated for
men in a state of civilization, and who already

have, or are anxious to have, a country and fellow-citizens.

It was highly important to collect all the proofs which were likely to infuse the wished for success; it was necessary to convince all sovereigns that it was incumbent on their justice to follow the example which France had given in 1791; it was necessary to prove that the ill conduct of some Jews proceeded from the unfavourable opinion by which they were degraded, and from those acts of oppression, frequently renewed with additional cruelty, by which the whole nation was held up to public contempt, and experienced the torment of a kind of slavery, the bane of every generous sentiment.

A work, entitled *An Appeal to the Justice of Kings and Nations*, written and published at Strasburgh in 1801, pointed, at the same time, the steps which the congress was to take to accelerate the moral regeneration of the Jews, and the proofs which, by removing prejudices long prevailing in Europe, and perpetuated sometimes by blind hatred, and sometimes by lawless cupidity, clearly shewed to all powers, that it was equally their duty and their interest to give all the Jews residing in their territories the rank and rights of citizens, as a means to induce them to devote themselves to the service of the country.

The hope of success was grounded, in a great
measure, on the example given by France; this
was further strengthened by historical truths,
which, by tracing a faithful picture of all the horrors of intolerance, solicited, in the name of a
God of peace, those sentiments of benevolence
and of love which men ought to have for each
other, whatever may be the principles of their religious belief.

It is a duty I owe to our brethren of all countries, to preserve, in a collection of general interest like this, the remembrance of truths, which,
after having promoted the return of happiness and
benevolence to France, cannot fail of bringing the
whole earth under the guidance of that justice,
which the wisdom of the Creator has made the
common duty of all men.

" Soon after the establishment of Christianity,"
says this writer, " the Jewish nation, dispersed
" since the second destruction of its temple, had
" totally disappeared. By the light of the flames
" which devoured the monuments of its ancient
" splendour, the conquerors beheld a million of
" victims dead or expiring on their ruins. The
" hatred of the enemies of that unfortunate na-
" tion raged longer than the fire which had con-
" sumed its temple; active and relentless, it still
" pursues and oppresses them in every part of the

" globe over which they are scattered. Their per-
" secutors delight in their torments too much to
" seal their doom by a general decree of proscrip-
" tion, which would at once put an end to their
" burthensome and painful existence. It seems as if
" they were allowed to survive the destruction of
" their country, only to see the most odious and
" calumnious imputations laid to their charge, to
" stand as the constant object of the grossest and
" most shocking injustice, as a mark for the insult-
" ing finger of scorn, as a sport to the most invete-
" rate hatred; it seems as if their doom was inces-
" santly to suit all the dark and bloody purposes
" which can be suggested by human malignity,
" supported by ignorance and fanaticism.

" Weighed down by taxes, and forced to contri-
" bute more than Christians for the support of so-
" ciety, they had hardly any of the rights which it
" gives. If a destructive scourge happened to
" spread havock among the inhabitants of a coun-
" try, the Jews had poisoned the springs, or those
" men, cursed by Heaven, had, nevertheless, in-
" censed it, by their prayers, against the nation
" they were supposed to hate. Did sovereigns
" want pecuniary assistance to carry on their
" wars? The Jews were compelled to give up
" those riches in which they sought some consola-
" tion against the oppressing sense of their abject

K

" condition: as a reward for their sacrifices, they
" were expelled from the state they had support-
" ed, and they were afterwards recalled to be
" stript again. Compelled to wear exteriorly the
" badges of their abject state, they were, every
" where, exposed to the insults of the vilest popu-
" lace. When from his solitary retreat an enthu-
" siastic hermit preached the crusades to the na-
" tions of Europe, and a part of its inhabitants
" left their country to moisten with their blood
" the plains of Palestine, the knell of promiscuous
" massacre tolled before the alarm-bell of war.
" Millions of Jews were then murdered to glut the
" pious rage of the crusaders. It was by tearing
" the entrails of their brethren that these warriors
" sought to deserve the protection of Heaven.
" Skulls of men and bleeding hearts were offered as
" holocausts on the altars of that God who has no
" pleasure even in the blood of the innocent lamb,
" and ministers of peace were thrown into a holy
" enthusiasm by these bloody sacrifices. It is thus
" that Basil, Treves, Coblentz, and Cologn, be-
" came human shambles. It is thus that upwards
" of four hundred thousand victims, of all ages,
" and of both sexes, lost their lives at Cesarea and
" Alexandria. The recollection of these horrors
" draws tears of blood from my eyes, and I cannot
" help blushing for the whole race of mankind.

" And is it after they have experienced such treat-
" ment that they are reproached with their vices?
" Is it after being for eighteen centuries the sport
" of contempt, that they are reproached with be-
" ing no longer alive to it? Is it after having so
" often glutted with their blood the thirst of their
" persecutors, that they are held out as enemies to
" other nations? Is it, when they have been be-
" reft of all means to mollify the hearts of their
" tyrants, that indignation is roused if, now and
" then, they cast a mournful look towards the ru-
" ins of their temple, towards their country, where,
" formerly, happiness crowned their peaceful days,
" free from the cares of ambition and of riches?
" Is it when the career of arts and of industry has
" been completely shut against them, that the
" Jewish nation is represented as a lazy, indolent,
" useless race, a burthen to the country which
" supports them? But whither am I going? Our
" persecutors would have us to kiss our fetters, and
" hug to our hearts the murderers of our brethren,
" in return for the inveteracy which they manifest
" against us every where but in France. The
" slightest expression of grief wrung from us,
" marks us a ferocious people. They wish to take
" from us even the last distant hope of future hap-
" piness, to seize whatever belongs to us most legi-
" timately, and that, like senseless victims, we

" should in the mean time refrain from any sign of
" resentment, which, powerless in itself, excites on-
" ly derision or contempt.

" Since the light of philosophy began to dawn
" over Europe, our enemies have ceased to satisfy
" their revenge with the sacrifice of our lives;
" Jews are no longer seen, who, generously refu-
" sing to bend under the yoke of intolerance, were
" led with solemn pomp to the fatal pile: but al-
" though the times of these barbarous executions
" are past long ago, although the hearts of sove-
" reigns are now strangers to this cruelty, yet sla-
" very itself and prejudices are still the same.
" By what crimes have we then deserved this furi-
" ous intolerance? What is our guilt? Is it in
" that generous constancy we have manifested in
" defending the laws of our fathers? But this con-
" stancy ought to have entitled us to the admira-
" tion of all nations, and it has only sharpened
" against us the daggers of persecution. Braving
" all kinds of torments, the pangs of death, the
" still more terrible pangs of life, we alone have
" withstood the impetuous torrent of time, sweep-
" ing indiscriminately in its course nations, reli-
" gions, and countries. What is become of those
" celebrated empires, whose very name still excites
" our admiration by the ideas of splendid great-
" ness attached to them, and whose power embra-

" ced the whole surface of the known globe? They
" are only remembered as monuments of the va-
" nity of human greatness.........Rome and Greece
" are no more; their descendants, mixed with
" other nations, have lost even the traces of their
" origin; while a population of a few millions of
" men, so often subjugated, stands the test of thir-
" ty revolving centuries, and the fiery ordeal of
" fifteen centuries of persecution! We still pre-
" serve laws which were given to us in the first
" days of the world, in the infancy of nature!
" The last followers of a religion which had em-
" braced the universe have disappeared these fif-
" teen centuries, and our temples are still stand-
" ing! We alone have been spared by the indis-
" criminating hand of time, like a column left
" standing amidst the wreck of worlds and the
" ruins of nature. The history of this people
" connects present times with the first ages of the
" world, by the testimony it bears of the existence
" of those early periods; it begins at the cradle of
" mankind, and its remnants are likely to be preser-
" ved to the very day of universal destruction. All
" men, whatever may be their opinions and the
" party they have adopted, whether they suppose
" that the will of God is to maintain the people he
" has chosen, or whether they consider that con-
" stancy which characterises the Jews as a repre-
" hensible obstinacy, or if, at last, they believe in

" a God, who, regarding all religions with equal
" complacency, needs no other wonders to exem-
" plify his greatness, but the incessant and magni-
" ficent display of the beauties of nature, all, if
" their minds are susceptible of appreciating virtue
" and tried firmness, will not refuse their just ad-
" miration to that unshaken constancy unparallel-
" ed in the annals of any nation."

To this picture of the calamities which have so
long pressed on the Israelites, are joined plans and
views which seem calculated to induce all civilized countries to restore them to the rights which
they have recovered in France.

" The enquiry has three objects in view ; I wish
" to prove, that the exclusion of the Jews from the
" rights of citizens, is at the same time *immoral*,
" *unjust*, and *impolitic*.

" It is *immoral*, because no government can re-
" fuse an equal degree of protection and justice to
" all those inhabitants of the country who consent
" to become parties in the social contract, which
" alone constitutes the existence of legitimate go-
" vernment, whatever may be its form ; and because
" religion has nothing to do with the political and
" civil existence of citizens.

" It is *unjust*, because the vices with which many
" among the Jews have been reproached, with
" some truth, are not, as their enemies pretend, in
" their natural dispositions, but are certainly the fa-

" tal and unavoidable consequence of the abject
" state of slavery in which they have so long re-
" mained; and because they besides make up for
" those foibles by virtues which exclusively belong
" to them, and which the most inveterate foes have
" never as yet attempted to deny.

" It is *impolitic*, because the Jews have proved ve-
" ry useful citizens, whenever they have met with
" just and humane governments, and because the
" states of Europe, who often feel the necessity of
" increasing their population, deprive themselves,
" by this exclusion, of the industry of a people who,
" to prove that in zeal and patriotism they are in-
" ferior to no class of citizens, are only waiting for
" the liberty they solicit, to exert all their activity
" and to direct it to public advantage."

On each of these heads the author gave the arguments and proofs which brought about the memorable decree of 1791; and, at last, to move to pity
hearts hardened by prejudices, he gave the still
faithful picture of the virtues by which, at the example of France, the Israelites deserve to be considered by other nations as being capable of all the
sentiments and all the zeal which constitute useful
citizens.

" You," said he, " you who consider as depraved,
" men who are only unfortunate, come with me
" and study their passions and their private actions,
" not in books in which hatred has instilled its,

" venom, but in the circle of their families, and
" amidst the objects of their affections and, if the
" expression could be allowed, under the protection
" of their household gods. It is among these men,
" whom you consider as the refuse of nature, that
" you will find, in all their simplicity, the senti-
"ments of nature divested of the dross of luxury
" and of the refinements of wit. Their common
" sufferings, the enthusiasm produced by persecu-
" tion, have united them in the bonds of sacred
" friendship, which the most hardened man could
" not behold without shedding tears of sensibility.
" Tossed in the wide world by his evil fate, the
" Jew, wandering, often without assistance, a prey
" to misery, on an unknown shore, in meeting with
" a fellow sufferer, always meets with a brother,
" ready to sacrifice for him his fortune and his life.
" Morose philosophers pretend that misfortunes
" deaden sensibility; I believe, on the contrary, for
" the honour of mankind, that weeping over our
" own misfortunes, teaches us to weep over those of
" others. It is in the crucible of adversity that the
" Jew has acquired that feeling soul which is his
" characteristic. No where are the poor of that
" nation seen abandoned without assistance to be-
" come a burthen to the country; and while those
" very men, who regard as barbarians those who
" are strangers to the world and to its ways, reluc-

" tantly give a trifling portion of their superfluity
" to the wretched victims of misery, a people whose
" name is held almost synonymous with ferocity,
" would really think they should deserve the ap-
" pellation, if they could hesitate to share their
" moderate resources with the unfortunate who
" surround them. Those who delight in affixing
" guilty intentions to praise-worthy actions will
" see nothing in this union but a dangerous associ-
" ation; but the sentimental observer will never
" hold back his just approbation.

" It is also in this devoted nation that we must
" seek for that inviolable attachment among the
" members of the same family, too scarce among
" us, where gloomy jealousy, a spirit of contradic-
" tion and hatred, almost always divides those
" whom nature intended to bind in everlasting
" friendship. There, you will never see ungrate-
" ful children, unmindful of the last will of their
" parent, tearing each other to come at the spoils
" of their father.

" Luxury, that bane of virtue and of peace, is
" hardly known among them; their inclinations
" and their sentiments are unsophisticated, like na-
" ture, from whence they spring; they do not know,
" it is true, how to deck with all the ornaments
" of eloquence, actions which they consider as du-
" ties: but if they do not know how to extoll the

L

" charms of virtue, they have learnt to appreciate
" its intrinsic worth.

" You will see but seldom among them guilty
" husbands leaving their virtuous partners for aban-
" doned prostitutes, or shameless wives abandon-
" ing the care of their families, and the sacred du-
" ties of matrimony and maternity, to plunge heed-
" lessly into debauchery.

" It is there that lovely chastity follows the graces
" and enhances their charms; there an amiable blush
" still overspreads the face of the modest virgin.

" The dissolution of the sacred tie of marriage,
" altho allowed by their religion, always leaves the
" stamp of reprobation on him who gives the sad
" example of divorce. Vainly would you attempt
" to find among the Jews, people who coolly part
" after solemn oaths of eternal love, and who give
" up without emotion the blessing of ever behold-
" ing the innocent beings who owe to them their
" existence.

" But you will find among them couples united
" by the bonds of the most inviolable attachment,
" who, finding in their old age the first links which
" bring to their minds the beginning of their union,
" bedew with their tears those sacred pledges of love;
" you will find mothers who weep for joy when the
" solemn day approaches in which they are to lead
" an only daughter under the sacred nuptial veil;

" you will find fathers of families whose only care
" is to insure the happiness of dutiful children,
" who are one day to follow their example.

" Observe, ye philosophers, who delight in stu-
" dying the heart of man, and in penetrating in-
" to its inmost recesses; mark what distinguishes,
" among all others, the funeral of a father of a
" family of the Jewish nation : you will never re-
" mark there those forced tears which a trouble-
" blesome sense of propriety draws from men,
" who, for a great while before, were hastening, by
" their wishes, the moment when they would bar-
" ter for a vile metal even the picture of their fa-
" ther: there you will see real grief, surrounded by
" its darkest and heart-rending attributes; children
" frantic with despair, tearing their hair and their
" clothes, covering their forehead with dust and
" ashes, embracing the inanimate corpse of their
" father, and rending the air with their dismal
" cries.

" Come with me into their cemeteries, where
" every thing traces this idea, that death is the
" passage to immortality. Behold those friends,
" lying on the tombs of their departed friends,
" and kissing with transport their cold inanimate
" remains. There, at least, if an envious fate de-
" prive me of the object of my affections, I shall
" bedew his tomb with my tears......In this dreary

" and silent abode I shall exclaim, ' Consoling im-
" mortality? no, thou art not a chimera.' The
" souls of those benevolent beings, whose endear-
" ing intercourse made the delight of my life, are
" not surely returned to non-entity ; they exist, no
" doubt, in a better and purer world; they are ho-
" vering around me; they hear me; and they are
" the judges of my actions. If ever I should
" swerve from the path of virtue, if ever I should
" forget my duties, I would go to this abode of
" melancholy, and, bedewing the sacred tomb
" with tears of repentance, I should again become
" worthy of visiting these monuments of my love.

" Will you learn how to appreciate still better a
" nation which owed its abject state solely to its
" misfortunes? Reflect on the part the Jews have
" acted in the French revolution, and during the
" reign of terror; when, suddenly made free, they
" dared to look in the face those who lately had a
" right to insult them with impunity. I ask those
" men who know how the multitude is inclined to
" pass without reflexion from one extreme to ano-
" ther, and how much persecution sours even the
" mildest tempers—I ask them, I say, in what class
" was it likely to find the greatest number of
" those, who, regardless of the most sacred and
" inviolable duties, have shewn to what excesses
" men may be hurried by the violence of passion?

" How natural it was to expect that the Jews, in
" frantic delirium, would have laid destructive
" hands on the very last traces of a form of go-
" vernment under which they had suffered so
" much! Well! let the blood-stained annals of the
" infamous reign of Roberspierre be opened, and
" if, in the number of his supporters, you find the
" name of one of these men, who alone could be
" justified by the sense of their former sufferings,
" I abandon every one of them to their sad fate.

" Neither will you find among them those
" unnatural children who carried sword and
" flames into their country, which ought always
" to have been dear to them, who incurred the ha-
" tred of their countrymen and the contempt of
" sovereigns, forced by circumstances to assist
" them for a while, though they could never esteem
" traitors and perjurors, men very different from
" those who left their country only in those disas-
" trous times when no one could be just or virtu-
" ous with impunity. But you will find the Jews
" in the path of true honour and of military glo-
" ry; you will see them shedding their blood in
" the service of their country; obtaining, by their
" bravery, the admiration of generous enemies;
" deserving, in short, to be considered as men and
" as citizens, wherever those titles are granted to

" them, as they are elsewhere patient and submis-
" sive under the yoke which bears on them.

" Shall the pecuniary advantages, which go-
" vernments derive from the extraordinary contri-
" butions levied on the Jews, be put in the scale
" against the glory of proclaiming an act of jus-
" tice, which is required by so many powerful
" reasons? Should we even suppose for a moment
" the truth of that fallacious assertion of the
" friends of anarchy, that interest is the sole spring
" of kingly governments, still it would be evident,
" to every enlightened mind, that the pecuniary
" advantages accruing to the state from the extra-
" ordinary contributions which lay heavy on the
" Jews, can by no means compensate for the losses
" which sovereigns experience by depriving them-
" selves of the industry of so numerous a class.
" The greatest part of the European states cannot
" increase their resources as much as they wish;
" most frequently, and without a doubt, from want
" of a sufficient population: and while many of
" them collect, at a vast expence, thousands of co-
" lonists, who cannot be thoroughly incorporated
" with the people, but after many generations, and
" who, for a great length of time, consider them-
" selves as foreigners, they refuse to naturalize
" men, who could not but consider that as their

" country which has given them birth, since there
" alone they could expect to lead a happy and
" quiet life.

" But is it impossible that the views even of the
" present government, should tend to the abolition
" of the Jewish religion, whose existence is loath-
" some to many? Is it not with an intention to
" force the Jews to a complete union with other
" nations, not only by the tie of friendship, but
" by those of blood and of religion, that the
" remnants of the ancient settled system of per-
" secution is so constantly followed up against
" them? I think that I have proved, in the begin-
" ning of this work, that I am far from imputing
" views so intolerant to the sovereigns of the
" eighteenth century; and besides, where is the
" man so little acquainted with the human heart,
" as not to know, that at all times, martyrs have
" sprung up at the fierce cries of persecution, and
" that man prizes the objects of his love only from
" the extent of the sacrifices they cost him? The
" hope of detaching the Jews from the religion of
" their fathers must be extravagant and ground-
" less, as long as they shall be obliged to endure
" the greatest hardships to follow it.

" Is it not owing to the rage of the Inquisition
" and to *Auto da fez*, that we must principally at-
" tribute the miraculous existence of this nation

" through the greatest revolutions which have
" changed the face of the globe? When religi-
" on shall have ceased to be for them the dear
" bought consolation of so many sacrifices, usher-
" ed into the busy scenes of life, Will they not
" begin to experience the workings of ambi-
" tion, superseding in their hearts their religious
" sentiments? Then, and then only, some hopes
" may be entertained that they may, at some fu-
" ture period, renounce their ancient faith. What-
" ever, in short, may be the just or unjust views
" which are supposed to actuate governments, it is
" an undoubted fact, that the abject state in which
" the Jews are kept, even now, is excessively impo-
" litic, and contrary to the interests of those who
" might put a stop to it. Every thing proves that
" even their regeneration, which was thought to
" be the work of centuries, will be equally sudden
" and complete. The rapid progress which the
" French Jews have already made in the career of
" civilization, are the surest pledges of this pro-
" mise ; the greatest number of them have already
" got rid of that timid crouching demeanour,
" which excluded them from company, or made
" them appear ridiculous. The greater part,
" throwing off perjudices of all kinds, intend
" their children for honourable professions, in-
" stead of limiting their views, as they hither-
" to have done. Many attend the national

" schools with the most brilliant success, and bid
" fair to increase the demesne of sciences by their
" labours and by their genius. The Jew avoided
" the Christian, only because he saw in him a fero-
" cious and inveterate enemy; the Christian avoid-
" ed the Jew, only because he considered him as a
" being devoted from his brith to contempt and
" slavery ; friendship has been the mutual wish of
" both, as soon as they have learnt to esteem each
" other. What should we mind if a few men still
" preserve hatred against us? They alone are to
" be pitied, since they are strangers to the sweets of
" reconciliation.

" I shall not deny that many among us, still deaf
" to the voice of reason, persist in drawing all their
" resources from a shameful and dishonest traffic:
" but this obstinacy of a few individuals will ap-
" pear astonishing only to men unacquainted with
" the force of habit, and with the time and cares
" necessary to change the manners and the dispo-
" sitions of a whole nation. I must add, that in
" other European countries, the Jews must ad-
" vance more rapidly in civilization than they have
" done in France, where, since the revolution, each
" succeeding government, intent only on the de-
" struction of its predecessors, could not accele-
" rate their progress, nor gradually encourage
" them. It is incumbent on every government to

M

" shew the ridiculousness of prejudices, without
" openly and violently attacking them; to engage
" Jewish parents, or even to compel them, to send
" their children to share the advantages of public
" instruction; to grant signal rewards to the first
" who should prove, by their success, that they are
" susceptible of emulation; to punish with seve-
" rity whoever, by his discourses or by his actions,
" should betray lurking symptoms of suspicion or
" hatred; such, once more, are the duties of all
" governments towards a class of men, who must,
" at last, be restored to happiness; duties which
" the French government has not till now been
" able to fulfil, and which are well worthy of the
" monarchs of the eighteenth century."

The manner in which these several measures
should be put in activity has been already detailed in many publications I have quoted, and
principally in the excellent dissertation of M.
Dohm, which, for its logic, precision, and sound
reasoning, I shall here quote again.

" The eternal principles of morality, on which
" monarchies, as well as republics, are grounded,
" those even of a sound and true policy, require
" that an end should be put, for ever, to the shame-
" ful slavery of the Jews; that they should be freed
" from personal tributes, that the career of indus-
" try, of arts, and of sciences, should be opened for

" all; that they should reassume the rank they are
" entitled to from nature, and from whence they
" never ought to have been degraded; and in short,
" following the example of justice given by France,
" in the first days of the revolution, governments
" should irrevocably make them real and useful
" citizens: then only shall the Jews, who, although
" scattered on the face of the earth, have, till
" now, formed a separate nation, begin really to
" mix and to be incorporated with other nations;
" they shall cease to form, as it has been often re-
" proached to them, a state within a state, when
" once they shall have, at last, really acquired a
" country, and when they shall consider themselves
" no longer as the slaves, but as the subjects of go-
" vernments. Seeing that by mixing with society,
" they may acquire consideration, they will first
" necessarily discontinue the practice of those re-
" cent, nonsensical, and absurd customs, which
" would then become impracticable to them, and
" would make them appear justly ridiculous.
" In the different stations of life, they will suc-
" cessfully exert that activity and that penetra-
" tion which they are acknowledged to possess,
" and which, till now, only tended to facilitate
" their pursuits in that degrading branch of traf-
" fic, which was in a manner left to them; all citi-
" zens will become the object of their affections,

M 2

" formerly concentrated among themselves; they
" will consider as brethren not only those who
" worship God in the same manner, but all these
" to whom the same country has given birth, who
" defend the same cause, who live under the pro-
" tecting influence of the same laws and of the
" same authority: then only they will consider
" themselves as belonging to the immense family
" of mankind.

" It is by such a glorious deed that Europe must
" crown the century just elapsed, and in which
" posterity will behold events of such a magni-
" tude, and succeeded by consequences so dread-
" ful."

Nothing in this was intended for France, where
the progress of knowledge, and sound views of national interest had already removed those prejudices which had brought oppression and hatred on
the Jews.

It may be expected that those observations will
produce on the other states of Europe those sentiments of justice and benevolence on which alone
can rest the happiness and stability of empires.

We see, not far distant, the moment when the
genius of a great and glorious Emperor will, in his
benevolence, make us reap all the advantages of
our new situation. We must redouble our prayers, to obtain from the God of our fathers that he

may be pleased to direct the attention of kings to the Israelites living under their dominion, and to inspire them with the resolution of distinguishing themselves by deeds of greatness and of national utility.

I shall also be entitled myself to the blessings of my brethren scattered in all the states of the world, since my collection will expose to all kings and to all nations, the truths which have opened for us the way to happiness, and will record acts which most certainly will lay the grounds for a general regeneration.

On the first of these two points, I must add to the proofs I have already adduced, two kinds of testimonies in our favour, which will acquaint the public with the opinions entertained by the wise, even before our august Emperor had called us together to establish the basis of our future prosperity.

The first of these testimonies is a letter, replete with force and truth, written in the *Sorbonne* the 30th of August, 1762, by M. l'Advocat, Doctor, Librarian, and Professor in that University. It contains his ideas on the *Apologie des Juifs*, just then published, in answer to Voltaire's writings.

The second is the letter which M. Simon Mayer, Jewish deputy for the, department of *La Seine*, wrote the 30th of July, 1806, to the editor of the *Journal de l'Empire*, to prove that the Israelites re-

siding in France, far from considering themselves
foreigners in the territory of the French empire,
were, in truth, devoted to the country which had
granted them an honourable adoption and which
did not cease to contribute to their happiness.

Sovereigns and nations will see in the letter of
M. l'Advocat, what they are to think of the unjust
judgments which the vulgar passed indiscriminately on the Israelites.

In that of M. Simon Mayer, they will see the
absurdity of the calamities, lately reiterated against
us, for want of consideration, or by the impulse of
hatred.

And if M. de Bonald and M. Poujol do not
abandon their unjust prepossessions, they will have
these two antagonists more, whose testimonies in
favour of truth and justice they must strive to do
away.

*Letter of M. l'Advocat, Doctor, Librarian, and
Professor of Sorbonne.*

Sorbonne, 30th of August, 1762.
" I am very sorry, Sir, to have been absent from
" Sorbonne, when you did me the honour of call-
" ing upon me there. I have received in the coun-
" try the little Apology of the Jews, in answer to

" Voltaire. I have read it, and I have affixed my
" approbation (8) to it, making, however, some
" slight alterations, which, as you will own your-
" self, do not in the least hurt your cause. No-
" thing can be more unjust than the contempt in
" which the Jews are held: this sentiment is repre-
" hensible even in the mob, which is hurried to ha-
" tred or contempt, often without knowing why;
" but it is much more so in a thinking or honest
" man, since humanity teaches us that we must
" avoid hatred and contempt for every one of our
" fellow creatures, whatever may be his country,
" his religion, or his profession. If M. de Voltaire
" gloried in being a Christian, I would tell him,
" that Christianity obliges him absolutely to re-
" tract every thing he has advanced against the
" Jews, since Jesus Christ has ordered us to con-
" sider all men, without distinction, as our bre-
" thren, and to love them as we love ourselves:
" a direction which is incompatible with hatred
" and contempt towards the Jews.

" But this famous poet prides himself more on
" being a philosopher than on being a Christian,
" and it was right to refute him in that point of
" view in your Apology; nothing being farther

(8) Every one knows that in the ancient government of France
books could not be published without the *approbation* of the censors

" removed from true philosophy than blindly to
" give up to popular prejudices and prepossessions.
" The reproach of ignorance and barbarism, which
" he lays to the charge of ancient and modern
" Jews, arising in reality from his own ignorance
" of the language and of the writings of the He-
" brews.   It is not from barbarous and tame
" translations that original writings can be judged.
" If M. de Voltaire's translations were again to be
" translated, word for word, into barbarous Latin,
" these translations would make M. de Voltaire
" appear more ignorant and more barbarous than
" he is aware of, and he would find himself in the
" garb of a Vandal or an Ostrogoth (9).   Job,
" Moses, David, Solomon, Isaiah, and most of the
" Hebrew poets, are by no means inferior to the
" Greek, Latin, and French poets, without except-
" ing even M. de Voltaire.   The poetic writings of
" the Hebrews are superior to those of every other
" nation, by the pomp of the expressions, the
" grandeur of the images, the sublimity of
" thought, in short, by all the genuine characteris-
" tics of true genius and of poetry ; and M. de
" Voltaire will no more succeed in his attempt to
" bring them into disrepute, than Perrault in his

(9) Favourite expressions of M. Voltaire, by which he compared his
antagonists to those northern barbarians.

" attacks on Homer and the other Greek poets.
" The Proverbs of Solomon are preferable to the
" *Gnomai* of the Greeks, and they contain at least
" as much philosophy, and as much knowledge of
" the human heart, as the writings of Voltaire.
" Maimonides, Abenesdra, Abarbanel, Kimchi,
" and many other Hebrew writers, were fully
" equal, in their times, to the contemporary writers
" of other nations. Raschi, or Solomon Jarchi,
" was the best commentator of the age he lived
" in; and we might mention some modern Hebrew
" poets, whose productions M. de Voltaire would
" admire, and by which he would even be impro-
" ved, were he able to understand them. What he
" says of the cheats of the inferior Jewish merchants
" and traders, is what is commonly to be met with
" in the conduct of inferior dealers of other na-
" tions. But, at least, Jews do not bring them-
" selves to untimely death by their robberies, or it
" happens very seldom. I can bear witness, that
" during these thirty years that I have resided in
" Paris, there has not been three Jews condemned
" to death for robbery or other crimes; so that,
" taking all together, the manners of the Jews in
" general are not worse than those of other people
" in similar stations. The superstition which M.
" de Voltaire lays to the charge of the Jews, does
" not go to prove that they are or ever were equally

N

" ignorant and barbarous as the Egyptians are
" represented to have been. Neither the Greeks
" nor the Romans were barbarous nations, and
" they had superstitions more dangerous, more
" absurd, more ridiculous, than those which the
" Jews are supposed to retain. David, after ha-
" ving conquered the Syrians, the Ammonites, the
" Moabites, the Idumeans, and part of the country
" of the Philistines, did not condemn to the flames
" or otherwise put to death, a single individual,
" on account of religion or of superstition ; he rest-
" ed satisfied with making these nations tributary,
" and he treated them with the humanity of a fa-
" ther as soon as they became his subjects. Na-
" tions are beside naturally more inclined to super-
" stition than to irreligion, and this disposition
" turns to the advantage of society. The super-
" stitious practices of a people are never hurtful
" to mankind, like the impious maxims of the athe-
" ists. Let our pretended philosophers, instead of
" blaspheming the Divinity, offer their thanksgi-
" vings that nations are so averse to Atheism ; *for if*
" *the nations now existing were impious or atheistical,*
" *neither the property nor the lives of these pretended*
" *philosophers would be safe* (10). Superstition is

---

(10) If we bear in mind that this letter was written in 1762, this sentence will look like a prediction, too well fulfilled in the untimely death

" like those weeds we carefully pluck up from our
" gardens, without hurting the corn or the useful
" vegetables. But our pretended philosophers
" want to tear up every thing by the roots. Let
" not M. de Voltaire exclaim so much against the
" superstitions of the Jews in particular. This
" is, Sir, my opinion as to the hatred and unjust
" contempt to which the Jews are exposed. Some
" years ago I was applied to for advice on this sub-
" ject by the ministry of Poland. My memorial
" confounded their accusers, and their chief was
" arrested and punished by order of the King of
" Poland. I keep a copy of this memorial, and
" shall with great pleasure communicate it to you.

I am, sincerely,

L'ADVOCAT.

Doctor, Librarian, and Professor in Sorbonne.

Letter of M. Simon Mayer, *Vice Deputy of the Departments of* La Seine *to the* Jewish *Assembly, to
the Editor of the* Journal de l'Empire.

" Sir,

" The Jews, filled with respect and gratitude for
" the august Sovereign who deigns to take their

of the leaders of the philosophical party who were at the head of the
French revolution.

" situation into his consideration, were far indeed
" from expecting that periodical writers would
" presume, without any authority, to judge ques-
" tions which are on the point of being discussed
" in the assembly, where their deputies are called,
" and still less that those premature judgments
" should be such as to establish, as an incontro-
" vertible fact, the greatest reproach to which a
" class of men can be liable, that *of not acknow-*
" *ledging the laws of their country.*

" This assertion, which is represented as an un-
" doubted truth in your paper of the 26th of Ju-
" ly instant, might have frightened the Jews in
" those times, when, excluded from every class of
" citizens, their keeping apart was nevertheless
" considered as a crime—when the most absurd
" inculpations were sought for with avidity, were
" adopted and employed against them as pretexts
" for proscription. It cannot cause the smallest
" uneasiness at a time when our hearts are opened
" to the liveliest gratitude for the benefits we de-
" rive from those laws which have put us on an
" equal footing with all citizens, under a prince
" equally just and firm, whose genius dispels the
" clouds of ancient prejudices, and whose councils
" are actuated by truth, justice, reason, humanity,
" and the ardent wish of making all Frenchmen
" happy.

" But accusations, made in so public a manner
" and on so important an occasion, must neverthe-
" less be confuted ; because they may lead into
" error a few credulous men, afford pretences to
" the evil intentions of others, excite ill-will
" against us, and throw difficulties in the way of
" that union of all Frenchmen, which is the aim of
" government, and the wish of every wise and en-
" lightened man.

" On examining the article of your journal al-
" ready alluded to, it becomes evident that the sole
" object the writer had in view was to present, as
" an incontrovertible truth, the following suppo-
" sition :

" *The Jews do not acknowledge the laws of France;*
" and that, without much minding whether or no
" his commentary on this assertion afforded any
" meaning, he has run his chance of meeting with
" credulous readers.

" In this century," says the writer, " the only
" questions at issue between the friends of the Jews
" and those who are against them are—to know if
" France, for instance, must reckon those men who
" do not acknowledge her laws, in the number of her
" children, till such a time as they have pledged
" themselves to assimilate their manners, as much
" as possible, to those of the rest of the nation ; or if
" sound policy requires that government, before

" it admits the Jews to share all the advantages
" common to all other Frenchman, should acquire
" the certainty that they shall make use of them
" only for the general interests of the empire ?"

" The absurdity of the first question is evident.
" Can government put in question *whether it should*
" *consider as children of the same country men who*
" *would refuse to acknowledge its laws, should they*
" *even engage to change their manners?*

" Whoever refuses to acknowledge the laws of a
" country must be excluded from it, let his man-
" ners be what they may; and if it were true, as the
" author pretends, *that the Jews refuse to acknow-*
" *ledge the laws of France*, their proposed admission
" among the children of France would not de-
" serve the slightest consideration. Luckily the
" falsehood of that assertion will be hereafter
" proved by facts.

" And how could the author suppose that the
" object of discussion was *whether France should*
" *admit the Jews among her children?* Do not Jews
" enjoy already that advantage? Have they not
" been called by the laws to the full enjoyment of
" all civil rights, common to all Frenchmen? Did
" not the same laws grant them the free exercise
" of their mode of worship? Did they not, in short,
" adopt them in the number of the children of
" France?

" Was the writer ignorant of all this? or does
" he refuse himself to acknowledge the laws of
" France while he inconsiderately urges that re-
" proach against the Jews?

" The question, then, is not to know if Jews are
" to be admitted among the children of France.
" It might be asked, at most, if they have made a
" bad use of the advantages they have received by
" their adoption? if they are become worthy or
" unworthy of retaining them? and if there are
" grounds to hope that the facility they have re-
" ceived, in common with all Frenchmen, to avail
" themselves of the protection of the laws, shall
" gradually induce them to adopt the general
" manners of the nation and at last level that
" barrier which the barbarism of antient legisla-
" tors had raised between them and other nations?

" The Jews do not shun the discussion of these
" questions: well authenticated facts speak in
" their favour on all these points; and the present,
" if examined without prejudice, will be deemed
" a sufficient pledge for the future.

" The second question is as absurd as the first;
" for, *to propose advantages to men on condition that
" they shall make use of them only for the interest of
" the public*, would prove a total want of knowledge
" of the human heart and of the true aim of legisla-
" tion, and I venture to say, that there has never

(96)

" existed on earth a nation capable of fulfilling
" such an engagement.

" Self interest is in man the first and principal
" spring of action; the advantages he derives
" from the laws must tend to favour this inclina-
" tion; but the grand art, I might almost say the
" cunning of the legislator, consists in regulating
" the use of each of these advantages in such a
" manner as to be naturally productive of the ge-
" neral welfare. It might be asked, then, if, in the
" opinions of the Jews, in their manners, in the
" professions to which they usually give the pre-
" ference, some particular obstacles may not be
" found which prevent the advantages they share
" in common with all Frenchmen from tending
" so directly to the public welfare as when in
" other hands? Inquiries might be set on foot to
" ascertain the nature of these obstacles, and laws
" or regulations might be afterwards adopted to
" lessen or to do them away altogether; but Jews
" are only men; and, surely, efforts above the
" strength of human nature will not be required
" of them.

" There is then, in reality, no reasonable meaning
" in the two questions about the Jews which the
" author supposes are to come under discussion.
" These set aside, there remains only this gratui-
" tous supposition:

" *The Jews do not acknowledge the laws of France.*

" Let us examine this assertion:

" A common and grand mistake in writers, pass-
" ing judgment on different societies of men, is,
" that they confound times, places, and other cir-
" stances, according to the side they have taken,
" and to the opinion they wish to establish on this
" or that society. In thus confusing every thing,
" there exists no nation, no community, no religi-
" ous association, which may not be represented
" at pleasure, as virtuous or vicious, just or unjust,
" brave or cowardly, atrocious or generous, loyal
" or rebellious, useful or dangerous, as deserving
" the highest praise, or as the fittest object of
" contempt.

" Certainly, if you consider the Jews at a time
" when, as says a writer you quote, *they were de-*
" *barred from possessing lands, from commerce,*
" *from industry,* when, in short, they were in a
" manner outlawed, it may be said that they did
" not acknowledge the laws of France, or, to speak
" more correctly, that they had been placed in the
" impossibility of acknowledging them. Exclud-
" ed from all the advantages of general society,
" they were forced to withdraw into their own
" particular community, and to seek in their cus-
" toms, their institutions, the doctrine of their
" doctors, support and consolations they could

o

" find no where else. But, it would be the height
" of injustice to alledge against them as a crime,
" the state to which they had been reduced by
" others, and to accuse them of having refused to
" acknowledge the laws of a society from which
" they had been expelled. I will go still farther :
" it would be unjust, now, to reproach them with
" some remaining attachment to those custou.s
" and to those manners, the common source from
" which generations after generations have drawn
" assistance, hope, and some alleviation of the
" hardships heaped upon them.

" Certainly the Jews would have been reprehen-
" sible, they would have justified the severity of
" the laws by which they were excluded from so-
" ciety, and even deserved to be excluded again,
" if, when governments more enlightened have
" taken them under their protection, have called
" them into the bosom of general society by giving
" them a country, they, in return, had ungrateful-
" ly rejected the proffered benefits, violated the
" laws under whose protection they were allowed
" to live, and disdained all the advantages of civil
" society, to give obstinately the preference to the
" customs and manners of their particular society ;
" then, indeed, it might have been said, that their
" abhorrence of the laws of other nations was, to
" this day, an inherent principle of their associa-

" tion, as it was in those days when the politics of
" their first lawgiver made this abhorrence a fun-
" damental maxim of their government.

" But considering the Jews, such as they are in
" in modern times, we shall see that every where
" their hatred has ceased with persecution; that
" wherever they have been admitted to share the
" benefits of the laws, they have gradually been
" united with those nations who have consented
" to adopt them; that every where they have re-
" spected the laws under whose protection they
" were allowed to live,

" It has been asserted, that the Jews have be-
" haved well in Holland, and that, far from giving
" occasion to complaints against them, they have,
" by their industry, contributed to the prosperity
" of the country. The cause of this difference
" between the Jews of Holland and those of other
" countries is evident; it is because in Holland
" they participate in all the advantages from which
" they were excluded elsewhere; in that country,
" facts have proved, that when they are considered
" as men and citizens, they shew themselves, like
" others, men and citizens. The particular ad-
" vantages they obtain become in their hands con-
" ducive to public welfare.

" Let us now consider them in France: since
" they have obtained the advantages common to

" all Frenchmen, can it be said that they have re-
" fused to obey the laws? Can it be said that, spurn-
" ing these advantages and the institutions of their
" new country, they have remained, as before, ex-
" clusively attached to their particular society?

" On the contrary, many among them have
" abandoned the exclusive professions to which
" they had been condemned, to follow others which
" bring them nearer their new fellow-citizens; they
" have acquired considerable landed property, they
" have formed vast commercial establishments, and
" erected manufactories; among them are to be
" seen artists and mechanics, practising me-
" chanical arts and following trades. They have
" sought for a new education in the national
" schools. Called to the armies, they have zea-
" lously taken up arms, they have fought with
" courage; and many, under the very eyes of the
" hero, who now governs France, have deserved
" the recompence of the brave.

" Can it be said that men who behave thus *do*
" *not acknowledge the laws of France?*

" Can it be a matter of doubt that their man-
" ners will gradually blend with those of nations
" who admit them to share their advantages and
" their civil rights?

" Certainly the change is not yet general, nor is
" it the work of a day; but it is wished for by all

" enlightened Jews: many among them have spon-
" taneously given the example. The impulse is
" given; wise regulations will do the rest; and I
" doubt not but we shall be indebted for them to
" the assembly which is now sitting.

" I shall not examine here into the means cal-
" culated to accelerate this happy change, and
" oblige the Jews to follow, more especially, profes-
" sions from which they were excluded by former
" laws. But I think that it is absolutely necessa-
" ry to adopt some efficacious measures to obtain
" this result, and I would even venture to propose
" some, if I did not place the most implicit confi-
" dence in the intentions and in the talents of those
" who compose and lead the assembly.

" You would not have received this long letter,
" Sir, if, instead of unjustly inculpating the
" Jews, you would have proposed means to make
" them what government wishes them to be. But
" what did you expect in affirming *that Jews do not*
" *acknowledge the laws of France?* No doubt you
" wanted to represent them as bad citizens, as
" men whom it is impossible to bring under the
" yoke of the laws. Such avowed intentions
" sour the mind, instead of mending the manners,
" and increase the evil instead of effecting a cure.

" I would, to conclude, answer M. de Bonald,
" whom you quote towards the end of your article:

" but the production of this writer does not threat-
" en much danger; the nature of his intentions is
" too evident, and the acrimony of his zeal acts as
" an antidote to his opinions.   M. de Bonald sees
" the present in the past and the past in the pre-
" sent. This illusion may contribute to his hap-
" piness; but it cannot seduce men of sound minds
" and enlightened understandings; and whatever
" he may do, he will not, in this age of knowledge,
" and under a government equally wise and firm
" in its resolutions, form a party very formidable
" to the Jews."

(Signed)   " SIMON MAYER."

Thus, in a word, every thing is disposed to insure the complete success of measures, by which
Israelites will, at last, receive manners and habits
capable of raising them to the rank of citizens
eminently useful.

Nations will know, more generally, how to appreciate those vicious prejudices which, till now,
have been the prolific sources of manifold persecutions, to which they attribute their incessant misfortunes, not objected to them as crimes.

Truths placed beyond a doubt, will prove to
every one that the Jews are capable of fulfilling
all social duties, and that they zealously support

all those measures which are likely to produce and insure their happiness.

In France, the grand act of justice announced by our august Emperor was totally unexpected.

Memorials were transmitted calling the attention of His Imperial and Royal Majesty to a number of bond-debts which were represented as likely to ruin many unfortunate land-holders.

The history of past centuries induces a belief, that, in other times, and under the reign of a weak or irresolute sovereign, rigorous coercive measures would have been proposed as the means of redressing wrongs, whose existence is not even yet legally ascertained.

Those of our brethren who are accused of injustice, and the Jews altogether, would have been, once more, exposed to the rigour of sanguinary laws, similar to those which too often have exposed our ancestors to the hatred of nations, and thrown them into all the horrors of misery.

A soul formed for great things; a mind incessantly bent upon thoughts the best calculated to accelerate the happiness of mankind; a genius accustomed to conceive whatever can consolidate the basis, the stability, and the prosperity of an empire created by a provident wisdom; virtues which constitute the greatness of sovereigns, up-

held by all the qualities which form the states-
man, have produced the memorable example of a
resolution heretofore unparalleled, and whose utility will excite in all the powers of Europe a generous emulation.

Let us place and preserve in our annals the imperial decree of the 30th of May, 1806. Soon
will this collection spread it through all the states
of Europe.

It gives us an immediate right to the esteem of
mankind; it lays the grounds of our future happiness; and will afford us the means of proving worthy of our country.

The acts to which it has given birth do not relate it; and it is rather surprising that the editor of
the *procès verbal* of the sittings of the assembly,
did not affix it at the head of his work.

This imposes on me the duty of giving it here at
full length. It is the work of protecting benevolence, a deed of a magnanimity unknown before
on earth; it bears the stamp of the decrees of Providence. It will carry to the most distant generations the pleasing conviction, that, in our times,
we beheld in our august Emperor the living image
of the Divinity.

(105)

Imperial Decree, given at the Palace of St. Cloud,
May 30, 1806.

" Napoleon, Emperor of the French, King of
" Italy.

" On the report which has been made to us, that
" in many of the northern departments of our em-
" pire, certain Jews, following no other profession
" than that of usurers, have, by the accumulation
" of the most enormous interests, reduced many
" husbandmen of these districts to the greatest
" distress :

" We have thought it incumbent on us to lend
" our assistance to those of our subjects whom ra-
" pacity may have reduced to these hard extremi-
" ties.

" These circumstances have, at the same time,
" pointed out to us the urgent necessity of revi-
" ving, among individuals of the Jewish persua-
" sion residing in our dominions, sentiments of
" civil morality, which, unfortunately, have been
" stifled in many of them by the abject state in
" which they have long languished, and which it
" is not our intention either to maintain, or to re-
" new.

" To carry this design into execution, we have
" determined to call together an assembly of the

P

" principal Jews, and to make our intentions
" known to them by commissioners whom we
" shall name for that purpose, and who shall, at
" the same time, collect their opinions as to the
" means they deem the fittest, to re-establish
" among their brethren the exercise of mechanical
" arts and useful professions, in order to replace,
" by an honest industry, the shameful resources to
" which many of them resorted, from generation
" to generation, these many centuries.

" To this end,

" On the report of our Grand Judge, Minister
" of Justice, of our Minister for the interior,

" Our Council of State being heard,

" We have decreed, and do decree as follows;

" Art. I. There is a suspension for a year, from
" the date of the present decree, of all executions
" of judgment and bond-obligations, except so far
" as to prevent limitation, obtained against hus-
" bandmen, not traders, of the departments of La
" Sarre, La Roer, Mont Terrible, Upper and
" Lower Rhine, Rhine and Moselle, and Vosges,
" whenever the bonds entered into by these hus-
" bandmen are in favour of Jews.

" II. There shall be formed, on the 15th of July
" next, in our good city of Paris, an assembly of
" individuals professing the Jewish religion and
" residing in the French territory.

" III. The members of this assembly, of the
" number fixed in the annexed List, shall be cho-
" sen in the departments therein named, and no-
" minated by the prefects from among the rabbis,
" the land-holders, and other Jews, the most dis-
" tinguished by their integrity and their know-
" ledge.

" IV. In all the other departments of our em-
" pire, not mentioned in the aforesaid table, and
" where men of the Jewish persuasion should re-
" side to the number of one hundred, and less
" than five hundred, the prefect may name a depu-
" ty for every five hundred, and for a higher num-
" ber, up to one thousand, he may name four
" deputies, and so on.

" V. The deputies thus named shall be in Pa-
" ris before the 10th of July, and shall send no-
" tice of their arrival, and of their place of resi-
" dence, to the secretary's office of our Minister of
" the Interior, who shall acquaint them of the
" place, day, and hour of the meeting.

" VI. Our Minister for the Interior is charged
" with the execution of the present decree.

(Signed)   " NAPOLEON.

" By the Emperor.

(Signed)   " H. B. MARET.

" Secretary of State."

P 2

List of the Number of Jews *to be returned to the Assembly of Individuals of the* Jewish *persuasion, whose Meeting has been ordered by His Majesty.*

Names of the Departments.	Number of Deputies to be sent.
Upper Rhine	12
Lower Rhine	15
Mont Tonnerre	9
Rhine and Moselle	4
Sarre	1
Roer	1
Moselle	5
Meurthe	7
Vosges	7
Gironde	2
Lower Pyrenees	2
Vaucluse	2
Cote-d'Or	1
Seine	6
	74

(Signed) H. B. MARET.

Secretary of State.

A true copy.

The proclamation of this decree produced that enthusiastic satisfaction which the sudden hopes of lasting prosperity always excite in men who consider themselves as abandoned by the whole world.

His excellency the minister of the interior, MM. the Prefects of all the departments, have manifested, in the execution of the orders of His Imperial Majesty, those sentiments of universal justice which, they know, dwell in the bosom of His Majesty, and which themselves consider as the first of their duties.

They have proved solicitous to make use of the best means to direct their choice so as to fulfil the intentions of His Majesty and to answer the expectations of the Jews.

In the beginning of July, 1806, the deputies arrived in Paris where they have proved worthy of the reputation they had acquired by their principles and their conduct, and of the great trust which had been reposed in them.

Their names and their places of abode in Paris were known by the declarations they made, in conformity to the fifth article of the imperial decree, to the Secretary's office of the minister of the interior.

List of MM. the Deputies of the Jewish *Nation, in the alphabetical Order of the Departments of the Empire.*

Adige.

Girolamo Bazizea.
Israel Coen.

Adriatic.

Aaron Tatis, Land-holder, Venice.
Abraham Tedesco, Merchant, Venice,
Jacob Samuel Cracovia, Rabbi, Venice.

Maritime Alps.

Isaac Samual Avigdov, Nice.

Bouches du Rhone.

Sabaton Costantini, Merchant, Marseilles.

Cote d'Or.

David Blum, Merchant, Dijon.

Crostolo.

Jacques Carmy, Rabbi, Reggio.

Doire.

Joseph Vita Monmilien.

Doubs.

Nathan Lippmann, Land-holder and Clock Manufacturer, Besançon.

Gironde.

Abraham Furtado, Land-holder, Bourdeaux.
Isaac Rodrigues, Merchant, Do.

Herault.

Moise Naquet Vidal, Silk Merchant.

Landes.

Abraham Andrade, Rabbi, Saint Esprit
Castro, jun.   Do.
Patto, jun.   Do.

Marengo.

De Benedetti.
Donato-Afeu-Lelio-Saloman Vitate.
Emilie Vitta.
Joseph-Benoist Pavia.

Meurthe.

Berr-Isaac-Berr, Tobacco Manufacturer, Nancy.
Elias Salomon, Land-holder, Sarrebourg.
Gumpel Levy, Merchant, Nancy.
Jacob Brisac, Land-holder, Lunéville.
Lazare Levy, Land-holder, and Mayor of Donnelay.

Leon Cohen, Land-holder, Toul.
Moïse Levy, Merchant, Nancy.

Meuse Inferieure.
David Joseph.

Mincio.
Abraham Cologna, Rabbi.
Benoit Fano, Merchant, Mantua.

Montenote.
Israel Emmanuel Ottolenghi.

Mont Tonnerre.
Aaron Friedberg, Manufacturer, Burgen.
Benjamin Jacob, Mentz.
Herz-Loep Lorech, Land-holder, Mentz.
Henz Oppenheim, Deux-Ponts.
Jacob Herz, Merchant and Land-holder, Rotskir-
    chen.
Jacob Lazare, Merchant, Otterburg.
Joseph Bloch, Land-holder, Hombourg. '
Moise Kauffman, Land-holder, Neu-Leingen.

Moselle.
Aaron-Marc Levy, Merchant, Metz.
Cerf Jacob Gondchaux, Correspondent of the Bank
    of France, Metz.
Jacob Gondchaux Beer, Landholder, Metz.

Joseph Hertz, Land-holder, Sarguemines.
Scawab, jun. Merchant, Metz.

Nord.

Salomon, Merchant, Lille.

Alona.

David Samson, Pavia.
Moise Formiggini.

Panaro.

Benjamin Uzigli.
Bonavetura Modena, Rabbi.

Po.

David Levy, Deputy Mayor of Quiers.
Jacques Todros, Turin.
Samuel Jacob Ghidiglia, Turin.

Po (Lower).

Bondi Zammorani, Rabbi, Ferrara.
Grazziadio Nappi, Rabbi and Physician, Ferrara.

Pyrenees (Lower).

Furtado, jun. Ship Owner.
Marg Foi, sen. Merchant.

Reni.

Felice Levy.

B.

Lazaro Coen.

Rhine (Lower).

Abraham Cahen, Saverne.
Abraham Piccard, sen. Strasbourg.
Auguste Ratisbonne, Cloth Merchant, Strasbourg.
Baruch Cerf Bar, Land-holder.
Cerf Salomon, Merchant, Strasbourg.
Daniel Levy, Merchant, Strasbourg.
David Zinsheimer, Rabbi, Ssrasbourg.
Hirsch Bloch, Land-holder, Diebolshuheim.
Israel Rhens, Strasbourg.
Jacques Meyer, Rabbi, Niederhuheim.
Joseph Deyfoss, Haguenau.
Hirsch Lazare, Rabbi, Haguenau.
Lazare Wolff, Merchant, Neuwiller.
Ruesse Picard, Strasbourg.
Samuel Witersheim, Merchant, Haguenau.

Rhine (Upper).

Abraham Jacol, Colnac.
Baruch Lang, Land-holder, Fierentz.
Calmau, Rabbi, Beishem.
David, Rabbi, Hegenheim.
Heymann Picqart, Land-holder and Leather Ma-
    nufacturer, Belfort.
Hirtz Salomon, Land-holder and Horse-dealer,
    Colmar.
Jacob Brunswieg, Rabbi.

Lipman-Cerf-Berr, Paris.
Mayer Samuel, Strasbourg.
Meyer Manheimer, Uffholtz.
Solomon Rabbi, Colmar.
Wolff Baruch, Manufacturer, Turkheim.

Rhine and Moselle.
Emmanuel Deutz, Rabbi, Coblentz.
Lion Marx, Land-holder, Bonn.
Mayer Marx, Municiple Council-man, Bonn.
Wolf Bermann, Merchant, Mayen.

Roer.
Saloman Openheim, Banker, Cologn.

Sarre.
Meyer Nathan Berncastel, Merchant, Treves.
Jeremie Hirsch, Land-holder, Sarrebruk.

Seine.
Michel Berr, Paris.
Theodore Cerf-Berr, Land-holder, Paris (named
    also for Nancy).
Saul Cremieaux.
Lazare Jacob.
Olry Hayem Worms.
Rodrigue, Banker.
Rodrigue, jun.

Aaron Schmoll, Paris.

Simon Mayer, formerly in the Army, Government
      Inspector in the Military Administration.

C. L. Wittersheim, Land-holder.

Sesia.

Segre, Rabbi, Land-holder, Municipal council-man
      of Verceil.

Stura.

Lattes Elie Aaron, Rabbi, Savigliano.

Lattes Solomon, jun. Land-holder, Coni.

Vaucluse.

Joseph Montaux, Silk Merchant, Avignon.

Moise Millaud.

Vosges.

Isaac-Louis May.

Michel Lazare, Land-holder, Charreau.

Moise May, Land-holder, Neufchateau.

All the deputies being arrived at Paris, His
Majesty the Emperor and King was pleased
to give orders for the speedy meeting of the assembly.

It was by a circular letter of the 13th of July,
that His Excellency the Minister of the Interior

made them acquainted with the place of their sittings, and the day on which they should meet to form an assembly under the presidency of one of their members.

The 26th of the same month was the day fixed for their first meeting; but His Excellency, having remarked that it happened to be on a Saturday, sent word to the deputies that if they thought themselves bound to abstain from every kind of labour, on such a day, they were at liberty to adjourn their first meeting.

The deputies, however, wishing to prove that they observe faithfully their antient laws, which command, above all things, a prompt obedience to all orders whatever from their sovereign, have fulfilled, on that very day, 26th of July, the intentions of His Majesty the Emperor and King.

Sitting of the 26th of July, 1806.

This day, the 26th of July, 1806, at eleven o'clock in the morning, the French deputies of the Jewish persuasion, called to Paris by the decree of His Imperial and Royal Majesty dated the 30th of May last, have assembled in a hall adjoining the town-house, according to the invitation contained in the circular letter of His Excellency the Minister of the Interior, of the 13th of this month, in order to name a president, two secretaries and three scrutineers (10).

In order to proceed to these nominations, the assembly has been formed under the presidency of M. Solomon Lipman, as the oldest member, assisted by MM. Moses Levy and Henry Castro jun. as secretaries.

It began its proceedings by calling over the names of the members; at the same time a scrutiny began for the nomination of a president, M. Abraham Furtado, having obtained the majority of votes, has been proclaimed president by the oldest member. But before taking the chair he addressed the assembly to return thanks for the honour they had conferred upon him, warning them, at the same time, to avoid tumult and dissentions, which too often take place in deliberating assemblies. " A sad experience, he " said, has too well proved that men, assembled " together in great numbers, oftener bring into " contact their passions than their virtues." He spoke with the most profound respect, and the liveliest admiration of the protecting hero who governs us, and invited the assembly to second

(10) Members chosen to examine the numerous scrutinies which always take place in French assemblies.

his magnanimous views by its steadiness and its vigilance.

The assembly rapturously applauded the speech of its President, and the cries of *long live the Emperor, long live the Imperial Family,* resounded through the hall.

The assembly having proceeded afterwards, by way of scrutiny, to the nomination of two secretaries, MM. Rodrigues, Junr. and Samuel Avigdoo obtained the majority of votes.

The President proclaimed them secretaries, and they took their places at the table accordingly. The nomination of scrutineers began afterwards; MM. Olry Bayem Worms, Theodore Cerf-Berr, and Emilie Vitta, having obtained the majority of votes, the President proclaimed them scrutineers, and they also took their places at the table accordingly.

The nominations being over, a member proposed to name a deputation, with the President at its head, to go to Saint Cloud, and carry to the foot of the throne the expression of the sentiments of respect, love, and loyalty, which warmed the heart of every member of the assembly towards the sacred person of his Imperial and Royal Majesty, and to assure the august monarch, under whose laws we live, of the eager

zeal with which this part of his faithful subjects
will strive to fulfil the benevolent intentions
which may be communicated to them by his
commissioners.

Another member said, " Yes, Gentlemen, our
" most ardent wish must be to carry to the foot of
" the throne the expressions of our gratitude and
" of our dutiful respect; to take into the august
" presence of our sovereign, the engagement of
" furthering, by all the means in our power, the
" grand designs which His Majesty entertains in
" respect to us, and to renew our oath to be faith-
" ful and devoted to our Emperor, even till death."
He concluded by demanding that His Excellency
the Minister of the Interior, should be requested
to transmit to His Majesty this wish of the Jewish
deputies; and that, in the expectation of this
favour, on which the assembly could never set
too great a value, His Excellency would have the
goodness to express to His Majesty the sentiments which animated the whole assembly.

A third member read a motion to the same
purpose; but as it contained various articles, the
assembly agreed, on the proposition of the President, to put off the discussion to the next meeting.

Several members having delivered their opinions, the assembly agreed to express its wish of

being collectively admitted into the presence of
his Imperial and Royal Majesty, to express the
sentiments of respect, love, and loyalty for his
sacred person, which penetrate the heart of every
individual member; and to take the solemn engagement of furthering, by all the means. in its
power, the benevolent and paternal intentions
which his great soul had conceived, and of which
the meeting of the assembly was the first pledge.

The assembly adjourned to Tuesday next, 29th
inst. at twelve o'clock precisely; the President
closed the sitting, to wait immediately on His Excellency the Minister of the Interior, to give him
the report of the proceedings of the assembly,
of its adjournment, and of the wish it had expressed, to be enabled to carry to the foot of the
throne the expression of the sentiments by
which it was animated towards the sacred person
of His Imperial and Royal Majesty.

This first sitting naturally introduces observations which will throw a greater light on the several
acts I am about to record.

It is not astonishing that at their first meeting,
the Deputies should have manifested a zeal truly
enlightened.

The Prefects had made such a choice as honours
their discernment, and which will be a source
of blessings to the Jews.

R

Attachment to their duties, extensive knowledge, wise principles, and an ardent desire to serve the country, characterise the Deputies, and have produced these resolutions, to which they will adhere, of furthering by all the means in their power, the magnanimous designs of our August Emperor. They are strengthened in these resolutions by a wish of proving useful to their brethren, and by the praise-worthy ambition of fulfilling the hopes entertained of their ability to consolidate, on firmer grounds, the happiness arising from our new condition.

By chusing M. Furtado of Bourdeaux for President, a most worthy choice in every respect, the assembly has proved its judicious intentions, and given a pledge of the line of conduct it intends to follow.

Portuguese Jews, in general, are, both in theory and in practice, far superior to other Jews in the habits of social virtues.

M. Furtado is well known among merchants, and has obtained a distinguished rank among those useful writers who consider accurately their ideas and diffuse salutary knowledge.

And lastly, the qualities of his heart, would, without any other merit, amply justify the choice of the assembly.

He has given the first example of zeal; he encourages and employs for the general advantage the various talents of the several members.

Many others, advantageously known already, are also distinguished by their extensive knowledge: their conduct justifies the opinion entertained of them, and they honourably deserve all the gratitude of their brethren, the esteem and the consideration of their contemporaries.

M. Avigdov, one of the secretaries of the assembly, author of several writings in favour of the Jews, has every day given fresh proofs of his zeal.

M. Michel Berr, councellor at law, member of several academies, one of the deputies for the department of *La Seine*, author of a pamphlet entitled *An Appeal to the Justice of Kings and Nations*, from which I have given ample extracts in this collection, continues still to exert all his talents in defence of the rights and interests of the Jews, whom he proved, in 1801, entitled to the benevolence of all sovereigns.

M. Segre, Rabbi, deputy for the department of *La Seine*, is highly commendable for his extensive learning which he zealously employs in promoting the interests and the wishes of his brethren.

Other deputies have confirmed the hopes contained in the letter of M. Berr Isaac Berr, (11) by

(11) See page 11.

a remark which proves that this production, published in 1791, has really been productive of some good effects. It is very true, as they have advanced, and I have ascertained the fact, that, in April, 1803, an establishment was formed in Copenhagen for the instruction of Jewish youth; that at the end of the year 1805, the number of the pupils was forty; that, by a public examination, held in June, 1806, their success in their studies had been ascertained; that they had made great progress in the Hebrew, French, and German languages, in geography, and in natural history; and in short, that this establishment was in a very flourishing condition.

A writing published in France at the epocha of the first meeting of the assembly, whose acts I am now recording, has proved that the Jewish nation in Germany, is greatly indebted to the public establishment of M. Jacobson, Privy Councellor of Finances at Brunswick, for the instruction of Jewish youth.

It is very certain, then, that, to the principles contained in this letter, and published by M. Michel Berr, in 1801, these first advantages are to be attributed. The learning and the views of this last writer will assist powerfully in the completion of the great work which the enlightened benevolence of a beloved monarch is preparing to effectuate in the French empire.

Immediately after the first sitting of the assembly, M. Berr-Isaac-Berr published observations which afford a new proof and a new pledge of his praise-worthy zeal.

M. Lipmann Cerf-Berr has also contributed his share, by ideas and reflexions which have obtained universal approbation.

M. Baruch Cerf-Berr, emulous of his father's constant zeal, has adopted the sentiments and opinions of those distinguished writers, whom he quotes honourably, in a publication well entitled to notice, and which I should introduce in this collection, if I was not apprehensive that it would interrupt too much the account of the sitting of the assembly.

The works of the deputies I have just mentioned, the zeal of all, are the honorable pledges of their intentions, and prove that they place their happiness in their efforts to deserve the gratitude of their brethren.

Could the French Jews have been assembled to name themselves their representatives their choice could not have been happier.

The whole of the acts of the assembly has proved that their interests could not be placed in the hands of men better entitled to their confidence.

Second Sitting, *July* 29, 1806.

The president opened the sittings precisely at twelve o'clock. He named, as Commissioners for the maintainance of order, MM. Rodrigue, sen, Lipmann Cerf-Berr, and Castre, jun.

One of the secretaries read a letter addressed to the President by His Excellency the Minister of the Interior, dated the 28th of this month, in which he informs him, that " MM. Mole, Portalis, " jun.and Pasquier, *Maitres des Requêtes*, (12) and " chosen by His Majesty as Commissioners to " transact whatever belongs to us, will attend the " assembly, this day, at three o'clock, to impart " the intentions of His Majesty the Emperor and " King.

" The Minister, at the same time, desires the " President to acquaint the assembly, that, before " proceeding further, it is necessary to name a " commission, which shall prepare the ground- " work of the discussions which are to take place " on the communications which the commissioners " have received directions to make."

The President opened the discussion on the formation of this commission.

(12) Law officers attached to the Council of State, with functions nearly similar to those of our Masters in the Court of Chancery.

A member proposed that it should be composed of twelve members named by the President.

Another observed that it would be better to defer forming the commission till the Commissioners have acquainted the assembly with the nature of the questions which shall be submitted to its judgment, in order to select members accordingly.

A third thought that, " even from the contents " of the letter of His Excellency the Minister for " the Interior, it is possible to put off the forma- " tion of the commission till the commissioners of " His Majesty have acquainted the assembly with " the nature of their communications."

A deputy observed, that, " as several members " of the northern departments are not thoroughly " acquainted with the French language, it would " be proper to name two members to translate for " them, verbally and literally, the several opini- " ons, that they may," says he, " deliberate with " some knowledge of the subject."

The assembly adopted this resolution, and the President named MM. Lyon Marx and Joseph Benjamin to translate for them.

These two members acquainted those northern deputies, who were not sufficiently acquainted with the French language, with the several opinions relative to the formation of the commission, which have been expressed in the course of the present debate.

A member observed, that, " as the President " and the members, officers of the assembly, form " naturally part of the commission, twelve mem- " bers added to them, will be sufficient to compose " it".

The assembly divided on the question by shew of hands, and it was agreed that " the commission " shall be composed of twelve members, besides " the President and the officers, and that they " shall be named by the President, after the Com- " missioners shall have acquainted the assembly " with the nature of the questions to be submit- " ted to its opinion.

A dispatch was brought to the President, directed to MM. Mole, Portalis, jun. and Pasquier, *Mai- tres des Requetes*; it was laid on the table. The minutes of the meeting of the 26th were read.

A member demanded leave to speak, and ob- served that " our sentiments of loyalty, respect, " and love, for the sacred person of His Royal and " Imperial Majesty, have not been expressed with " that warmth and enthusiasm which animate the " whole assembly."

This member was reminded that it would be a

difficult task to express those sentiments with the enthusiasm they excite.

Another observed that, in the journal of the minutes, the number of votes which the President, the Secretaries, and the Scrutineers had obtained, had been omitted.

The assembly ordered " that the observations " of these two members should be mentioned in " the minutes, as well as the number of votes al- " luded to."

It appeared, from notes taken of the sitting of the 26th, " M. Solomon Lipmann, as the oldest " member, being President, and MM. Moses Levi " and Castro, jun. as the youngest, being Secreta- " ries, that out of ninety-four votes, M. Furtado, as " candidate for the Presidency, had obtained sixty- " two, and M. Berr-Isaac-Berr thirty two ; that, " for the office of Secretaries, M. I. S. Avigdor had " obtained forty-four votes, and M. J. Rodrigues " forty-three ; that for that of Scrutineers, MM. " Olry-Hayem-Worms, Theodore Cerf-Berr, and " Emilie Vitta had obtained, the first seventy votes, " the second sixty-three, and the third twenty-nine."

The President named afterwards a deputation of fifteen members, viz. MM. Berr-Isaac-Berr, Lipmann, Cerf-Berr, Saul Cremieux, Patto, jun. Castro, jun. Cadet Carcassonne, Costan- tini, David Zinzheimer, Mayer, Samuel Rodrigues, sen. Moses Levy, Marx, jun. Jacob Lazare, Levy, and Baruch Cerf-Berr, to go and meet the Commissioners of His Majesty.

The President then suspended the proceedings of the assembly until the arrival of the Commissioners.

At three o'clock, it was announced that the Commissioners of His Majesty were coming to the assembly, by a door facing that by which the deputies are admitted.

Immediately, the fifteen members of the deputation, with the President and the officers at their head, went to meet them.

The Commissioners of His Majesty were introduced into the hall, amidst repeated acclamations of *Long live the Emperor, Long live the Imperial Family*. The most profound silence succeeded to this spontaneous effusion; the members remained standing to hear His Majesty's intentions read.

M. Mole, *Maitre des Requetes*, one of the Commissioners of His Majesty, opened the letter directed to them which laid on the table, took out the documents it contained, and pronounced the following discourse to acquaint the assembly with the intentions of His Majesty.

" Gentlemen,

" His Majesty, the Emperor and King, having

" named us Commissioners to transact whatever
" relates to you, has this day sent us to this as-
" sembly to acquaint you with his intentions,
" Called together from the extremities of this vast
" empire, no one among you is ignorant of the
" object for which His Majesty has convened this
" assembly. You know it, The conduct of many
" among those of your persuasion has excited
" complaints, which have found their way to the
" foot of the throne: these complaints were found-
" ed on truth; and nevertheless, His Majesty has
" been satisfied with stopping the progress of the
" evil, and he has wished to hear you on the means
" of providing a remedy. You will, no doubt,
" prove worthy of so tender, so paternal a conduct,
" and you will feel all the importance of the trust,
" thus reposed in you. Far from considering the
" government under which you live as a power
" against which you should be on your guard, you
" will assist it with your experience and co-
" operate with it in all the good it intends; thus
" you will prove that, following the example of
" all Frenchmen, you do not seclude yourselves
" from the rest of mankind.

" The laws which have been imposed on indi-
" viduals of your religion have been different in
" the several parts of the world : often they have
" been dictated by the interest of the day, But,

s 2

" as an assembly like the present, has no precedent
" in the annals of Christianity, so will you be
" judged, for the first time, with justice, and you
" will see your fate irrevocably fixed by a Christian
" Prince. The wish of His Majesty is, that you
" should be Frenchmen; it remains with you to
" accept of the proffered title, without forgetting
" that, to prove unworthy of it, would be renounc-
" ing it altogether.

" You will hear the questions submitted to you;
" your duty is to answer the whole truth on every
" one of them. Attend, and never lose sight of
" that which we are going to tell you ; that, when a
" monarch equally firm and just, who knows every
" thing, and who punishes or recompences every
" action, puts questions to his subjects, these would
" be equally guilty and blind to their true interests,
" if they were to disguise the truth in the least.

" The intention of His Majesty is, Gentlemen,
" that you should enjoy the greatest freedom in
" your deliberations: your answers will be trans-
" mitted to us by your President, when they have
" been put in regular form.

" As to us, our most ardent wish is to be able to
" report to the Emperor, that, among individuals
" of the Jewish persuasion, he can reckon as many
" faithful subjects, determined to conform in every
" thing to the laws and to the morality, which

" ought to regulate the conduct of all French-
" men."

One of the Secretaries read afterwards the following twelve questions proposed by the Commissioners.

*Questions proposed to the Assembly of the Jews by
the Commissioners named by His Majesty the Emperor and King, to transact whatever concerns them.*

1st. Is it lawful for Jews to marry more than
one wife?

2nd. Is divorce allowed by the Jewish religion?

Is divorce valid, although not pronounced by
courts of Justice, and by virtue of laws in contradiction with the French code?

3d. Can a Jewess marry a Christian, or a Jew a
Christian woman?

Or has the law ordered that the Jews should
only intermarry among themselves?

4th. In the eyes of Jews are Frenchmen considered as brethren or as strangers?

5th. In either case what conduct does their law
prescribe towards Frenchmen not of their religion?

6th. Do the Jews born in France, and treated

by the law as French citizens, acknowledge France as their country?

Are they bound to defend it?

Are they bound to obey the laws, and to follow the directions of the civil code?

Who elects — 7th. What kind of Police-jurisdiction have the *Rabbis?* Rabbies among the Jews?

What judicial power do they exercise among them?

9th. Are the forms of the elections of the Rabbies and their police-jurisdiction, regulated by the law, or are they only sanctioned by custom?

10th. Are there professions from which the Jews are excluded by their law?

11th. Does the law forbid the Jews from taking usury from their brethren?

12th. Does it forbid or does it allow usury towards strangers?

During the reading of these questions, the assembly manifested by unanimous and spontaneous emotions, how deeply it was affected by the doubt which the questions seemed to convey, as to the attachment of Frenchmen, following the law of ‘Moses, for their fellow citizens, and for their country, and as to their sense of the duty by which they are bound to defend it.

The assembly was not able to conceal the emotions caused by the sixth question, in which it

ERRATA.—In p. 134, after line 5, read, "7th. Who elects the Rabbies?" The succeeding question should be numbered 8.

is asked if Jews born in France and treated by the law as French citizens, acknowledge France as their country, and if they are bound to defend it. The whole assembly unanimously exclaimed,— *Even to death.*

The reading of the questions being ended, the President addressed the following discourse to the Commissioners of His Majesty the Emperor and King.

" Gentlemen Commissioners,

" We have listened with all the attention we " could command to the intentions of his Majesty " the Emperor, which you have just communicated " to us.

" Chosen by this assembly as the interpreter " of its sentiments, I must assure you, in the name " of all those who compose it, that, when His Majes- " ty determined to call us together in his capital, " in order to further the accomplishment of his " glorious designs, we saw, with inexpressible " joy, this occasion of doing away many errors and " putting an end to many prejudices.

" The benevolent intentions of His Majesty " have offered us an opportunity, most fervently " desired this great while, by all honest and en- " lightened men of the Jewish persuasion, residing " in France.

" We had, however, but a distant prospect of the
" epocha which would completely reform habits
" occasioned by a long state of oppression. Now
" the moment seems almost at hand, and we owe
" this precious advantage to the paternal goodness
" of His Majesty. It was impossible that his ex-
" alted mind could, even for an instant, entertain
" a thought on our situation, without its being
" materially improved.

" We shared, in common with all Frenchmen,
" the sentiments inspired by that protecting genius
" which had saved this empire from the rage of par-
" ty spirit, from the horrors of a bloody anarchy,
" and from the ambitious designs of its exterior
" enemies.

" We could not suppose that after so many be-
" nefits, it could be still possible for him to acquire
" new rights to our gratitude, or to increase our
" love for his sacred person. Times of ignorance
" and of anarchy had always been, for us, days of
" trials and of misfortune. His Majesty had freed
" us from any apprehension as to the return of the
" first of these scourges, the other was chained by
" his powerful hand. His laws, the establish-
" ment of his dynasty, and the return of order, had
" calmed all the fears we might have entertained
" of a retrograde motion in the progress of the
" great science of social economy in France; we flat-

" tered ourselves with the hope of progressively
" enjoying the sweets of so many blessings.. The
" slow but sure regeneration of some of our bre-
" thren would have been the result of our new con-
" dition. His Majesty wishes to hasten the preci-
" ous moments, and, through his protecting good-
" ness, we shall enjoy, under his reign, social ad-
" vantages, which we could expect only from cen-
" turies of perseverance.

" It is thus that the greatest of heroes becomes
" the common father of all his subjects; whatever
" religion they follow, he only sees in them chil-
" dren of the same family.

" The enterprize His Majesty undertakes is such
" as might have been expected from the most
" astonishing man whose deeds were ever record-
" ed by history. Methinks I see the muse hold-
" ing her immortal *burin*, and tracing on her ada-
" mant tables, amidst so many deeds, which make
" this reign so conspicuous, that which the hero of
" the age has done to destroy utterly the barrier
" raised between nations and the scattered re-
" mains of the most antient people.

" Such is, Gentlemen Commissioners, the point
" of view under which we consider, with compla-
" cency, the communications we have received
" from you. It confirms us in the idea that no
" practicable good escapes the penetration of
T

" His Majesty, which can be equalled only by
" his goodness, and by the generosity of his heart.

" The choice which His Majesty has been pleas-
" ed to make of you, Gentlemen Commissioners, to
" convey to us his intentions, adds a new value to
" the favour he intends for the Jews. The most
" unlimited confidence will reign between us, in
" the course of our communications.

" While this confidence pleads some excuse for
" our involuntary errors, it will be a pledge of the
" purity of our intentions.

" Have the goodness, Gentlemen Commissioners,
" to convey our sentiments to His Majesty, and to
" assure him that he does not reign over subjects
" more faithful, or more devoted to his sacred per-
" son, than we are."

The discourse of the President being ended,
the hall resounded with repeated cries of *Long live
the Emperor.*

The Commissioners of His Majesty have requested an official receipt for the questions they laid on
the table.

It was given by the President.

Many members manifested their intention of
delivering their sentiments before the Commissioners. But they left the assembly amidst the
cries of *Long live the Emperor?* They were conduct-

ed by the same deputation which had introduced them into the hall.

The assembly proceeded afterwards to form a commission to prepare the ground work of the discussions, which are to take place on the Communications which the Commissioners of His Majesty have made to the assembly. The President names to compose it --- MM. Berr-Isaac-Berr, Segre, Rabbi, David Zinzheimer, Rabbi, Abraham Andrade, Rabbi, Jacob Lazare, Jacob Gondehaux Berr, Moses Levy, Rodrigues, Samuel Jacob Guediglia, Michel Berr, Baruch-Cerf-Berr, and Lyon Marx.

Previous to the rising of the assembly, the President observed, that it was useless for him to observe, that no answer will be sent to the Commissioners, without having been previously submitted to the deliberation of the assembly.

The President closed the sitting at four o'clock, and announced to the deputies that they will be acquainted, by letters of convocation, with the day and hour of the next meeting.

Sitting of the 4th of August, 1806.

The President took the chair at twelve o'clock; one of the Secretaries read the minutes of the

t 2

sitting of the 29th of July last, which passed without any objection.

The President named MM. May, of Paris, Samuel Wittersheim, and Gumpel Levy: as Commissioners to maintain order in the assembly.

The President read a letter from His Excellency the Minister of the Interior, acquainting him, that His Majesty the Emperor and King had consented to admit the assembly into his presence, in a body, whenever its labours shall be sufficiently forwarded to promise some results. The reading of this letter was followed by repeated acclamations of *Long live the Emperor, long live the Imperial Family.*

The President informed the assembly that a secretary would read the answers which the commission, named to prepare the ground-work of the discussions of the assembly, on the questions proposed by His Majesty's Commissioners, had thought fit to return to the three first questions. He intreated the assembly to remain calm during the discussion, and invited those members who may chuse to deliver their sentiments, to give in their names at the table.

One of the Secretaries read the answer proposed by the commission to the first question. M. Lyon Marx, one of the interpreters of the assembly and member of the commission, read the literal translation he had made of it into German. The discussion opened on the first question.

A member ascended the tribune, and said, that though the answer was within the meaning and sense of the law, yet the wording of it was not sufficiently clear. The President ased if he had another to propose in its stead; he answered in the negative.

Another member expressed his surprize, that the member who had just sat down should not point out in what particulars he found the wording reprehensible. A third observed that the French word in the question, which means *lawful*, more particularly alluded to religious law; the answer should be made with a view to this meaning.

"Nobody," said another, "having offered to speak " against the sense of the answer proposed by the " commission, it ought to be put to the vote." This proposition was seconded, and put to the vote; and the answer to the first question, was adopted almost unanimously, without any alteration.

The answer to the second question was read. M. Lyon Marx read, as before, the translation he had made of it into the German language; no one offering to speak on the answer proposed by the commission, it was put to the vote, and passed unanimously.

One of the secretaries read the answer to the

third question ; M. Lyon Marx read the German literal translation he had made of it. A. Rabbi proposed that whenever principles purely theological should be presented for discussion, his brethren the Rabbies should be more particularly consulted. " Is it not evident," says he, " that if astronomical " subjects were proposed, you would consult only " astronomers? Why then should you not leave to " theologians, whatever relates to religion ?" He thought that questions of this nature should not be determined by the majority of votes.

The President observed to this speaker, that the principle of the majority of votes was inherent to the nature of every deliberative assembly, and that it was impossible to depart from it.

One of the Secretaries read the written opinion of the Rabbies, members of the assembly, on the third question.

A member said, that government, in forming that assembly, had not composed it entirely of Rabbies; it had selected also land-holders and other persons known by their integrity and by their learning; that, on the other hand, the two answers were written nearly on the same principles; since both acknowledged that Christians were our brethren. He thought that the two answers might be combined together, so as to make only one. A Rabbi expressed as his opinion that the answer did not include all the bearings of the question; he thought that it should contain observations on the probable consequences of such marriages.

A member said that certainly government should be made acquainted with all the obstacles which stood in the way of unions of that nature.

Another thought that all the members who composed that assembly were sufficiently enlightened on their religion, to deliver their opinion according to their conscience. He deemed the answer of the commission perfectly correct, and demanded that it should be put to the vote in the same mode as the others had been.

A member declared, that, in questions of this importance, the Rabbies should be more particularly consulted, in order to be better fixed in the true principles.

Another observed, that Rabbies delivering their opinion like other members, must rest satisfied with the influence their profession gave them, without attempting to increase it.

A Rabbi intreated his fellow-doctors to discuss the question with moderation and docility, as became true disciples of Moses; he declared that he too would stand forth the champion of religion, but that he thought it also a duty incumbent upon him to expose publicly the additions which degrade it, and which he attributed, with the celebra-

ted Mendelshon, to the pestilent breath of superstition, which had often shewn itself openly.

A member said, " We shall always hear the
" Rabbies with pleasure; but their opinion must
" not have more authority than that of the other
" members."

Another added, that a commission having been
named to prepare the answers, and this commission presenting them afterwards to the assembly,
every member was at liberty to deliver his sentiments, and that, consequently, in the deliberations,
one vote could not have more weight than another.

A Rabbi said, that, whenever his fellow-doctors
delivered an opinion, they should adduce proofs to
support it; and consequently that the assembly
should not admit contrary opinions, unless supported by arguments which should refute theirs.

Several members spake in support of the answer
proposed by the commission, and at the same time
approved the principles laid down by the last
speaker.

A Rabbi said, that marriage is a religious act,
and that the persons united in wedlock, must be
of the same religion.

A member stated that it did not appear to him,
that this necessary condition is expressed in any
law. " The difference of religion," says he, " cer-
" tainly makes those unions more difficult, but
" they cannot be considered as forbidden on that

" account ; it will be sufficient to point out these
" obstacles in the answer."

Another observed that, since no law forbade that
kind of marriages, they must be lawful.

A member said that the first precept of the law
is *increase and multiply*; that in the sacred writings
he finds no religious ceremonies relative to marriage; that some, indeed, are prescribed in the
Talmud, but only to enliven the festivity of the
day, and make it more agreeable to the married
couple, to their parents, and to their friends.

A Rabbi thought that marriages with Christians were forbidden. He requested the assembly
to consider that when Moses forbad those unions
with the proscribed nations, he gave, as the motive of this prohibition, the fear and apprehension
lest, by the seduction of women, men should be led
astray from the the law of the God in whose name
he spoke; that, consequently, the probability of seduction still existing in unions with other nations,
the prohibition still existed likewise.

Another member spake on the same side of the
question; he begged of the assembly not to hurry
the decision, but to give time to the deputies to
weigh the question maturely; he proposed to adjourn the deliberation to the following day.

Another began by reading the four first verses
of the 7th chapter of Deuteronomy; then he said,

U

" Why should we apply to Christians the prohibi-
" tion contained in these verses? Are we com-
" missioned to destroy them? not to give them any
" quarter? Do they not worship the same God we
" adore? Surely if God were to send us a second
" Moses, far from tracing a line of separation be-
" tween us, he would tell us—'Love the Christians ;
" cherish them as your brethren ; unite with them ;
" consider them as children of the same family.
" You all acknowledge that they are no idolators ;
" that they worship, as you do, the Creator of hea-
" ven and earth ; that they are your brethren and
" your benefactors.' What more is necessary to
" make marriages lawful between Jews and Chris-
" tians? Will you say that the present Rabbies do
" not consider them as such ? The answer framed
" by the commission contains this declaration.

" Great stress has been laid on the domestic in-
" conveniences which would result from such
" marriages; but has a word been said of the great
" political advantages they would produce? If
" both should be put into the scale, could the su-
" periority of the last be doubted? Certainly not :
" we must, then, adopt the answer proposed by the
" commission, which contains the whole truth."

This opinion was strongly supported by many
members.

A Rabbi answered that truth must be told, let

the consequences be what they may. He declared, as his opinion, that marriages with Christians are not lawful.

A member said that it would be a difficult matter to come to a resolution, if the question be not regularly proposed. He demanded that the President should put the first part of it to the vote.

Several Members demanded the priority for the answer of the Rabbies, others for that of the commission.—[*Some tumult took place.*]

A member proposed to adjourn the discussion.

Another proposed, on the contrary, that the debate should be closed, and that the assembly should proceed to a division.

Another insisted that the assembly could not rise till the question was decided.

Another proposed to suspend the discussion; to call the Rabbies to the table, in order to unite the two answers into one, in such a manner, as to conciliate the principles advanced on both sides of the question.

This proposition was adopted; the President suspended the discussion, and prepared a new answer with the assistance of the Rabbies and the members of the commission.

After a lapse of three-quarters of an hour, the President announced that the discussion was resumed; he read the new answer to the third question. M. Lyon Marx translated it verbally into German, The question was called for on every side. The President put the new answer to the vote, and it was adopted almost unanimously. The President then called for the reading of a declaration which he thought should be affixed to the answers: the assembly approved it by, acclamation, and with shouts of *Long live the Emperor!* This declaration was translated into German by M. Lyon Marx.

The assembly also ordered that this declaration, and the answers to the three first questions, should be inserted in the minutes of the proceedings of the day. In consequence these four documents were annexed to that day's minutes.

The President proposed afterwards to name a commission to prepare the ceremonies of a festival to be celebrated in the synagogues, on the 15th of August next, in commemoration of His Majesty's birth day, and of the re-establishment of religious worship, as one of the greatest blessings of his reign.

The assembly adopted this proposition unanimously, and the President named as Commissioners to prepare this festival, MM. J. Rodrigues, sen. of La Gironde; Gumpel Levy, of Nancy, May, jun. of Paris, Sabaton Constantini, of Marseilles, and Aaron Schmol, of Paris, who are to consult with the Administrators of Synagogues.

A member reminded the assembly that in the sitting of the 26th of July, he made a proposition analogous to this subject, the discussion of which had been adjourned to another meeting; he demanded that it should be now taken into consideration.

The President referred the propositions of this member to the Commissioners, whose report would be received at the next meeting, which the President fixed for Thursday the 7th. instant. The sitting closed at half past five.

Declaration adopted by the Assembly, and the Answers to the three first Questions.

DECLARATION.

Resolved, by the French deputies professing the religion of Moses, that the following Declaration shall precede the answers returned to the questions proposed by the Commissioners of His Imperial and Royal Majesty.

" *The assembly, impressed with a deep sense of* " *gratitude, love, respect, and admiration, for the*

" sacred person of his Imperial and Royal Majesty,
" declares, in the name of all Frenchmen professing
" the religion of Moses, that they are fully deter-
" mined to prove worthy of the favours His Majesty
" intends for them, by scrupulously conforming to
" his paternal intentions; that their religion makes
" it their duty to consider the law of the prince as
" the supreme law in civil and political matters; that,
" consequently, should their religious code, or its
" various interpretations, contain civil or political
" commands, at variance with those of the French
" code, those commands would, of course, cease to in-
" fluence and govern them, since they must, above all,
" acknowledge and obey the laws of the prince.

" That, in consequence of this principle, the Jews
" have, at all times, considered it their duty to obey
" the laws of the state, and that, since the revolution,
" they, like all Frenchmen, have acknowledged no
" others."

FIRST QUESTION.

Is it lawful for Jews to marry more than one wife?

ANSWER.

It is not lawful for Jews to marry more than one

wife : in all European countries they conform to the general practice of marrying only one.

Moses does not command expressly to take several; but he does not forbid it. He seems even to adopt that custom as generally prevailing, since he settles the rights of inheritance between children of different wives. Although this practice still prevails in the East, yet their antient doctors have enjoined them to restrain from taking more than one wife, except when the man is enabled by his fortune to maintain several.

The case has been different in the West; the wish of adopting the customs of the inhabitants of this part of the world has induced the Jews to renounce Polygamy. But as several individuals still indulged in that practice, a synod was convened at Worms in the eleventh century, composed of one hundred Rabbies, with Guerson at their head. This assembly pronounced an anathema against every Israelite who should, in future, take more than one wife.

Although this prohibition was not to last for ever, the influence of European manners has universally revailed.

SECOND QUESTION.

Is divorce allowed by the Jewish Religion? Is di-
vorce valid when not pronounced by Courts of Justice
by Virtue of Laws in Contradiction with those of the
French Code?

ANSWER.

Repudiation is allowed by the law of Moses;
but it is not valid if not previously pronounced
by the French code.

In the eyes of every Israelite, without exception, submission to the prince is the first of duties. It is a principle generally acknowledged
among them, that, in every thing relating to civil
or political interests, the law of the state is the supreme law. Before they were admitted in France
to share the rights of all citizens, and when they
lived under a particular legislation which set them
at liberty to follow their religious customs, they
had the facility of repudiating their wives; but it
was extremely rare to see it put into practice.

Since the revolution, they have acknowledged no
other laws on this head but those of the empire.
At the epocha when they were admitted to the
rank of citizens, the Rabbies and the principal
Jews appeared before the municipalities of their

respective places of abode, and took an oath to conform, in every thing to the laws, and to acknowledge no other rules in all civil matters.

Consequently they can no longer consider as valid the repudiation pronounced by their Rabbies, since, to make it valid, it must have been previously pronounced by competent tribunals; for, in like manner as by an *arrete* of the Consular Government, the Rabbies could not impart the matrimonial benediction till it appeared to them that the civil contract had been performed before the civil officer, in like manner they cannot pronounce repudiation, until it appears to them that it has already been pronounced by a sentence which gives it validity. Supposing even that the aforesaid *arrete* had been silent on this head, still the rabbinical repudiation could not be valid; for, according to Rabbies who have written on the civil code of the Jews, such as Joseph Carro in the *Abeneser*, repudiation is valid only, in case there should be no opposition of any kind. And as the law of the state would form an opposition, in point of civil interests---since one of the parties could avail himself or herself of it against the other---it necessarily follows that, under the influence of the civil code, rabbinical repudiation cannot be valid. Consequently, since the time the Jews have begun to enter into engagements before the civil officer,

no one, attached to religious practices, can repudi-
ate his wife but by a double divorce---that pronounced by the law of the state, and that prescribed
by the law of Moses; so that under this point of
view, it may be justly affirmed, that the Jewish religion agrees on this subject with the civil code.

THIRD QUESTION.

*Can a Jewess marry a Christian, and a Jew a
Christian woman? or does the law allow the Jews to
intermarry only among themselves?*

ANSWER.

The law does not say that a Jewess cannot
marry a Christian, nor a Jew a Christian woman;
nor does it state that the Jews can only intermarry
among themselves.

The only marriages expressly forbidden by the
law, are those with the seven Canaanean nations,
with Amon and Moab, and with the Egyptians.
The prohibition is absolute concerning the seven
Canaanean nations: with regard to Amon and Moab,
it is limited, according to many Talmudists, to the
men of those nations, and does not extend to the
women; it is even thought that these last would
have embraced the Jewish religion. As to Egyp-

tians, the prohibition is limited to the third generation. The prohibition in general applies only to
nations in idolatry. The Talmud declares formally that modern nations are not to be considered
as such, since they worship, like us, the God of
heaven and earth. And, accordingly, there has
been, at several periods, intermarriages between
Jews and Christians in France, in Spain, and in
Germany: these marriages were sometimes tolerated, and sometimes forbidden by the laws of those
sovereigns, who had received Jews into their dominions.

Unions of this kind are still found in France;
but we cannot dissemble that the opinion of the
Rabbies is against these marriages. According to
their doctrine, although the religion of Moses
has not forbidden the Jews from intermarrying
with nations not of their religion, yet, as marriage,
according to the Talmud, requires religious ceremonies called *Kiduschim*, with the benediction
used in such cases, no marriage can be *religiously*
valid unless these ceremonies have been performed. This could not be done towards persons who
would not both of them consider these ceremonies
as sacred; and in that case the married couple
could separate without the *religious* divorce; they
would then be considered as married *civilly* but
not *religiously*.

x 2

Such is the opinion of the Rabbies, members of this assembly. In general they would be no more inclined to bless the union of a Jewess with a Christian, or of a Jew with a Christian woman, than Catholic priests themselves would be disposed to sanction unions of this kind. The Rabbies acknowledge, however, that a Jew, who marries a Christian woman, does not cease on that account, to be considered as a Jew by his brethren, any more than if he had married a Jewess *civilly* and not *religiously*.

After the sittings of the 26th and 29th of July, I should naturally have placed many discourses, some of which, from unforeseen circumstances, could not be delivered in the assembly. I was forced, much against my intention, by the press of matter, to notice them briefly, as may have been already remarked; but many persons having expressed a wish to see them inserted in this collection, I have been induced to accede to it, particularly as the sentiments which they contain are honourable to the authors, and prove their zeal for the interest of our brethren whom they represent, and their dutiful attachment to the wise government which protects them.

I shall, then, with pleasure, introduce them here.

I shall, in the like manner, and immediately after each sitting, give the different writings relative to the questions debated.

Reflections of M. Baruch Cerf-Berr, *Deputy to the* Jewish *Assembly convened at* Paris *by Order of His Majesty the Emperor.*

" It is under the auspicious protection of Napo-
" leon the Great, of that hero whom Providence
" has sent in his mercy to regenerate the French
" empire—that hero, equally wonderful by his
" profound genius and by his promptitude in ex-
" ecution, and who was destined to fix irrevocably
" the fate of Europe, that this assembly was formed:
" it is to our august Sovereign's tender solicitude
" for the welfare of his faithful subjects, that we
" are indebted for the happiness of being, for the
" first time, assembled together to represent a
" part of the nation which, differing from their fel-
" low citizens in religious opinions, are not sur-
" passed by them in love for the sacred person of
" our august Sovereign, or in zeal for the public
" welfare.

" At the same time General and Soldier, pro-
" found Legislator and consummate Politician,
" His Majesty has formed, in his high wisdom, the

" means of conciliating the diversity of religions
" with the public welfare, and binding together
" those divergent opinions, which, nevertheless,
" tend to the same aim through different ways.

" Catholics and Lutherans, Jews and Calvinists,
" are considered by His Majesty as children of the
" same father: he leaves to the Supreme Being the
" right of calling them to account for their opini-
" ons; they enjoy in safety the same rights and
" protection, and share equally his paternal atten-
" tion; His Majesty acknowledges no difference
" among them, except that which results from vir-
" tue and from talents.

" In reading the annals of history, the most ob-
" durate heart must feel for the misfortunes which
" we have experienced ; but tears are dried up; the
" heart is relieved when the reader reaches the age
" of Napoleon. His Majesty has been pleased not
" only to make us forget hardships which degrade
" mankind, but also to put us in full enjoyment
" of all the rights of French citizens: his wish is
" to unite us more closely with the greatest nation
" on earth, so as to form but one people.

" But, to second the benevolent views of His Ma-
" jesty, how many reforms must be made !....How
" many abuses are to be corrected !....All those in-
" conveniencies, produced, no doubt by the vari-
" ous political systems under which we have

" groaned, have been deeply felt by the celebrated
" writers of our persuasion, and by distinguished
" persons among our brethren, who have noticed
" them long ago, but who did not judge them in-
" superable.

" And truly under what pretence can a man re-
" fuse his whole support to a government which in-
" sures him the enjoyment of his rights and of his
" property? The venerable father, Cerf-Berr, proved
" that his heart was truly French; that he knew the
" obligations which men contract in forming part of
" society, when he sought for, when he courted,
" the honour of being useful to his country, even
" at a period when the Jewish nation was groaning
" under an oppressive system.

" If the tomb which contains the ashes of those
" virtuous men, who have written, who have
" thought, who have served their country with
" zeal and disinterestedness, who have been
" sought after by sovereigns, who have diffused
" instruction or encouraged those who propagated
" learning---if the tombs of Blien, of Gradix,
" Humbert, Mendelshon, Aaron-Mayer, of Cerf-
" Berr, could now open, and that their inhabitants,
" once more visiting this world, could sit with us in
" this august assembly, how eagerly would they pay
" their tribute of admiration to the benevolent de-
" signs of His Majesty! How zealously would they

" contribute to further his regenerating views! But
" why did they enjoy only the dawn of happiness?
" Why are we deprived of their assistance as guides,
" in deliberations which are to realize our hopes and
" consolidate our happiness? But if we have not
" inherited their talents and their extensive learn-
" ing, we can, like them, boast of hearts truly
" French. We are animated by the same attach-
" ment to public welfare, which entitles us to the
" confidence of government. Have we not, be-
" sides, among us Zinzheimer, Moses Lipmann,
" Eneishem? And who is there among us, who
" could hesitate to contribute to the great work,
" by all the means in his power, when he consi-
" ders that, in the military career, His Majesty has
" indiscriminately placed eagles and laurels within
" the reach of our children? That he has opened for
" them the sanctuary of the law, the temple of arts
" and sciences, manufactures, &c.? Some of our
" children are even entitled to our praises, by their
" efforts to justify the good opinion His Majesty is
" pleased to entertain of us. But how small their
" number is still! Yet my heart tells me that the
" Jewish people will prove worthy of the tender
" regard of His Majesty: and, if wishes and good
" intentions only were wanting, we are all disposed
" to give our brethren that impulse which has been
" rendered necessary by the torpid state in which

(161)

. " we have so long languished ; and our grand child-
" ren, for I durst indulge in the consoling idea,
" will one day mark the meeting of this august
" Synod, as the epocha of the regeneration of the
" people of God, and will bless the memory of
" those wise and learned interpreters of the law,
" who, by their example, their erudition, their
" virtues, and their writings, have opened for us the
" road to happiness.

" B. C. B."

Discourse at the Opening of the general Assembly of the Jews, delivered by M. Lipmann Cerf-Berr, *Deputy for the Department of the* Upper Rhine.

" An ever-memorable imperial decree has called
" us together in this hall. I ascend this tribune to
" express those sentiments of gratitude which I
" owe to our august Emperor, and to assure you,
" my dear brethren, of my most inviolable and
" most sincere affection.

" Government has called us round it, as a father
" calls his children; let us prove worthy of the
" benefit; let us prove worthy of the trust reposed
" in us; let us prove worthy of ourselves in
" entering this hall: let us forget from whence we

Y

" came; let there be no longer distinction between
" Alsatian, Portuguese, or German Jews.

" Scattered on the face of the globe, we form
" only one people, worshipping the same God, ad-
" hering religiously to the obedience which our
" law commands towards the power under whose
" protection we live; and this obedience, which,
" towards princes in general, is only the expression
" of our duty, is when, paid to Napoleon, the
" genuine offspring of love and gratitude. Who
" does not feel these sentiments for a benevolent
" and enlightened monarch, equally active in dis-
" covering the misfortunes of his subjects, and in
" applying the proper remedy? This union of
" wisdom and goodness particularly distinguishes
" the decree by which we are this day assembled.
" It is new for us, it is even unprecedented in his-
" tory. No sovereign has ever done what Napo-
" leon has now affected for the people of God. A
" new career is open for us, and the doors which
" lead to it are unbarred: all the Hebrews
" residing in this vast empire, and in Europe, have
" their eyes fixed on us. If our cotemporaries ex-
" pect their happiness from us, we also must expect
" to be judged by posterity. Our conduct will be
" recorded in history; the evil-intentioned watch
" and observe us; let us be on our guard, not to
" afford any hold to their malignity.

" Moses and Joshua always recommend *Rac,*
" *chazac veametz — strength and courage.* Now that
" we have nothing to fear, let us get rid of that
" timidity which has overcome us ever since we
" have lived for ages in slavery. This day the
" Grand Napoleon extends towards us his power-
" ful, protecting hand; what have we to fear but
" God and Posterity?

" Let us be calm in our discussions, wise in our
" deliberations, attentive and indulgent to those
" who deliver their sentiments. We all meet here
" with the purest intentions, of this let us never
" loose sight, and let this truth, which we all ac-
" knowledge, plead excuse for whatever may escape
" us in the warmth of debate.

" I am the first to lay claim to the indulgence I
" recommend: the time I take up, in addressing
" you, is precious: you will excuse me for having
" trespassed on it, as I am conscious of having ex-
" pressed sentiments congenial to your own.

" These sentiments have suggested to me the
" following outlines of an *arrete* which I have the
" honour of submitting to your judgment.

OUTLINES OF AN *Arrete.*

" Art. I. The 2nd. 3rd. 4th. 5th. and 6th. arti-
Y 2

cles of the imperial decree of the 30th. of May
" last, shall be engraved on a marble tablet to be
" hung up in this hall, during the course of our
" sittings, and to be afterwards placed in the me-
" tropolitan temple of the Jewish worship.

" II. The bust of His Majesty the Emperor and
" King shall be placed in this hall,

" III. An address of thanks, expressive of our
" gratitude, shall be presented to His Majesty by
" the whole assembly,

" IV. The Saturday next after the 26th of July,
" shall, every year, be commemorated as an ex-
" traordinary festival by all the Jews residing in
" the French empire.

" V. The Rabbies, sitting among us, are re-
" quested to compose a new prayer, in form of a
" benediction, for the welfare of His Majesty the
" Emperor, Her Majesty the Empress, and their
" august family, which shall be solemnly addressed
" to God on that day.

" VI. A copy of this present *Arrete*, shall be
" most humbly presented to His Majesty, with the
"Address of the whole assembly,"

Discourse of M. Berr Isaac Berr *Deputy of the Department of* La Meurthe.

" Gentlemen,

" More than seventeen centuries have elapsed
" since the ever memorable epocha when, by victo-
" rious and foreign legions, the Jewish people was
" subjugated and reduced from a tributary to a
" servile condition, and scattered by the storm of
" adversity, over the face of the habitable globe;
" always unfortunate, always persecuted, always
" faithfully adhering to the religion of its ances-
" tors, in spite of tortures and of sufferings, it af-
" fords, to this very day, a striking phenomenon
" incomprehensible to human reason; it stands
" like a column, erect amidst the wrecks of suc-
" ceeding centuries; and while, in tracing the origin
" of this people, we reascend to the cradle of man-
" kind, it should seem as if its remains are to
" be preserved until the day of universal destruc-
" tion.

" Our ancestors, for a considerable time, had to
" encounter injustices and the misfortunes produ-
" ced by oppression; we ought to admire their
" conduct while we congratulate our brethren on
" their better fate; we ought, above all, to return
" our thanks to Providence, who has not suffered

" that the aged tree should be torn up by the roots,
" though it has often permitted that its branches
" should severely suffer.

" The Jews have been alternately persecuted and
" degraded as a punishment for their faithful adhe-
" rence to the religion of their fathers; they ceased
" to be considered as men in proportion as they wish-
" ed to remain Jews. Mixed among civilized na-
" tions, they would have proved useful citizens, had
" they not been prevented by a barbarous policy.
" In fact, humiliation and misfortune did often real-
" ly degrade us. To these baneful causes is to be
" attributed the degraded state in which many
" of our brethren still languish in some countries.
" The progress of reason and of justice among
" the nations of Europe will put an end to these
" sufferings; but, during our misfortunes, and in the
" times of our slavery, religious constancy was not
" the only characteristic of our fathers. The
" splendid light of talents, the sacred flame of vir-
" tue, shone among the unfortunate Israelites,
" under the iron-hand of oppression. Our annals
" are stained with blood, since the taking of Jeru-
" salem by Titus; in reading them over, we do not
" once meet with a monarch who called to the foot
" of his throne those who might have been able to
" help him in relieving the misfortunes and heal-
" ing the wounds of Israel.

" We live, thanks be to God, in happier times;
" we live under the salutary influence of philoso-
" phy and of reason ; under the most astonishing,
" the most sublime of legislators and of heroes ;
" under the greatest of mortals, whether consider-
" ed as to his heart, his virtues, his fortune or his
" genius : it is to him that we are indebted for the
" unprecedented appearance of this assembly, of
" which I am proud to form a part. It is the first
" time, since the fatal epocha of our misfortunes
" and of our dispersion, that a monarch convenes
" such an assembly, and that he thus shews, in our
" favour, his regard for the principles of reason.
" If, after the regenerating laws already existing,
" the last traces of our humiliation and of our sla-
" very are not completely erased from among all
" our brethren, if the reprehensible conduct of
" some of them, still hardened against these enlight-
" ened and renovated sentiments, has occasioned
" complaints which have found their way to the
" foot of the throne, yet, on the other hand, our
" august monarch deigns to consult and to associ-
" ate, in the views of reform conceived in his wis-
" dom, the principal persons of the Jews, distin-
" guished by their zeal, their learning, and their
" integrity; it is by acting in concert with us
" that he wishes to bring back all our brethren to
" a sense of their duty, and to make them all wor-

" thr of the indefeasible rights of men, of subjects,
" and of citizens.

" We will fulfil the expectations of His Majesty;
" we will undertake with zeal the noblest task
" which could be imposed upon us, by the love
" of our country, of our Sovereign and of our re-
" ligion. Who but He could be destined to ac-
" complish such designs? Is he not the only mortal
" according to God's own heart, to whom he has
" intrusted the fate of nations, because he alone
" could govern them with wisdom? He has car-
" ried his triumphant eagles into the three parts
" of the ancient world; he has overcome, as con-
" queror, the ancient land of the eternal pyramids,
" the scene of our ancestors' captivity; he has ap-
" peared on the banks of the once sacred Jordan;
" he has fought in the valley Sichem, in the plains
" of Palestine. He alone could conceive this
" sublime idea to which we are indebted for our
" being assembled in this place, this idea so well
" calculated to do away the last traces of misfor-
" tune, of shame, and of that ancient oppression
" which has ceased first in France.

" As *Frenchmen* and as *Jews*, then let us indulge
" all the gratitude which fills our hearts. Let us
" swear never to separate these sacred titles: as
" *Frenchmen* we will defend the country we love,
" and strictly observe the laws of the empire; as

" *Jews* we will remain attached to the faith and to
" the religion of our ancestors: as *Jews* and
" *Frenchmen* let us swear an inviolable attachment
" to our august Emperor.

" Let us all together invoke the Almighty, the
" God of Armies, the Guide of Kings, terrible in
" his judgments, and return our grateful thanks,
" that he has been pleased to pour incessantly on
" the great Napoleon the unspeakable treasures of
" his grace, of his wisdom, and of his might.

" As to you, Gentlemen Commissioners, who
" have been intrusted with so important and so
" interesting a mission, deign to convey to govern-
" ment, and to its august and immortal head, our
" sentiments and our wishes; assure him of our
" dutiful and profound gratitude, and our readi-
" ness to further, by all the means in our power,
" his benevolent views and his salutary designs.

" A noble task has been imposed on you, Gen-
" tlemen; you are here, sent by His Majesty to
" communicate to the assembly the questions sub-
" mitted to its judgment; this mission is for you
" an honourable testimony of the esteem of a So-
" vereign, who knows how to appreciate talents,
" services, and virtue. Reason, justice, and the
" love of public weal will guide your steps: we,
" too, shall strive to make these the grounds of
" our dutiful communications. Happy will be our

z

" fate, if, on leaving this hall, we carry with us
" the heart-soothing consciousness of having con-
" tributed to increase, in the bosom of the general
" civil society, the number of just, laborious, vir-
" tuous, and useful men; and in having assisted in
" doing away the traces of eighteen centuries of
" persecution, from among a class of men, who
" have always been, and always will be, attached
" to the religion of their fore-fathers; this new
" benefit will, in future times, mark the most bril-
" liant period of our history!"

Sitting of August 7, 1806.

The President took the chair at three quarters
past twelve. One of the Secretaries read the minutes of the sitting of the 4th of the month.

The President demanded if any member had
any observations to make on them.

No one offering to speak, they were put to the
vote, and adopted unanimously.

The President named, as Commissioners to
maintain order in the hall, MM. Auguste Ratisbonne, Cadet Carcassonne, and Schawb, jun.

M. Moses Levy, of Nancy, was requested, by
the President, to give in the report of the Commission on the answers to be returned to the fourth,
fifth, sixth, seventh, and eighth questions.

He ascended the tribune, and submitted to the assembly the draft of the answer to the fourth question.

M. Lyon Marx read the German translation, and M. Avigdor verbally translated the answer into Italian.

A member thought that the answer was considerably too long, and contained matters quite foreign to the question; he demanded that it should again be referred to the Commission, with directions to prepare another.

Another member said, that the too great length of this answer is not its only fault; it establishes a difference between Portuguese and German Jews, which ought to be suppressed; he concluded by supporting the motion of the last speaker.

A member complained that the Jews of the northern departments were particularly pointed at in the answer: he declared that, in the department in which he resided, although a northern one, Jews are as much esteemed and as much considered as those of the south: he therefore requested that these distinctions should be expunged from the answer, which, with this alteration, he should approve.

Another member proposed to refer the draft of the answer to another Commission, which should examine all the details it contained, and suppress whatever did not immediately fall within the meaning of the question.

Another ascended the tribune; he laid down the principles on which, according to his opinion, the answer ought to be framed, and read to the assembly the draft of another answer.

A deputy observed, that the second part of the answer only had been the subject of animadversion; he therefore proposed to suppress it altogether, and to adopt the first part alone, which, by itself, fulfilled every purpose.

This proposition was supported by several members. The President observed, that when the Commission established a difference between the Jews of the north and those of the south, it only meant to remark that these last have made greater progress in civilization, because their hardships were much less than the others; he thought, in the mean time, with the last speaker, that the first part of the answer might be adopted by itself.

The President accordingly read a second time the first part of the answer prepared by the Commission. He afterwards requested M. Lyon Marx to inform, in German, those members who were not sufficiently acquainted with the French language, that he was going to put to the vote the answer to the fourth question, consisting only of the first part, which he had just read,

A member obtained leave to speak; he observed, that, in the circular letter of the 23d of July, addressed by His Excellency the Minister of the Interior to all the deputies, mention is made of three Scrutineers, who have been named accordingly. He was surprized that the assembly should not vote by ballot, and demanded that that mode of collecting votes should be exclusively adopted in the present discussions.

The President observed to the last speaker, that recourse was had to that mode, (which occasioned great delay) only when the shew of hands left some doubt; but that it was useless when the majority was evident.

The same speaker replied, that there was a great difference between deliberations on principal points, and those on accessory objects; that, for the last, the shew of hands might be admitted, but that the twelve questions, being of the highest importance, the assembly ought to vote on the answers by way of ballot.

The order of the day was called for.

The President put to the vote, by shew of hands, the new draft of the answer to the fourth question: it was adopted unanimously.

One of the Secretaries read the answer proposed by the Commission to the fifth question. M. Lyon

Marx read it in German, and M. Avigdor translated it into Italian.

A member wished to see an expression altered,
which was done accordingly. After this correc-
tion, the President put the answer to the vote, and
it was adopted unanimously.

The same Secretary read the answer to the sixth
question. MM. Lyon Marx and Avigdor translated it verbally, the first into German, the second
into Italian. No objections being made to this
answer, it was put to the vote, and adopted unanimously.

The President called afterwards for the reading
of the answer to the seventh question. MM. Lyon Marx and Avigdor translated it likewise into
German and into Italian.

A member observed, that, in the answers to the
former questions, allusions had been made to the
order of things previous to the revolution, whenever the case made it necessary; he thought that, in
this answer, government should, in like manner, be
made acquainted with the mode of choosing Rabbies before the revolution, and with that which
has prevailed since.

A member said, that a difference should be
made between the officiating Rabbi who holds
the first rank in a Jewish society, and the man

having only the title of Rabbi, who, although equally learned as the first, is not distinguished from the rest of the Jews; that, in this last point of view, the Rabbi was only an individual, like all others, while in the first instance, the Rabbi became entitled to the consideration annexed to this rank, only by the votes of those who named him, whether simple individuals or administrators of charities.

The board framed a new answer, which was also translated into German and into Italian.

The President afterwards put it to the vote, and it was adopted by the majority.

One of the Secretaries read the answer prepared by the Commission to the eighth question.

M. Lyon Marx translated it into German, and M. Avigdor into Italian.

One of the members observed, that these translations contained contradictions, as to the functions of Rabbies, and demanded that the mistake might be rectified.

Another said, that the answer was not sufficiently explicit. One of the Secretaries attempted several alterations, which he read successively; they were all rejected. The answer was sent back to the Commission for revision.

A deputy mentioned a writing circulated among the members by a stranger, and which had ap-

peared in several news-papers; he thought that
the assembly should publicly disown the propositions it contained. Some members seconded this
motion; others called for the order of the day.
In the midst of the tumult which ensued, a member exclaimed that the assembly should be perfectly indifferent to writings which did not originate
with its members. Others maintained contrary
opinions.

The President quitted the chair at five o'clock,
and announced the next meeting for Tuesday the
12th inst. at nine o'clock.

Here follow the answers adopted to the fourth,
fifth, sixth, and seventh questions proposed to the
assembly by the Commissioners of His Royal and
Imperial Majesty.

FOURTH QUESTION.

*In the eyes of Jews, are Frenchmen considered
as their brethren? Or are they considered as strangers?*

ANSWER.

In the eyes of Jews Frenchmen are their brethren, and are not strangers.

The true spirit of the law of Moses is consonant
to this mode of considering Frenchmen.

When the Israelites formed a settled and independant nation, their law made it a rule for them to consider strangers as their brethren.

With the most tender care for their welfare, their lawgiver commands to love them, (13) " Love ye " therefore the strangers," says he to the Israelites, " for ye were strangers in the land of Egypt."

Respect and benevolence towards strangers are inforced by Moses, not as an exhortation to the practice of social morality only, but as an obligation imposed by God himself. " *When ye reap* " *the harvest of your land,*" (14) says he to them, " *thou shalt not make clean riddance of the cor-* " *ners of the field when thou reapest, neither shalt* " *thou gather any gleaning of thy harvest;* " *thou shalt leave them unto the poor and to the* " stranger; *I am the Lord thy God.* (15) *When* " *thou cuttest down thy harvest in the field, and hast* " *forgot a sheaf in the field, thou shalt not go back* " *again to fetch it: it shall be for the* stranger, *for* " *the fatherless, and the widow: that the Lord thy* " *God may bless the work of thy hands.* (16) *Thou* " *shalt neither vex a* stranger, *nor oppress him.*

(13) Deut x. 19. Lev. xix. 34. Exod. xxii. 21. xxiii. 9.
(14) Levit. xxiii. 22.
(15) Deut. xxiv. 19.
(16) Exod. xxii. 21.

" (17) *The Lord your God doth execute the judg-*
" *ment of the fatherless and widow, and loveth the*
" stranger, *in giving him food and raiment.* Love
" *ye therefore the stranger; for ye were* strangers *in*
" *the land of Egypt.*"

To these sentiments of benevolence towards the *Stranger*, Moses has added the precept of general love for mankind: " *Love thy fellow creature as thyself.*"

David also expresses himself in these terms: (18) " The Lord is good to all: and *his tender mercies are over all his works.*" This doctrine is also professed by the Talmud.

" We are bound," says a Talmudist, " to love as " our brethren all those who observe the (19) " *Noachides,* whatever their religious opinions may " otherwise be. We are bound to visit their sick, " to bury their dead, to assist their poor, like those " of Israel. In short, there is no act of humanity " which a true Israelite is not bound to perform to- " wards those who observe the *Noachides.*" What are these precepts? To abstain from idolatry, from blasphemy, from adultery, not to kill or hurt our neighbours, neither to rob or to deceive, to eat only

(17) Deut. x. 18. 19.
(18) Psalm, cxlv. 9.
(19) The precepts given by the Patriarch Noah.

the flesh of animals killed ; in short, to observe the rules of justice; and therefore all the principles of our religion make it our duty to love Frenchmen as our brethren.

A Pagan having consulted the Rabbi Hillel on the Jewish religion, and wishing to know in a few words in what it consisted, Hillel thus answered him: " Do not to others what thou shouldst not " like to have done to thyself. This," said he, " is " all our religion; the rest are only consequences " of this principle."

A religion whose fundamental maxims are such —a religion which makes a duty of loving the stranger—which enforces the practice of social virtues, must surely require that its followers should consider their fellow-citizens as brethren.

And how could they consider them otherwise when they inhabit the same land, when they are ruled and protected by the same government, and by the same laws? when they enjoy the same rights, and have the same duties to fulfil? There exists, even between the Jew and Christian, a tie which abundantly compensates for religion—it is the tie of gratitude. This sentiment was at first excited in us by the mere grant of toleration. It has been increased, these eighteen years, by new favours from government, to such a degree of energy, that now our fate is irrevocably linked with the com-

mon fate of all Frenchmen. Yes, France is our
country; all Frenchmen are our brethren, and
this glorious title, by raising us in our own esteem,
becomes a sure pledge that we shall never cease to
be worthy of it.

FIFTH QUESTION.

*In either case, what line of conduct does their law
prescribe towards Frenchmen not of their religion?*

ANSWER.

The line of conduct prescribed towards Frenchmen not of our religion, is the same as that prescribed between Jews themselves; we admit of no
difference but that of worshipping the Supreme
Being, every one in his own way.

The answer to the preceeding question has explained the line of conduct which the law of Moses and the Talmud prescribe towards Frenchmen
not of our religion. At the present time, when the
Jews no longer form a separate people, but enjoy
the advantage of being incorporated with the
Great Nation, (which privilege they consider as a
kind of political redemption) it is impossible that
a Jew should treat a Frenchman, not of his reli-

gion, in any other manner than he would treat
one of his Israelitish brethren.

SIXTH QUESTION.

*Do Jews born in France, and treated by the laws
as French citizens, consider France as their country?
Are they bound to defend it? Are they bound to obey
the laws and to conform to the dispositions of the civil
code?*

ANSWER.

Men who have adopted a country, who have resided in it these many generations---who, even under the restraint of particular laws which abridged
their civil rights, were so attached to it that they
preferred being debarred from the advantages
common to all other citizens, rather than leave it,
cannot but consider themselves as Frenchmen in
France; and they consider as equally sacred and
honourable the bounden duty of defending their
country.

Jeremiah, (chapter xxix.) exhorts the Jews to
consider Babylon as their country, although they
were to remain in it only for seventy years. He
exhorts them to till the ground, to build houses,
to sow, and to plant. His recommendation was so

much attended to, that Ezra, (chapter ii.) says,
that when Cyrus allowed them to return to Jerusalem to rebuild the Temple, forty-two thousand three hundred and sixty only, left Babylon; and that this number was mostly composed of
the poorer people, the wealthy having remained in
that city.

The love of the country is in the heart of Jews a
sentiment so natural, so powerful, and so consonant to their religious opinions, that a French Jew
considers himself, in England, as among strangers,
although he may be among Jews; and the case is
the same with English Jews in France.

To such a pitch is this sentiment carried among
them, that, during the last war, French Jews have
been seen fighting desperately against other Jews,
the subjects of countries then at war with France.

Many of them are covered with honourable
wounds, and others have obtained, in the field of
honour, the noble rewards of bravery.

SEVENTH QUESTION.

Who names the Rabbies?

ANSWER.

Since the revolution, the majority of the chiefs of

families names the Rabbi, wherever there is a sufficient number of Jews to maintain one, after previous inquiries as to the morality and learning of the candidate. This mode of election is not, however, uniform; it varies according to place, and, to this day, whatever concerns the elections of Rabbies is still in a state of uncertainty.

Sitting of the 12th of August, 1806.

The President took the chair precisely at eleven. He named as Commissioners to maintain order, MM. Baruch Cerf-Berr, Pato, jun. and Michel Berr.

One of the Secretaries read the minutes of the sitting of the 7th of this month.

A member said, that it was useless to mention the remarks made on the difference established between German and Portuguese Jews by the draft of the answer to the fourth question. He said it was equally superfluous to insert the remark made on this head by a deputy from a northern department.

The President observed, that the minutes must take notice of whatever is said in the assembly.

A member called for the order of the day.

Another seconded the motion of the first speaker.

A loud cry of *Question.*

The President put the minutes to the vote, and they were adopted by the majority.

One of the Secretaries read the draft of the answer to the eighth question. M. Avigdor translated it into Italian, and M. Lyon Marx into German.

A member requested leave to speak; he observed, that if in the north most marriages were blessed by the Rabbies, the case was different in the southern departments, where there were but few Rabbies; and that, even in places where Rabbies were maintained, the father, or one of the elders of the family, frequently took pleasure in performing himself the marriage ceremony.

It was resolved that this remark should be inserted in the journal.

A member observed that the words *Kingdom of Italy*, should be added to those of *French Empire*, as the customs of both countries were similar.

The President had the words inserted; and, after a second reading, the draft of the answer was adopted almost unanimously.

A Secretary read the draft of the answer to the ninth question.

M. Lyon Marx translated it into German, and
M. Avigdor into Italian.

A member requested the explanation of a phrase.
The President explained it for him.

He then put it to the vote; it was adopted almost unanimously.

The President ordered afterwards the reading
of the draft of the answer to the tenth question.

M. Lyon Marx translated it into German, and
M. Avigdor into Italian.

No objections being offered, the President put
it to the vote, and it was adopted unanimously.

One of the Secretaries read the draft of the answer to the eleventh question.

M. Lyon Marx translated it into German, and
M. Avigdor into Italian.

A member requested leave to speak, and said,
that, as this answer explained the text of the 24th
chapter of Deuteronomy, it ought to be especially
recommended to the attention of Rabbies, who have
the care of preaching morality, in order that those
among the Jews who are ignorant of their duty in
their money transactions with other Frenchmen,
should be made acquainted with them, to be on
their guard against the temptation of cupidity.

The proposition was seconded.

Another member observed, that Rabbies, in

preaching morality certainly would not forget this essential exhortation.

A member ascended the tribune, and expressed his astonishment that the expression *Law of Moses* should always be used in speaking of the written law. " God," said he, " is our legislator, " and we must consequently say the *Law of God*, " and not the *Law of Moses*." He demanded that the expression should be altered accordingly.

Another member appeared in the tribune after him. He began by praising the scrupulous zeal of the last speaker, but he did not think that his amendment ought to be adopted. " I can safely " maintain," said he, " without a wish to offend " the last speaker, that my parents were, to the " full, as orthodox as he can possibly be. Yet I " well remember to have heard them say always " *Torat Mosse,* the *Law of Moses,* in speaking of the " written law." He demanded that the wording of the Commission should be maintained.

Some Rabbies delivered their sentiments in favour of the first speaker.

A member observed, that, whenever the expression, *the Law of Moses,* occurred, it was always understood to mean the *Law of God* transmitted to the Jews by Moses. He thought that the best way to reconcile the different opinions would be, to insert this explanation in the minutes,

This proposition was adopted.

Another member ascended the tribune and spoke on the word *ahiha*, in the 19th and 20th verses of the 23d chapter of Deuteronomy, which means *Brother;* he thought that the word *brother* could be applied only to a fellow Jew.

A member observed that this word was not exclusively applicable to men of the same religion; he quoted the 4th verse of the 49th chapter of Genesis, where it is used in the more general acception of *friend.*

He quoted also the 12th verse of the 15th chapter of Deuteronomy, in which the word *Hebrew* is joined with the word *ahiha.* Hence he concluded that, since the law joined the word *Hebrew* with that of *brother,* where it meant a man of the same religion, it clearly followed that, whenever these two expressions were not joined, the word *brother* had a more general acception. He quoted several other passages in support of this opinion.

Another member examined critically the 20th verse of the 23d chapter of Deuteronomy, already alluded to. He observed that the word *Nochri* which means a stranger, had no reference to religious belief, but only to the country or state; that the verb *tassich,* which means to make profit, was applicable to the *foreigner,* not to the *fellow-countryman.* And that the substantive *ahiha,* which means *brother*, was to be taken in the acceptation of *fellow-countryman* and not of *fellow Jew.* (18) He observed, that the law was purely political; and that what preceded and what followed proved sufficiently, that profit, and not usury, was meant. He concluded by demanding that the answer proposed by the Commission, which contained nearly the same principles, should be put to the vote.

A member observed that this answer being very long, it was fit it should be read a second time.

The President ordered the answer to be read a second time.

A Rabbi observed, that the answer admitted that interest was lawful; he declared that interest, of any kind, was forbidden by the law.

Another member observed, that, in fact, the law allowed of no interest, but that, since the Jews have ceased to be a nation, and are become mer-

(18) For the intelligence of this part of the debate, we shall subjoin here the two verses alluded to:

19. Thou shalt not lend upon usury to thy brother, usury of money, usury of victuals, usury of any thing that is lent upon usury.

20. Unto a stranger thou mayest lend upon usury; but unto thy brother thou shalt not lend upon usury, that the LORD thy God may bless thee in all that thou settest thine hand to, in the land whither thou goest to possess it.

It should seem that the Jewish doctors give a different meaning to the word usually translated by *usury.*

chants, they have been allowed to take a small profit; that the answer meant a moderate gain arising from a commercial speculation, and not usurious interest.

A member observed, that, by explaining this idea to the Rabbies, they would perceive that the answer was agreeable to the principles of the law.

Another demanded a third reading of the draft of the answer.

A Secretary read it for the third time.

A member moved that it should be put to the vote.

The President put it to to the vote, by shew of hands, and it was adopted almost unanimously.

A Secretary read the draft of the answer to the twelfth question.

M. Lyon Marx translated it into German, and M. Avigdor into Italian.

No objections being made against it, the President put it to the vote, and it passed unanimously.

The President read the draft of an address to His Majesty the Emperor and King, on the anniversary of his birth-day, couched in the following terms:

To His Majesty the Emperor of the French *and* King *of* Italy.

" Sire,

" Your French and Italian subjects, whatever
" religion they profess, celebrate this day the an-
" niversary of Your Majesty's birth-day; all im-
" plore the King of Kings in their respective tem-
" ples that he may be pleased to pour his most
" signal favours on your sacred person, and on the
" august imperial family. We, too, animated with
" the same sentiments, and impressed with a grati-
" tude still livelier, if possible, put up our fervent
" prayers to heaven in the same frame of mind.

" Providence, Sire, has given you this vast em-
" pire, to rescue it from the abyss into which it was
" apparently hurried by the selfish views of jar-
" ing factions.

" After rendering France illustrious by your
" victories, you have given it peace, the first bless-
" ing on earth; you astonish the universe, you ex-
" haust admiration by holding up to wondering
" mortals the model of the wisest, the most benevo-
" lent of lawgivers, and of the greatest of heroes.

" Deign, Sire, graciously to accept, on this day,
" the expressions of those sentiments of profound
" respect, love, and gratitude, towards your sacred

" person, which fill the hearts of your French and
" Italian subjects professing the religion of Mo-
" ses."

The Assembly received this address with loud
acclamations of *Long live the Emperor, long live the
Imperial family.* The President was directed to
transmit it to His Excellency the Minister for the
Interior, and to request, at the same, time that His
Excellency would have the goodness to lay it before His Majesty.

M. Rodrigues, of La Gironde, ascended the tribune, and gave in the report of the Commission of
five, who had been directed to prepare the ceremonies of the festival, to be celebrated on the
15th, in the Jewish Temple of *Rue Sainte-Avoie*, in
honour of His Majesty's birth day. He proposed
the ten following articles.

1st. Precisely at ten o'clock in the morning the
members shall assemble in the hall of meeting.

2nd. The sitting shall begin by reading the minutes of the sitting of the 12th, and the President
shall leave the chair immediately after they shall
be concluded.

3rd. At eleven o'clock the deputies, with the President at their head, shall proceed to the Temple;
on their entering it, the orchestra shall strike the
tune of *Where can a man be better than in the bosom*

of his family? The President shall deliver a discourse analogous to the festival.

4th. At twelve o'clock precisely an hymn of thanksgiving, in honour of His Majesty the Emperor and King, shall be sung by M. Andrade, accompanied by a chorus.

5th. M. Abraham Andrade, deputy of Bayonne, shall deliver a French discourse, M. Zinzheimer, Rabbi, deputy of the Lower Rhine, a German discourse; and M. Segre, Rabbi, deputy of Verceil, an Italian discourse.

6th. The orchestra shall play a symphony of Haydn. In the mean time Mlle. Caroline Wolf, who has had two brothers this great while in the army, the eldest decorated with the star of the legion of honour, the second a lieutenant in the 3d regiment of dragoons, wounded at Austerlitz, Mlles. Schmoll and Julie Theodore Cerf-Berr, the first accompanied by M. Rodrigue the eldest, the second by M. Castro jun. and the third by M. Avigdor, shall make a collection in the Temple.

The produce of this collection shall be distributed among the poor of all persuasions; and shall accordingly be divided between the several charitable institutions.

7th. The Temple shall be illuminated and ornamented with garlands and flowers; the Imperial Eagle shall be placed above the Altar.

8th. At night the outside of the Temple shall be illuminated as well as the hall in which the assembly meets.

9th. The President shall give the signal of departure, and the deputies shall return in the same order.

10th. To avoid confusion, carriages shall wait in the second yard.

The assembly approved these dispositions.

The reporter added, that the Commission had also taken into its consideration the discourse of M. Lipmann Cerf-Berr. His opinion was to adjourn the execution of the 1st, 3rd, 4th, and 5th articles of the proposed plan. There could be but one voice on the second article, which expressed a wish to see His Majesty's bust in this hall. The President was requested to transmit that wish of the assembly to His Excellency the Minister for he Interior,

The President quitted the chair at half past three. The answers adopted by the assembly to the eighth, ninth, tenth, eleventh, and twelfth questions.

EIGHTH QUESTION.

What police jurisdiction do Rabbies exercise

among the Jews? what judicial power do they enjoy among them.

The Rabbies exercise no manner of Police Jurisdiction among the Jews.

The qualification of *Rabbi* is no where to be found in the law of Moses, neither did it exist in the days of the first Temple; it is only mentioned towards the end of those of the second.

At these epochas the Jews were governed by *Sanhedrim* or tribunals. A supreme tribunal, called *the Grand Sanhedrim*, sat in Jerusalem, and was composed of seventy-one Judges.

There were inferior courts, composed of three judges for civil causes and for police; and another composed of twenty-two Judges, which sat in the capital to decide matters of less importance, and which was called *the Lesser Sanhedrim*.

It is only in the Misna and in the Talmu that the word *Rabbi* is found for the first time applied to a doctor in the law; and he was commonly indebted for this qualification to his reputation, and to the opinion generally entertained of his learning.

When the Israelites were totally dispersed, they formed small communities in those places where they were allowed to settle in certain numbers.

Sometimes, in these circumstances, a Rabbi and two other doctors formed a kind of tribunal, named *Bethin*, that is, House of Justice; the Rabbi fulfilled the functions of judge, and the other two those of his assessors.

The attributes, and even the existence of these tribunals, have, to this day, always depended on the will of governments under which the Jews have lived, and on the degree of tolerance they have enjoyed. Since the revolution those rabbinical tribunals are totally suppressed in France, and in Italy. The Jews, raised to the rank of citizens, have conformed in every thing to the laws of the state; and, accordingly, the functions of Rabbies, wherever any are established, are limited to preaching morality in the temples, blessing marriages, and pronouncing divorces.

In places where there are no Rabbies, the Jew who is best instructed in his religion, may, according to the law, impart the marriage-benediction without the assistance of a Rabbi; this is attended with an inconveniency, the consequences of which it certainly would be proper to prevent, by extending to all persons, called upon to bless a marriage, the restrictions which the consular *arrete* places on the functions of Rabbies in this particular.

As to judicial powers, they possess absolutely

none; for there is among them neither a settled ecclesiastical hierarchy, nor any subordination in the exercise of their religious functions.

NINTH QUESTION.

Are these forms of Election, and that police-judicial-jurisdiction, regulated by the law, or are they only sanctioned by custom?

ANSWER.

The answer to the preceding questions makes it useless to say much on this, only it may be remarked, that, even supposing that Rabbies should have, to this day, preserved some kind of police-judicial-jurisdiction among us, which is not the case, neither such jurisdiction, nor the forms of the elections, could be said to be sanctioned by the law; they should be attributed solely to custom.

TENTH QUESTION.

Are there professions which the law of the Jews forbids them from exercising?

ANSWER.

There are none: on the contrary, the Talmud
(*vide* Kiduschim, *chap.* 1*st.*) expressly declares
that " the father who does not teach a profession
" to his child, rears him up to be a villain."

ELEVENTH QUESTION.

*Does the law forbid the Jews from taking usury
from their brethren?*

ANSWER.

Deuteronomy (chap. xxiii. vers. 19,) says,
" thou shalt not lend upon *interest* (21) to thy
" brother, *interest* of money, *interest* of victuals,
" *interest* of any thing that is lent upon *interest.*"
The Hebrew word *nechech* has been improperly
translated by the word *usury:* in the Hebrew language it means *interest* of any kind, and not *usurious interest.* It cannot then be taken in the acceptation now given in the word *usury.*
It is even impossible that it could ever have had
that acception; for usury is an expression relative
to, and compared with, another and a lawful

(21) English Translation, *usury.*

interest; and the text contains nothing which alludes to the other term of comparison. What do
we understand by usury? Is it not an interest
above the legal interest, above the rate fixed by
the law? If the law of Moses has not fixed this
rate, can it be said that the Hebrew word means
an unlawful interest? The word *nechech* in the Hebrew language answers to the Latin word *fœnus:*
to conclude that it means *usury*, another word
should be found which would mean *interest*; and,
as such a word does not exist, it follows that all interest is usury, and that all usury is interest.

What was the aim of the lawgiver in forbidding
one Hebrew to lend upon interest to another? It
was to draw closer between them the bonds of fraternity, to give them a lesson of reciprocal benevolence, and to engage them to help and assist each
other with disinterestedness.

The first thought had been to establish among
them the equality of property, and the mediocrity
of private fortune; hence the institution of the
sabbatical year, and of the year of jubilee; the
first of which came every seventh year, and the
other every fifty years. By the sabbatical year
all debtors were released from their obligations:
the year of jubilee brought with it the restitution
of all estates sold or mortgaged.

It was easy to foresee, that the different qualities of the ground, the greater or lesser industry,
the untowardness of the seasons, which might af-
fect both, would necessarily make a difference in
the produce of land, and that the more unfortunate Israelite would claim the assistance of him
whom fortune should have better favoured. Moses did not intend that this last should avail himself of his situation, and that he should require
from the other the price of the service he was soli-
citing; that he should thus aggravate the misery
of his brother, and enrich himself by his spoils.
It is with a view to this that he says, *Thou shalt
not lend upon interest to thy brother.* But what
want could there exist among the Jews, at a time
when they had no trade of any kind? when so little money was in circulation, when the greatest
equality prevailed in property? It was, at most,
a few bushels of corn, some cattle, some agricultural implements; and Moses required that such
services should be gratuitous; his intention was
to make of his people a nation of husbandmen.
For a long time after him, and though Idumea
was at no great distance from the sea-shores, inhabited by the Tyrians, the Sidonians, and other nations possessing shipping and commerce, we do
not see the Hebrews much addicted to trade: all

the regulations of their lawgiver seemed designed
to divert their attention from commerce.

The prohibition of Moses must therefore be
considered only as a principle of charity, and not
as a commercial regulation. According to the
Talmud, the loan alluded to is to be considered
almost as a family loan, as a loan made to a man
in want; for in case of a loan made to a merchant,
even a Jew, profit adequate to the risk should be
considered as lawful.

Formerly the word *usury* carried no invidious
meaning; it simply implied any interest whatever.
The word usury can no longer express the meaning of the Hebrew text: and accordingly the Bible
of Osterwald and that of the Portuguese Jews,
call *interest* that which Sacy, from the Vulgate, has
called *usury*. (22)

The law of Moses, therefore, forbids all manner
of interest on loan, not only between Jews, but
between a Jew and his countryman, without distinction of religion. The loan must be gratuitous
whenever it is to oblige those who claim our assistance, and when it is not intended for commercial
speculation.

We must not forget that these laws, so humane and
so admirable at these early periods, were made for

(22) Vide Puffendorff de Jure Naturæ ac Gentium.

a people which then formed a state and held a rank among nations.

⊦ If the remnants of this people, now scattered among all nations, are attentively considered, it will be seen, that, since the Jews have been driven from Palestine, they no longer have had a common country, they no longer have had to maintain among them the primeval equality of property. Although filled with the spirit of their legislation, they have been sensible that the letter of the law could no longer be obeyed when its principle was done away; and they have, therefore, without any scruple, lent money on interest to trading Jews, as well as to men of different persuasions.

TWELFTH QUESTION;

Does it forbid or does it allow to take usury from strangers?

ANSWER;

We have seen, in the answer to the foregoing question, that the prohibition of usury, considered as the smallest interest, was a maxim of charity and of benevolence, rather than a commercial regulation. In this point of view it is equally condemned by the law of Moses and by the Talmud;

we are generally forbidden, always on the score of
charity, to lend upon interest to our fellow-citizens of different persuasions, as well as to our fellow-Jews.

The disposition of the law, which allows to take
interest from the stranger, evidently refers only to
nations in commercial intercourse with us; otherwise there would be an evident contradiction between this passage and twenty others of the sacred
writings.

" (23) *The Lord your God loveth the stranger, in*
" *giving him food and raiment; love ye therefore*
" *the stranger, for ye were strangers in the land of*
" *Egypt.* (24) *One law shall be to him that is*
" *home-born, and to the stranger.* (25) *Hear the*
" *causes between your brethren, and judge righteous-*
" *ly between every man and his brother, and the*
" *stranger that is with him.* (26) *If a stranger*
" *sojourn with thee in your land you shall not vex*
" *him.* (27) *Thou shalt neither vex a stranger nor*
" *oppress him, for ye were strangers in the land of*
" *Egypt.* (28) *If thy brother be waxen poor, or*

(23) Deut. x. 18, 19.
(24) Exod. xii. 49, &c.
(25) Deut. i. 16.
(26) Lev. xix. 33.
(27) Exod. xxii. 21.
(28) Lev. xxv. 15.

" *fallen in decay with thee, thou shalt then relieve*
" *him; yea, though he be a stranger, or a sojourner.*"

Thus the prohibition extended to the stranger
who dwelt in Israel; the Holy Writ places them
under the safe-guard of God ; he is a sacred guest,
and God orders us to treat him like the widow and
like the orphan.

It is evident that the text of the Vulgate, *Extra-
nei fœnaberis et fratri tuo non fœnaberis*, can be understood only as meaning foreign nations in commercial intercourse with us ; and, even in this case,
the Holy Writ, in allowing to take interest from the
stranger, does not mean an extraordinary profit,
oppressive and odious to the borrower. *Non li-
cuisse Israelitis*, say the doctors, *usuras immodera-
tas exigere ab extraneis, etiam divitibus, res est per se
nota.*

Can Moses be considered as the lawgiver of the
universe, because he was the lawgiver of the Jews?
Were the laws he gave to the people, which God
had intrusted to his care, likely to become the general laws of mankind? *Thou shalt not lend upon
interest to thy brother.* What security had he, that,
in the intercourse which would be naturally established between the Jews and foreign nations,
these last would renounce customs generally prevailing in trade, and lend to the Jews without re-
quiring any interest? Was he then bound to sa-

crifice the interest of his people, and to impoverish
the Jews to enrich foreign nations? Is it not absolutely absurd to reproach him with having put
a restriction to the precept contained in Deuteronomy? What lawgiver but would have considered
such a restriction as a natural principle of recipro-
city?

How far superior in simplicity, generosity, justice, and humanity, is the law of Moses, on this
head, to those of the Greeks and of the Romans!
Can we find, in the history of the antient Israelites,
those scandalous scenes of rebellion excited by
the harshness of creditors towards their debtors;
those frequent abolitions of debts to prevent the
multitude, impoverished by the extortions of lenders, from being driven to despair?

The law of Moses and its interpreters have distinguished, with a praise worthy humanity, the
different uses of borrowed money. Is it to maintain a family? Interest is forbidden. Is it to undertake a commercial speculation, by which the
principal is adventured? Interest is allowed, even
between Jews. *Lend to the Poor*, says Moses.
Here the tribute of gratitude is the only kind of
interest allowed; the satisfaction of obliging is the
sole recompence of the conferred benefit. The
case is different in regard to capitals employed in
extensive commerce: there, Moses allows the lend-

er to come in for a share of the profits of the borrower; and as commerce was scarcely known
among the Israelites, who were exclusively addicted to agricultural pursuits, and as it was carried
on only with strangers, that is with neighbouring
nations, it was allowed to share its profits with
them

It is in this view of the subject that M. Cler-
mont-Tonnerre made use of these remarkable
words in the first National Assembly : " It is said
" that usury is permitted to the Jews; this asser-
" tion is grounded only on a false interpreta-
" tion of a principle of benevolence and fraternity
" which forbade them from lending upon interest
" to one another."

This opinion is also that of Puffendorf and of
other writers on the law of nations.

The antagonists of the Jews have laid a great
stress on a passage of Maimonides, who seems to
represented as a precept, the expression *Anochri
tassih*, (make profit of the stranger.) But although
Maimonides has presumed to maintain this opinion,
it is well known that his sentiments have been
most completely refuted by the learned Rabbi
Abarbanel. We find, besides, in the Talmud, a
treatise of *Macot*, (Perfection) that one of the ways
to arrive at perfection, is to lend without interest
to the stranger, even to the idolator. Whatever

besides might have been the condescension of God to the Jews, if we may be allowed the expression, it cannot be reasonably supposed that the common father of mankind could, at any time, make usury a precept.

The opinion of Maimonides, which excited all Jewish Doctors against him, was principally con-demned by the famous Rabbies Moses de Gironda and Solomon Benadaret, upon the grounds, first, that he had relied on the authority of Siffri, a private doctor, whose doctrine has not been sanctioned by the Talmud; for it is a general rule that every rabbinical opinion which is not sanctioned by that work is considered as null and void. Secondly, because, if Maimonides understood that the word *Nochri* (stranger,) was applicable to the Canaanean people doomed by God to destruction, he ought not to have confounded a public right, arising from an extraordinary order of God to the Israelites, considered as a nation, with the private right of an individual towards another individual of that same nation.

It is an incontrovertible point, according to the Talmud, that interest, even among Israelites, is lawful in commercial operations, where the lender, running some of the risk of the borrower, becomes a sharer in his profits. This is the opinion of all Jewish doctors.

It is evident that opinions, teeming with absurdities, and contrary to all rules of social morality, although advanced by a Rabbi, can no more be imputed to the general doctrine of the Jews, than similar notions, if advanced by Catholic theologians, could be attributed to the evangelical doctrine. The same may be said of the general charge made against the Hebrews, that they are naturally inclined to usury: it cannot be denied that some of them are to be found, though not so many as is generally supposed, who follow that nefarious traffic condemned by their religion.

But if there are some not over-nice in this particular, is it just to accuse one hundred thousand individuals of this vice? Would it not be deemed an injustice to lay the same imputation on all Christians because some of them are guilty of usury?

———————————

I did not think fit to interrupt the discussions of the assembly on the answers to be returned to the questions proposed by His Royal and Imperial Majesty by mentioning a discourse delivered by M. Marg Foy, sen. deputy of the department of the Lower Pyrenees, on the nature of the answers to be returned on the fourth, fifth, and sixth questions.

M. Marg Foy, in submitting to the assembly

his observations on these three questions, which he considered as particularly intitled to his atten-tion, remarked that the answers to be return-ed to the august Chief of the French Nation ought to be founded on the sentiments which animated the Israelites in common with all Frenchmen their brethren. He observed, that the questions them-selves referred to the law of the prince and to ci-vil rights, rather than to principles of religion, and that, according to this mode of considering them, the assembly ought to frame the answers rather as Frenchmen than as men of any particu-lar religion. " I am confirmed in this opinion," said the orator, " because I see nothing in the " precepts of our divine lawgiver which militates " against our civil rights, and, in this case, we " cannot more correctly answer to the call of the " prince, than by expressing those lively sentiments " which fill our hearts. And indeed how can any " one of us remain unmoved when we reflect that " we are called upon to give a pledge to Frenchmen " that the fraternal love and friendship which they " have manifested for us have not been ill bestowed? " How sad would our situation be, if it were thought " possible that France could be indifferent to us; or " that a country which, in return for manifold bene- " fits, has received our oaths of fidelity and love, " could, for an instant, doubt our sincerity; that the

" French people could, in short, consider us as form-
" ing a particular body within the state! No, such
" a doubt cannot exist; or if it has existed, but for
" one moment, it must have been done away, when,
" by an energetic and spontaneous impulse, we
" all together manifested before the Commissioners
" of His Imperial and Royal Majesty, how dear and
" sacred France and Frenchmen were to our hearts.
" Notwithstanding this conviction, we must, never-
" theless, Gentlemen, give our Sovereign a pledge
" of our sentiments; let us satisfy his demands.

" We must give to Frenchmen a pledge of our
" sentiments of union and fraternity: Moses himself
" has pointed out our duties on this head, for he
" says, to the children of Israel, *The stranger that*
" *dwelleth with you, shall be unto you as one*
" *born among you, and thou shalt love him as thy-*
" *self, for ye were strangers in the land of Egypt.*"
" And, Gentlemen, if our divine lawgiver could in-
" still in the minds of his people ideas so liberal in
" favour of strangers, what obligations would he
" have imposed on us, had he foreseen, that at some
" future period, a part of the Israelites, long time
" wandering and despised, would have found pro-
" tection and an asylum in that fine part of Europe
" called *France!* What gratitude would he have
" prescribed to unfortunate children who thus found
" a second promised land! How strictly would he

E E

" have enjoined towards Frenchmen the indulgence
:" of those sentiments of affection dictated by na-
" ture! Yes, Gentlemen, our holy prophet, who in
" all his laws exhorts to union, to humanity, to the
" love of our neighbour, would have told us—Love
" Frenchmen; they who open their arms to you,
" and deliver you from oppression, are your bre-
" thren; let wreaths of friendship and fraternity be
" formed of those very fetters of ancient slavery
" in which prejudice had bound you."

" We will then say to His Majesty, " Yes, Sire,
" we can, according to religious principles, consi-
" der France as our country; share the rights of
" citizens of your empire; follow the dispositions
" of the civil code; and obey, in every thing, the
" will of the prince. Our duty is to defend the ter-
" ritory of France, to pay our share of the burthens
" of the state, and to use all the means in our power
" for the prosperity of the empire. The law of
" God commands whatever is just and good; it
" never can raise an obstacle to the obedience due
" to the laws; for although we have a different
" mode of worship, we are, nevertheless, bound to
" fulfil all the honourable duties which constitute
" good citizens."

" You see, Gentlemen, that I have considered
" the question as relating to civil rights; I could
" have quoted many passages of our holy law, but

" you know it as well as me, and I only made use
" of that particular precept which gives the great-
" est extent to our gratitude. I shall now submit
" to you the draft of an answer. May it prove agree-
" able to you! May His Majesty the Emperor and
" King find, in the expression of our sentiments,
" what can never be with him a matter of doubt,
" a proof of our inviolable attachment to France,
" and to his sacred person!"

As the answers adopted by the assembly, differ
but little from those proposed by M. Marg Foy, I
have thought it useless to insert them, as he has
not thought proper himself to have them printed.

I could also mention the answers sent by the
Rabbies of Turin, by the learned Rabbi Mardo-
chee Cremieux, of Aix, but they also differ but little from those adopted by the assembly. I shall
therefore add but one word: the unanimity in the
principles on which the declarations are grounded,
will be, to future ages, one of the strongest testimonies of their truth, and of the conspicuous loyalty which dictated the answers to all the questions.

Gratitude and respect have also produced demonstrations of a different nature on the day that
all Frenchmen were called upon to celebrate the
anniversary of the memorable period which, for the
happiness of the world, gave birth to the Great Napoleon.

The assembly had unanimously resolved to set a part the whole day of the 15th of August, for prayers, thanksgivings, and all the demonstrations of a pure and lively joy.

M. Rodrigues, of La Gironde, had been directed by the Committee of Five to give in his report on the means best calculated to fulfil, to the utmost, the intentions of the assembly.

He gave it in on the 12th of August, and it was adopted by the assembly as containing the means best calculated to manifest the sentiments which animated every member.

In consequence, on the 15th of August, at ten o'clock in the morning, the deputies met in the hall of their sittings. The bust of his Majesty the Emperor adorned the hall. At this sight cries of *Long live the Emperor* burst from every one.

The President presented to the assembly an ode in Hebrew composed by M. J. Mayer on the Festival of Napoleon the Great. This ode was received with acclamations by the assembly. At eleven o'clock the deputies began their procession for the grand Synagogue; they walked in silence, in the greatest order, with the President at their head. The Temple was ornamented with taste. The name of Jehovah, the cyphers, and the arms of *Napoleon* and of *Josephine* shone on every side. The ark, which contained the book of the law, was surrounded and over-shaded by shrubs and flowers; seats were prepared for the President and the officers of the assembly, for the Rabbies, and some other persons. The deputies formed a circle, into which were admitted many Jewish and Christian spectators, from among the most distinguished citizens. The ladies, according to custom, had a separate gallery. Order and serenity prevailed every where: every countenance exhibited the most heart-felt satisfaction, manifesting, on so glorious, so fortunate a day, our gratitude to a monarch, who, amidst so many labours, has made the fate and the social happiness of the descendants of Israel the special object of his attention. Chorusses and hymns began the ceremony. The President, M. Furtado, afterwards delivered a discourse, tracing a rapid sketch of the persecutions which the Jews had to encounter during two thousand years, till the epocha when, recalled in France to the enjoyment of their civil and political rights, they saw the first dawn of their complete regeneration. He concluded by exhorting his brethren to bestow the greatest care on the education of their children, in order to enable them to repay to the country the manifold benefits conferred upon them, and those which were still in expectation. This discourse of the President was received with loud plaudits.

MM. Segre, Zinzheimer, and Andrade, Rabbies and deputies, delivered sermons: thefirst in Italian, the second in German, and the third in French. M. Segre clothed the sentiments of a mild and persuasive morality in elegant language. The sermon of M. Andrade was marked by numerous and appropriate quotations from the Holy Writ. M. Zinzheimer traced a more detailed picture of the different epochas of Jewish history. The same Rabby, in taking from the ark the book of the law, and in presenting it round the temple, pronounced a prayer for the happiness of all Frenchmen, which excited the liveliest emotion. Psalmns and Hymns were afterwards sung; and when they came to the prayer which Jews are accustomed to put up, for sovereigns, enthusiasm knew no bounds. Cries of *Long live the Emperor and King*, in Hebrew and in French, proceeded from every mouth. Thus has this festival been rendered remarkable by all the peculiarities which characterise the most antient people on earth, blended with the patriotic effusions so natural to all Frenchmen. During a symphony of Haydn, collections were made by Mdlles. Julie-Theodore Cerf-Berr, Caroline Wolf, and Schmoll, accompanied by MM. Avigdor, Rodrigues, sen. and Castro, jun. The produce was distributed among the poor of all persuasions.

In the evening the synagogue, and the hall of the sittings of the assembly were illuminated: the deputies met afterwards in private parties, in which the health of the Emperor, and of his august family, were drank with fresh enthusiasm.

Translation of the Sermon delivered in Italian *by M.* Segre, *Rabbi, Municipal Counsellor of* Verceil, *Deputy of the Department of* La Sesia.

My son, fear thou the Lord and the King.
Prov. chap. xxiv. vers. 21.

" Scarcely were my eye-lids opened to the dawn
" of this day, when my mind was assailed by the
" crouded images of the victories of Montenotte, of
" the laurels of Marengo blended with palms, of
" the atchievements and triumphs of Austerlitz. It
" is not then a vain illusion, did I exclaim! A su-
" pernatural genius has really appeared on earth,
" surrounded with greatness and with glory infi-
" nite. *I saw in the night visions, and behold* one,
" *like the son of man, came, and there was given him*
" *dominion, and glory, and a kingdom.* Daniel,
" chap. vii. verses 13 and 14.

" Already this day of joy and of universal festi-
" vity arises in renewed splendour, marked in in-
" delible characters by predominant stars; pure

" and serene above all days; day for ever blessed,
" in which Heaven sent unto the earth the great
" NAPOLEON enthroned in glory, the restorer of
" piety, of justice, of good order, the father of na-
" tions, the friend, yea, the sincere friend, of peace;
" the only title dear to his heart, and the most
" grateful to his subjects.

" Amidst the far-sounding praises of the hero,
" amidst the joyful hymns of gratitude offered to
" the Eternal for so precious, so sacred a gift, I has-
" ten to the Holy Temple, with you, O venerable
" Deputies of France and of Italy. Deemed wor-
" thy to be heard among you, permit me to add
" some reflections to the discourse of our honour-
" able President, and to those of the two learned
" orators who have addressed you before me. Do
" not be depressed, if this day I call to your re-
" membrance our ancient calamities, and that
" flood of misfortunes which overwhelmed us be-
" fore we set our eyes on that *bow in the cloud,*
" which is for us a divine token of a covenant of
" calm and serenity.

" Compare, said Moses, the condition of your
" fathers and mothers, and that of your children:
" *Remember the days of old, consider the years of*
" *many generations,* (Deut. xxxii. vers. 7.) and
" you will know how to appreciate the invaluable
" blessings of the new order of things.

" The scourge of war, Gentlemen, is usually
" transitory; either the wisdom of government
" quickly repairs the losses it occasions, or an ho-
" nourable treaty soon relieves the people, and
" brings back peace and plenty. But as to us.....
" as to us.......O God!........the iron hand of op-
" pression under which we lived, or rather groan-
" ed, for so many centuries, crushed us down even
" in the bosom of peace, and hope itself could af-
" ford no relief by holding the prospect of future
" deliverance. *We looked for peace, and no peace*
" *came.* (Jerem. viii. 15.) We were like the leaf,
" which, torn from the parent bough, becomes the
" sport of the slightest rustling breeze, even after
" the rage of the tempest has subsided. And
" where is the man of any nation, even supposing
" him the most passive, who, on reflecting on his
" situation, on seeing himself thus condemned to
" sloth, and his talents become useless through
" contempt; where is the man, I say, who, in the
" bitterness of his anguish, would not renounce
" his native land as his country? Thus did King
" David express his thoughts in similar circum-
" stances: *I looked on my right hand, and beheld,*
" *but there was no man that would know me; refuge*
" *failed me; no man cared for my soul.* Psalm
" cxlii. 4.

F F

" Thanks be this day to the Most High dispenser
" of all things! Infinite thanks be to the Hero of
" France, the Solomon of our days! He looked
" down on the cedars of Lebanon; neither did the
" humble hyssop, which grows between rocks,
" among briars, escape his attention: high seated
" on his throne, surrounded with treasures, the
" hearts of his people are his sole delight. He has
" for ever erased those ancient marks of shame
" and of sorrow, whose baneful influence blasted
" in the bud the most sublime talents, and wither-
" ed the most virtuous hearts. The paternal hand
" of the monarch has removed our evils with their
" cause: he points out to us the road of glory and
" of honour, arts, and sciences. O Israel! no more
" shall your tears embitter your bread; he says to
" us with the pious Jehosaphat, *Deal courageously,*
" *and the Lord shall be with the good.* 2 Chron.
" xix. 11.

" Since our mild and heavenly religion recom-
" mends labour as an antidote to those vices which
" degrade man, and sciences as the worthy means
" by which we may arrive at the knowledge of
" God, and since the supreme orders of the Hero,
" whose wisdom fosters all sciences, are entitled to
" the most religious obedience, what further in-
" ducements do we want? What brighter exam-

" ples could we have to induce us to start in the
" noble career, than that of so many wise princes,
" so many brave generals, and men distinguished
" in every branch of science? What efforts shall
" we make to become, by our own talents, useful
" to the state, to the country, and to ourselves?
" Now that our fate is connected with that of the
" country, our heart is in a manner already enno-
" bled. Let us embrace, with eagerness, a happi-
" ness so long unknown to us; call for arms to de-
" fend from every insult that country so dear to
" us. Soon we shall see our sons passing from
" that state of uneasy listlessness which always
" accompanies idleness, to that happy calm which
" is always produced by the pursuit of useful
" scienes, and by praise-worthy occupations.
" *For thou shalt eat the labour of thine hands, hap-*
" *py shalt thou be, and it shall be well with thee.*
" Psalm cxxviii. 2.

" Were we to receive only temporal advantages
" from the political regeneration wrought by the
" wisdom and clemency of the Immortal Hero,
" what gratitude could ever repay such a blessing?
" But it goes much further, Brethren; a safe and
" permanent political existence will facilitate to
" us the practice of all religious and moral virtue
" towards God and his creatures; precious virtues!
" hardly within our reach in the state of degrada-

" tion into which we were plunged! Ennobled, I
" say it once more, by the career of sciences now
" opened to them, our sons will find within them-
" selves powerful incitements to virtue. What a
" field for instruction, for useful knowledge?
" Now they will gradually acquire ideas more
" worthy of God, of religion, of social virtues, and
" of good manners. Such, Israel, such is the des-
" tiny God has in store for thee. There remains
" but one wish for thee to form; it is to have thine
" eyes opened, that thou mayest discern thy true
" honour and thy true glory, and that the Most
" High, on whom every grace depends, might this
" day deign to enlighten thee. *And wisdom and*
" *knowledge shall be the stability of thy times, and*
" *strength of salvation.* Isaiah, chap. xxviii. vers.
" 6.

" Always impressed with a deep sense of the sa-
" cred duties of love and gratitude, let us renew
" in this august Temple, before the God of our fa-
" thers, and near that venerable monument of our
" ancient splendour, which we glory in preserving
" like the light of our souls, (the book of the law)
" let us, I say, renew here, in the plenitude of our
" hearts, those fervent prayers which every one of
" us, in the bosom of his family, addresses to the
" Most High, for the preservation of the august,
" imperial, and royal house.—*God save the King.*

(221)

" Powerful God, Father of Kings, may our pray-
" ers ascend to the foot of thy throne. God of
" justice, who rules the fate of nations, who gave
" this vast empire to a monarch according to thine
" own heart, a monarch who is BRAVERY, WIS-
" DOM, and CLEMENCY itself, and whose name is
" echoed by fame in all the countries which the sun
" vivifies by its rays, preserve him for the hap-
" piness of nations, as a mirror and a model for all
" kings; preserve him for us, and for our most
" distant posterity, with all that fulness of glory
" he has acquired by so many titles. May the
" scepter remain for ever in his powerful hand!
" His virtues, his wisdom, his name, that august
" name carries more dread in it than the splendid
" array of his formidable and victorious armies.
" *Bless, O Lord, his substance, and accept the work of*
" *his hands: smite through the loins of them that*
" *rise against him, and of them that hate him, that*
" *they rise not again.* Deuteronomy, chap. xxxiii.
" verse 11."

Translation of the Sermon delivered in German by
M. David Zinzheimer, Rabbi, Deputy from Strasbourg.

Behold my servant whom I uphold, mine elect in whom my soul delighteth: I have put my spirit upon him; he shall bring forth judgement on

the gentiles; he shall not fail nor be discouraged till he have set judgment in the earth, and the isles shall wait for his law. I the Lord have
called thee in rightousness, and will hold thine hand, and will keep thee,
and will give thee for a covenant of the people, for a light of the gentiles,

Isaiah, chapter xlii.

" Brethren,

" Assembled here by order of our incomparable
" Emperor and King NAPOLEON THE GREAT,
" this day is a day of joy, for us such as our nation
" has never witnessed, for which we are indebted to
" divine favour.

" Yet the joy of this glorious day will become
" livelier, it will make a much stronger impression
" on your hearts, if you will, with me, briefly com-
" pare the past with the present times.

" The history of the Hebrews is remarkable above
" that of all other nations, by the vicissitudes of
" events, the number and the cruelty of the per-
" secutions of which this unfortunate people has
" been the deplorable victim or the miserable
" sport, and still more by the unparalled constan-
" cy the immoveable firmness, which they have uni-
" formly opposed to oppression since the fatal day
" that they were forced to abandon the land pro-
" mised to their fathers, to Abraham, Isaac, Jacob,
" and to their posterity; since the destruction of
" the Holy Temple. Scattered over the face of the
" globe, we have been wandering from nations to

" nations, from kingdoms to kingdoms, without
" finding rest or safety any where; every where
" we saw enemies rising against us, because we
" remained faithful to our laws, to those laws which
" the Lord himself gave us by his revelation amidst
" thunder and lightning. (Exod. xix. and xx.)

" The Lord had designed to take us *a nation
" from the midst of* another *nation, by tempta-
" tions, by signs, and by wonders, and by war, and by
" a mighty hand and by a stretched out arm.* (Deu-
" ter. chap. iv. verse 34.)

" But, on the other hand, when our ancestors
" proved unfaithful to these laws, they experien-
" ced the effects of the terrible threats the Lord
" had denounced against them (29).

" Then, Brethren, then, the nations who had
" not yet received the light of wisdom, these na-
" tions said, *Come and let us cut them off from
" being a nation, that the name of Israel may be no
" more in remembrance.* Psalm. lxxxiii. verse. 4.

" And in fact, can any one read the history of
" our nation without shuddering at the unparal-
" leled series of calamities of every description

(29) Deuteronomy, chapter xxviii. verse. 64 and 65. " And the
" Lord shall scatter thee among all people from the one end of the earth
" even unto the other;—and among these nations shalt thou find no ease,
" neither shall the sole of thy foot have a rest."

" which befel our ancestors in France, in Italy, in
" Germany, in Spain, in other lands?

" But notwithstanding all these persecutions,
" admire, dear Brethren, the miracles and the
" power of the Most High : we escape through the
" wrecks of centuries, and Providence has, at last,
" saved us from the total oblivion into which those
" nations had determined to plunge us. Driven
" from one country to another, we always found
" some magnanimous and benevolent Prince whose
" heart God disposed to receive us, and allow us
" to remain faithful to our laws. Can any thing
" shew more clearly the fulfilment of the promi-
" ses of the Lord ? (30)

" In the midst of these calamities the Lord,
" about three centuries ago, took pity on our suf-
" ferings; he caused the dawn of philosophy to
" enlighten Europe especially, some rays of hope
" gladdened our sight, and enlivened our pros-
" pects; a dam was raised against the destructive
" torrent of fanaticism, and human blood no
" longer drenched the earth in the name of God.

" But persecution did not cease entirely; it was

(30) Leviticus, chap. xxvi. verse. 44. " And yet for all that, when they
" be in the land of their enemies, I will not cast them away, neither will
" I abhor them to destroy them utterly and to break my covenants with
" them, for I am the Lord their God."

" reserved for other times to see this dawn of hap-
" piness ushering in a brilliant morning. Philo-
" sophy now diffuses its light over Europe; hearts
" are now opened every where to the mild senti-
" ments of philanthropy and of tolerance.

" Men are sensible that their Creator himself
" allows every one to worship him according to
" the light of his reason. O Brethren, consider
" here the wonderful favours of the Most High:
" by re-establishing concord among mankind, he
" has prepared the end of our tribulations and of
" our misfortunes. If persecution has not yet en-
" tirely ceased, because too many men, hurried by
" baneful habits, which become a second nature,
" have refused to open their eyes to the true light
" of philosophy; if, till now we, have seen only the
" dawn of happiness, this dawn will at last usher a
" pure and glorious light which will dissipate the
" last dark shades of ancient prejudices; all hearts
" will open to the noble enthusiasm of humanity,
" and we shall see clearly the infinite wonders of
" the Supreme Creator as predicted by Daniel. (30)
" He has chosen Napoleon to place him on the
" throne of France and Italy; he has chosen him

(31) Daniel, chap. ii. verse 21. " And he changeth the times and the
" seasons; he removeth kings and setteth up kings: he giveth wisdom
" unto the wise and knowledge to them that know understanding."

" in the way I have marked in my text. And
" we must apply to him what Pharoah said to his
" servants, *Can we find* such *a one as this* is, *a*
" *man in whom the spirit of God is?* We must also
" apply to him these words of my text, *I have put*
" *my spirit upon him.*

" And what else can we say when we consider his
" wonderful works, his first campaigns in Italy, his
" his achievements in Asia and in Africa, his second
" campaigns in Italy, and, lastly, his astonishing
" campaigns in Germany, and that ever memorable
" victory of Austerlitz, which produced the glori-
" ous peace of Presburg? After these wonders, could
" we one moment hesitate to apply to our invinci-
" ble Emperor these words of Isaiah : *Thus said*
" *the Lord to his annointed Cyrus, whose right hand*
" *I have holden, to subdue nations before him; and*
" *I will loose the loins of kings, to open before him*
" *the two-leaved gates, and the gates shall not be*
" *shut. I will go before thee and make the crooked*
" *places straight; I will break in pieces the gates of*
" *brass, and cut in sunder the bars of iron.* Isaiah,
" chap. xlv. 1, 2.

" Thus our invincible Emperor overcame that
" inaccessible mountain, the great Saint Bernard,
" to gain the immortal victory of Marengo. The
" Lord straightens all ways before him, and he
" rushes on the land of the enemy ; he breaks those

" gates of brass, that strong hold of Ulm surround-
" ed with intrenchments. An innumerable nest of
" enemies occupied the strong hold, but as soon as
" the Lord's annointed appeared, the words of Isaiah
" were fulfilled, " *they that war against thee shall*
" *be as nothing, and as a thing of nought.* Isaiah,
" chap. vers. 12.

" O Brethren, I have hitherto pointed out to
" you only few of his glorious deeds; my voice is
" too weak to sing the praises of the mighty. I
" shall say with David, *My heart is inditing a good*
" *matter: I speak of the things which I have made*
" *touching the King; my tongue is the pen of a ready*
" *writer.* Psalm xlv. 1.

" I have, till now, spoken only of his military
" prowess; to celebrate his political virtues, I shall
" say again with David, " *thou lovest righteousness,*
" *and hatest wickedness: therefore God, thy God, hath*
" *annointed thee with the oil of gladness above thy*
" *fellows.* Psalm, xli. 7. Or with Solomon in
" his Proverbs, *The King by judgment establisheth*
" *the land.* It is not only for his own people,
" but also for all nations, whose eyes are fixed
" on that monarch, unparalleled in the annals of
" nations, and, as I have said it in my text, *the*
" *isles shall wait for his law.* In thus uniting all
" nations he opens their eyes to their true in-
" terests. Where could we find the model of such a

" sovereign? The Holy Writ says of David that he
" imparted justice to his people, and heaped fa-
" vors on his subjects.

" Surely these words are perfectly applicable to
" our august Monarch, who, high seated on his
" throne, keeps his eyes fixed on a small number of
" men professing the religion of Moses, and wish-
" es to better their fate and that of their children,
" that they may no longer be exposed to the injus-
" tice of other nations.

" O Brethren, to what height of enthusiasm
" must our gratitude rise towards so great, so vir-
" tuous a monarch, who heaps so many favours
" upon us? *The righteous shall be in everlasting re-*
" *membrance.* Psalm cxii. 6.

" As to us, called together by the great Empe-
" ror, it becomes our most sacred duty to labour
" with strength and unanimity according to his
" will, and to further his benevolent views by
" our co-operation. It is also our sacred duty to
" offer our thanks to the Most High, who has in-
" spired the heart of our Sovereign with the wish
" of relieving from misery men unjustly oppress-
" ed. Let prayers be poured night and day for
" the preservation of his precious life, for that of
" our august Empress, and of the royal and im-
" perial family.

" O God, hear the fervent prayers which our

" hearts pour before thee; let a ray of thine own
" glory rest on the brow of our august Monarch;
" preserve the empire in all its splendour; and
" pour thy blessings on our brethren of every per-
" suasion. *Amen.*"

BENEDICTION.

" O God, Creator of heaven and earth, and of
" whatsoever their vast extent containeth, King of
" Kings, who hast appointed them to rule nations,
" among which thou hast, in a peculiar manner,
" favoured the French and Italians by giving them
" a man according to thy heart, NAPOLEON, cloth-
" ed in glory, whose goodness equals his justice
" and his mighty valour, and whose fame embra-
" ceth both extremities of the world. Deign, O
" Lord, to continue the signal favours thou hast
" heaped upon him. Deign, on this day of his
" anniversary, to hearken to the prayers of the
" deputies of France and of Italy, imploring thy
" blessings on him. Grant him, and to the wor-
" thy wife of his bosom, the EMPRESS JOSEPHINE,
" and to their august family, a long and happy
" life. May they always behold the French and
" and the Italians living in peace and plenty, and
" rising into prosperity under their blissful sway,
" which thou approvest, O Lord. *Amen.*"

MM. Cologna, J. Mayer, and S. Wittersheim, sen. celebrated that happy day by Odes and Hymns in Hebrew, which are remarkable by pleasing sentiments and energetic thoughts, by the justness of ideas, the classical elegance of diction, and the harmony of versification.

M. Moise Milland, deputy of Vaucluse, gained · also much credit by a Canticle in Hebrew, replete with energy and poetical beauties; as did M. Elie-Aaron Lattes, a learned Rabbi of Sevigliano, deputy for the department of La Stura, by a beautiful Hymn composed in Hebrew, and translated into Italian with much fidelity and elegance.

These several compositions will do the greatest honour to their authors, not only among their brethren, but also among the learned of Europe, who are able to understand the originals; they will be read with pleasure by all lovers of belles-lettres in general, and of Hebrew poetry, and more especially by those men who see with interest the convocation made by our august Sovereign, with a view to impart the advantages and the duties of society to a class of men, who have been sometimes degraded, only because they were always oppressed, and who always reckoned true religion, humanity, and reason, as their auxiliaries against fanaticism, hatred, and violence.

I much regret the impossibility of giving my

readers the original Hebrew text of these compositions; I shall attempt to compensate for it by a translation of the most remarkable.

O D E

For the Birth-day of NAPOLEON THE GREAT, *composed in Hebrew by* M. A. Cologna.

I.

Arise, O Muse! and take a lofty flight. Soft-sounding be my voice, and grateful to the ear. My heart indites a song of things most high. Pour thou grace into my lips.

II.

My soul is raised to thoughts immortal. My song is of glory and of wonder. O that my lips might drop as the honey-comb at the fountains of the sacred springs, causing the tongue to flow with grace, and force, and brilliancy.

III.

On the deeds of the mighty will I raise a song; on the deeds of the hero, chief of men, unmatched in battles. Near him the glory of kings fades and vanishes: they hide before him their diminished heads. Their greatness is a thing of nought.

IV.

Which of his deeds shall first inspire the bard? Wonders upon wonders are engraved on glory's adamantine

tablet! Numberless are his victories and countless his triumphs. Who to each bright orb in the starry heaven can
assign a name, or fix a stedfast eye on the father of light,
blazing forth in his meridian glory?

V.

Early were his deeds in arms. The hills of Montenotte
beheld him victorious : Egypt, that ancient land of slavery,
felt the strength of his arm: Ulm, Marengo, Austerlitz witnessed his prowess, nor weak was there the strife of death.

VI.

Distant hills shook with his warlike thunder: by his
strong arm his enemies were humbled. The mighty of the
earth have bent before him. He has said to nations, " Let
" there be peace," and the universe is at rest.

VII.

Firmly on wisdom is his throne fixed on high; justice
and truth uphold his crown. He pours the balmy oil of
grace into the wounds of innocence ; he heals the galling
sores of oppression. The proud and the haughty he heeds
not ; they stand silent and abashed before him.

VIII.

He has placed in justice the delight of his heart: un-
born races shall hail him Father of his people. By him the
happiness of nations rests on the tables of the law as on a
rock. The wreaths of victory adorn his brow, the gracious
seat of law-inspiring wisdom.

IX.

Exult, O France! queen of queens! His powerful arm hath raised thee from the abyss, placing thee over nations! Rejoice, O Italy! thy days of greatness are near; the hero pours his spirit on thee. Raise, O my country, raise the song of joy! Rest and happiness await thee.

X.

Hail, bright dawn of gladness! A Monarch is this day born unto us; in this day shall all other days of the year be blessed! For a great light arose and shineth upon our age; a light of happiness, and distant generations shall be glad and rejoice in it.

XI.

But a voice, like the murmur of the breeze, whispereth in my ear, and saith: Cease the words of thy praise; unspeakable is his glory, and above thy strength are his deeds; too high for mortal man to sing. The name of him standeth aloft, proclaiming aloud glory and greatness infinite. He is NAPOLEON.

XII.

I said unto my soul, " Repress thy bold flight." Silent is my tongue, but high beats my swelling heart, while before thy glorious throne I bend my knee, O King beloved! in thy goodness I place my trust; weak is my voice, and untaught my song, but my heart is pure and my mind, O King, dwelleth in righteousness.

XIII.

Raise, Brethren, raise the song of gratitude to the hero; he hath fulfilled his promises to Israel : his promises of peace and happiness! Thanksgiving he loveth not. Let the mind of youth be trained to wisdom ! let it be its guide in the path of virtue ; in such deeds his soul delighteth.

XIV.

O God, eternal and terrible in thy judgments, hearken to the voice of thy people, to the prayers of the children of Jacob, pouring their souls at the foot of thy altar, in thy sanctuary: they cry unto thee, O Lord ! Preserve the life of our immortal immortal Emperor ; long and happy be his days.

XV.

Lengthen, O Lord, the happy days of his beloved spouse, virtuous among women and glorious among queens : of his mother, blessed among mothers, for her womb brought forth the hero of the age. As long as the bright orb of the night shall shed its pale light on earth, as long as light itself shall keep divided from darkness, as thou didst set it, may the mighty house of NAPOLEON flourish in splendour and in majesty.

ODE

Composed in Hebrew by M. J. Mayer.

I.

My heart is troubled within me, my soul is on fire, hurried by power resistless: tumultuous feelings confound my thoughts; wonders strike my eyes, wonders are echoed in my ears. Tune the lyre of mighty deeds surpassing mortal. I will raise a song to the sons of men. Why is thy tongue mute? Pale is thy cheek, weak man! Above thy strength is the praise of the hero.

II.

No mortal eye can look on the father of light when, in mid career, bursting from clouds and mists, dark rolling on each side, he pursues the brightness of his steps. The green hills lift their dewy heads, the flowers glitter in the valley, the soft gale wafts fragrancy around.

III.

Such is NAPOLEON in his career of glory. Weak are the bards of present days to raise the song of his fame: too high for them are his mighty deeds. In wonder their voice is lost; the untuned lyre drops from their uplifted hands. Thus the sun of wisdom and strength gladdens the world, rising above mortal praise.

IV.

How great thy destiny, O NAPOLEON! Who can be

H H 2

compared with thee among the glory of nations? Who among renowned warriors, among sage lawgivers, ever raised his fame near to thine, O first of mortal men?——— Bright in days of old was the glory of Athens and of Rome: dim is their light now before thee. On thee the eyes of nations are fixed; they wonder, and bless thy name.

V.

What light of joy bursts at once on my soul! It moves my heart and agitates my frame. Give, O give, the sacred lyre—I must pour forth the gladness of my soul. Hail, prosperous day of an immortal birth! Hail, happiest among days! Thy dawn is to France the dawn of glory. The stars which rule the divided year shall mark thy return. August shall be the harbinger of peace and happiness.

VI,

" To thee belongs the dominion of the worlds thou hast created :" so sing the celestial seraphs before the throne of God; " for thou hast made from nought the world and " its wonders." To thee, O NAPOLEON, we sing, Rule in peace the empire thy wisdom has established. On truth and justice its glory is founded. On kings and heroes thou sheddest thy brightness. Thus, revolving round the father of light, planets glitter with borrowed rays.

VII.

Who is like unto thee, O NAPOLEON, in the days of thy glory, when thou graspest the death-dealing steel, that thy allies might rest behind its lightning! Like the eagle of the rock was thy flight over Germany's plains. Thy heroes innumerable crouded around thee; the thunder of war was in their hands, carrying destruction among the foe. Thus the cloud, rising from the abyss, borne along by the western wind, dark, vast, terrible, overspreads the blackened field.

VIII.

My soul abhorreth the snares of the wicked; their shafts were levelled at thee. They heard the shouts of victory, the voice of our rejoicings, and were no more. From distant shores the song of peace was heard, mingled with warlike praise. We mourned, like the tender youth lamenting the absence of his beloved sire, and behold he comes, high seated on his car, clad with glory.

IX.

The earth trembled, but now rests in peace. Far distant nations bent before the majesty of thy brow. Ulm, Marengo, Austerlitz, the plains of Egypt, beheld the feats of Napoleon. " Raise altars to the God of battles," he said, and altars arose from their ruins; bitterness fled from our hearts, at the dawn of his grace. Happy, happy are the children of France. Nations had but a glimpse of the star of our pride, swiftly gliding through the mist tinged with its glory.

X.

Bards of Israel, let your harmonious songs thrill in my soul, that, amidst the voice of nations, the fame of the hero may be raised in the ancient words of Jacob, the words of the youth of our people. The great NAPOLEON looked down on the children of woe, sport of the proud and of the oppressor: he gathered them round him like a tender father: from the dust he raised them to stand as a mark of his might. Just are his judgments; great and big with gladness is the propitious light of his wisdom. Before it, the darkening cloud of shame retires, rolling back on the foes of our people.

XI.

Sons of Israel, children of happy France, let songs of joy mark the birth of your king! An eagle, O Israel, shelters thee under his wings. Hills and mountains melt before him; he raiseth and keepeth thee on high: joy and comfort fill thy heart; to the noble chiefs of thy tribes he imparteth knowledge and wisdom. The glory of Israel returneth; clothe thyself with gladness and strength. The stormy cloud of misfortunes has retired behind the hills. The proud race of ancient France joins their friendly hands with their brethren of Israel.

XII.

Exult, O my country! Thy ships, big with riches, shall fly to distant shores; the bright day of happiness shall enliven thy fruitful plains; plenty and prosperity shall dwell in the land: for ever shall this song of gratitude be echoed through thy hills —Long, long may he live, our great, our powerful King, first of a thousand heroes! May the beam of his joy, the wife of his bosom, comfort his happy lengthened years. O God of the starry heavens, take them under the protecting shade of thy hand! On their lives hangs the fate of nations, O Creator of the World.

HYMN,

Sung by the French *Deputies of the Religion of* Moses, *composed in Hebrew by M.S.* Wittersheim, *and dedicated to M.* Furtado, *President of the Assembly.*

Come ye all, O children of Israel; make a joyful noise unto God, with voices and instruments of music : give thanks to the Eternal, and make his praise glorious, for he hath shewn mercy unto us this day---therefore shall this day be a day of joy unto Israel.

In the space of a year the sun performeth his course, and the moon begins a new career each month ; but these lights of Heaven do not mark a brighter day than this ; for on this day, NAPOLEON, the greatest of kings, was given unto us.

Let us all sing and rejoice! Be comforted, ye elders; for you have witnessed the wonder of this day, the marvellous works, above man's understanding! Rejoice, O youth! the King is the dawn of gladness. Happy and blessed shall be the reign of our glorious Emperor and King.

His name fills the universe; none have been like him among the sons of men! The fathers of praise cannot raise up their voices to the greatness of his deeds, to the glory of his works: they stand mute, lost in wonder!

Eminent in war is the hero among chiefs. The Nile and

the Jordan have beheld his deeds, terrible in battles. The lightning of his steel gleams on the proud in arms----but he exulteth not over the fallen foe : his mighty hand raiseth the fallen in the strife.

In vain the nations of the earth united against him; weak was their arm, and powerless their blows. In Marengo's and Austerlitz's bloody plains he broke the bow of the strong; the thickened phalanxes of his enemies were scattered before him. Grateful to humbled kings was the olive-branch of peace, mildly shining in the magnanimous hand of the conqueror.

To imperial France he bent his victorious steps; his faithful subjects greeted his return. Thus a father beholds his children, the pride of his heart, dutiful and affectionate : they rejoice in the firmness of his throne : it rests on victory---clemency---virtue---humanity---justice.

Let thy shouts, O Israel, proclaim thy gladness. Unmatched are the designs of NAPOLEON for thee; among the sons of his glory thou shalt be remembered. Away, ye scoffers of my people! no longer shall the head of Israel be humbled in dust before the pride of the wicked.

A mournful captive, weighed down by fetters, groaned in the dark dwelling of the dungeon ; the sun had hid him from his eyes, nor did the mild beams of the moon cheer his sleepless eye---no light shone on his captivity.

He heard a voice, as from the darkly-rolling cloud, and his soul arose. Is there an end to my sorrows? Shall the fetters be loosed from my hands? Shall I again behold the light of the heavens? Shall I visit, once more, the haunts of the living? Shall I be one among them?

Such was Israel since he dwelled among nations; a prey to misfortune, the sport of scorn : his mind failed within him; oppressors sought after his soul; he bowed himself down heavily, as one sorely troubled with fear.

Is it a vain illusion---or a vision from above :---Doth the dawn of happier days for him rise in the heavens? Is he delivered from bondage? Will the glory of his former days return, the honour of his name? Shall he be numbered among the children of magnanimous France?

It was a messenger from above; truth is in his tidings; NAPOLEON hath undertaken our deliverance---in him is our trust: he will fulfil his words. Have we not beheld the wonders of his sublime genius? He that has laid low the thrones of his enemies, he that has exalted others in their stead, and fixed them as on rocks, shall raise us from affliction and from shame. Under the shield of his wisdom we shall prosper in peace.

From afar he called thee, O Israel, from his distant dominions; in the first of cities, queen of the world, he gathered thy chiefs around him : the wings of the eagle are spread over the lamb ; their shadow is the shield of the weak.

His voice sounded in our ears, pronouncing mercy; like

a powerful blast it silenced the evil tongues of the wicked.
The dawn of happiness shone upon us, ushering the bright
day of Israel's glory.

May his fame, like his goodness, fill the universe! May
our AUGUST EMPEROR live for ever----May our AUGUST
EMPRESS live for ever. This is our constant prayer, the
dearest wish of our hearts: and may the Eternal pour his
holy blessings on the *Imperial Family. Amen.*

Sitting of the 18*th of September,* 1806.

The President took the chair at twelve o'clock;
he named three deputies to maintain order, and
announced that MM. Mole, Portalis, jun. and Pasquier, were to come to the assembly with some
fresh communications from His Royal and Imperial Majesty. He named MM. Formiggini, Cologna, Cracovia, Gondchaux, Dreyfoss, Rodrigues,
sen. Scawb, jun. and Lorich, to go to meet them
and introduce them into the hall.

At one o'clock the Commissioners of His Majesty
arrived, and took their places at the table.

M. Mole, one of them, read the following discourse :

" Gentlemen,
" His Majesty the Emperor and King is satis-
" fied with your answers; we are commanded by

" him to say, that he has approved the sense in
" which they are written; but the communications
" we are going to make in his name will prove,
" much better than our words, to what extent this
" assembly may depend on his powerful protec-
" tion.

" In entering this hall for the second time, Gen-
" tlemen, we are impressed with the same senti-
" ments, and the same ideas which occurred to us
" when we were first admitted into it. And who
" could behold without astonishment such a so-
" ciety of enlightened men, chosen among the
" descendants of the most ancient people of the
" world? If one of those, who lived in former
" years, could again visit this world, and were to
" be introduced into such an assembly, would he
" not think himself brought into the middle of the
" Holy City, or would he not suppose that a terri-
" ble revolution had renewed, from the very founda-
" tions, the state of all human things? In this he
" would not be mistaken, Gentlemen. It is after a
" revolution which threatened to swallow up all
" nations, thrones, and empires, that altars and
" thrones are raised every where from their ruins
" to protect the earth; a furious multitude attempt-
" ed to destroy every thing: a man has appeared,
" and has restored every thing; his eye embraces
" the whole world and past centuries even to their

" very origin; he has seen the wandering remnants
" of a nation, rendered as famous by its fall as
" others are by their greatness, scattered over the
" face of the earth : it was just that he should
" consider their situation; and it was right to ex-
" pect that these same Jews, who hold such a dis-
" tinguished place in the memory of mankind,
" should fix the attention of the man who is to
" occupy it eternally.

" The Jews, exposed to the contempt of nations,
" and not unfrequently to the avarice of princes,
" have never, as yet, been treated with justice.
" Their customs and their practices kept them afar
" from society, by which they were rejected in their
" turn; they have always attributed the ill-con-
" duct and the vices, laid to their charge, to the
" humiliating laws which oppressed them. Even
" to this day they attribute the backwardness for
" agricultural pursuits and useful employments,
" manifested by some of them to the little reliance
" which they can place on futurity, after having
" been, for so many centuries, the sport of circum-
" stances, and seeing their very existence depend
" on the whim of men in power: they will have no
" cause to complain in future, and this ground of
" defence will be taken from them.

" His Majesty's intention is, that no plea shall be
" left to those who may refuse to become citizens;
" the free exercise of your religious worship and

" the full enjoyment of your political rights, are
" secured to you. But, in return for his gracious
" protection, His Majesty requires a religious
" pledge for the strict adherence to the principles
" contained in your answers. This assembly, con-
" stituted as it is now, could not of itself give such
" a security. Its answers, converted into decisions
" by another assembly, of a nature still more dig-
" nified and more religious, must find a place near
" the Talmud, and thus acquire, in the eyes of the
" Jews of all countries and of all ages, the great-
" est possible authority. It is also the only means
" left to you to meet the grand and generous views
" of His Majesty, and to impart, to all of your
" persuasion, the blessings of this new æra.

    " The purity of your law has, no doubt, been
" altered by the croud of commentators, and the
" diversity of their opinions must have thrown
" doubts in the minds of those who read them. It
" will be then a most important service, conferred
" on the whole Jewish community, to fix their be-
" lief on those points which have been submitted
" to you. To find, in the history of Israel, an assem-
" bly capable of attaining the object now in view,
" we must go back to the Great Sanhedrim, and it
" is the Great Sanhedrim, which His Majesty this
" day intends to convene. This senate, destroyed
" together with the temple, will rise again to en-

" lighten the people it formerly governed : although
" dispersed throughout the whole world, it will
" bring back the Jews to the true meaning of the
" law, by giving interpretations, which shall set
" aside the corrupted glosses of commentators; it
" will teach them to love and to defend the country
" they inhabit; it will convince them that the land,
" where, for the first time since their dispersion,
" they have been able to raise their voice, is intitled
" to all those sentiments which rendered their an-
" cient country so dear to them.

" Lastly, the Great Sanhedrim, according to an-
" cient custom, will be composed of seventy mem-
" bers, exclusive of the President. Two thirds, or
" thereabout, shall be Rabbies, and among them, in
" the first place, those who sit among you, and who
" have approved the answers. The other third
" shall be chosen, by this assembly itself, among
" its members, by ballot. The duties of the Great
" Sanhedrim shall be to convert into religious
" doctrines the answers already given by this as-
" sembly, and likewise those which may result
" from the continuation of your sittings.

" For you will observe, Gentlemen, your mission
" is not yet fulfilled; it will last as long as that of
" the Great Sanhedrim, which will only ratify
" your answers and give them a greater weight;
" His Majesty is, besides, too well satisfied with your

" zeal and with the purity of your intentions, to
" dissolve this assembly before the accomplish-
" ment of the great work in which you were cal-
" led to assist.

" In the first instance it is fit that you should
" name by ballot a committee of nine members to
" prepare, with us, the ground-work of your future
" discussions, and of the decisions of the Sanhe-
" drim. You will observe that the Portuguese,
" German, and Italian Jews, are equally repre-
" sented in this committee. We also invite you to
" acquaint the several Synagogues of Europe of
" the meeting of the Great Sanhedrim without
" delay, that they may send deputies able to give to
" government additional information, and worthy
" of communicating with you."

After the reading of this discourse, which was
loudly applauded, the President answered as follows:

" Gentlemen,
" The new communications you have transmit-
" ted to this assembly from His Imperial and Roy-
" al Majesty, confirm, more and more, the hopes we
" had entertained of his paternal views in our be-
" half.

" Any man, endowed with an enlightened mind

" and a benevolent heart, might conceive the idea
" of a political reform useful to mankind; but
" these philanthropic conceptions usually remain
" dormant; they are considered as the idle dreams
" of benevolent men, either because these, being
" too much taken up with the object in view, do
" not possess minds sufficiently expanded to em-
" brace the means of execution, or because these
" means are generally beyond the reach of private
" individuals.

" The case is widely different in regard to a
" powerful and venerated Prince, one of those ex-
" traordinary beings who carry every thing along
" with them in their vortex, who give their name
" to the age in which they reign, and who are in-
" cessantly hurried by an ardent desire of doing
" good.

" When Heaven grants such sovereigns for the
" felicity of nations, no magnanimous designs
" escape them; there are none which cannot be
" fully carried into execution by their just and
" powerful determination.

" By the ascendancy of their energy, they give
" to all their establishments a character of strength
" and stability, which places them, as it were,
" above the reach of human instability and of hu-
" man passions.

" Such is the Prince under whose laws we live :

" by his bravery he has obtained the appellation of
" *Great*—that of *Beneficent* will be the reward of
" his benevolence, To him alone belonged the
" power to heal for ever the wounds which
" eighteen centuries of proscriptions and anathe-
" mas had inflicted on the unfortunate children of
" Israel.

" Ever since their dispersion they have been the
" victims of a false and wavering policy, the sport
" of prejudices and the caprice of the moment ; and
" it is a matter of wonder that, among so many dif-
" ferent princes who reigned in various countries,
" even among those who seemed inclined to better
" our fate, not one has been found who conceived,
" in their full extent and greatness, the idea and
" the means of raising sober, industrious, and active
" men from the civil and political nullity in which
" they were kept, Outcasts of society, the butt of
" calumny, the innocent victims of injustice, has
" uniformly been, for centuries, to suffer in silence
" their melancholy fate.

" His Majesty, amidst the great interests which
" might absorb the whole attention of a man,
" could not look on our situation with indiffe-
" rence; our regeneration has occupied his thoughts;
" this is abundantly proved by the new communica-
" tions we have just received. From the source of
" the evil itself the Emperor has drawn forth the

" remedy ; in some of the sad remains of the baneful
" effects of ancient oppression, still lurking among
" the Jews of the north, he has found an opportunity
" of bringing about the happiness of all the Israelites
" of the western world. It is like the rod of Moses
" bringing forth living waters from the barren rock.

" Here let us stop for a while, and consider that,
" according to the principles of political right, all
" forms of religion must submit to the Sovereign
" authority, inasmuch as they can depend from a
' temporal power: this super-inspection of govern-
" ment is necessary, first, lest they should split
" into different sects ; for if, from the nature of
" things, several established religions are suf-
" fered in the same state, public order and social
" morality require, on the other hand, that none of
" these religious should branch out into particular
" sects, which would disturb the internal peace of
" empires.

" To prevent this danger, reason and the great
" law of public interest require that each esta-
" blished religion should give the sovereign a re-
" sponsible pledge, and the means of super-inspec-
" tion; to this end, it must possess men who, by
" their profession, should study its principles,
" preach its morality, and preserve its purity, and
" thus become, in a manner, its trustees and its

" guardians ; and such are the duties imposed on
" all ministers of religious worship.

" These principles coincide with and sanction
" the first communications which have been made
" to us.

" The question was, at first, to know in what par-
" ticulars our religious dogmas coincided or were
" at variance with the law of the state, to ascertain
" whether these dogmas, too long considered as in-
" tolerant and inimical to society at large, were,
" really, either the one or the other. Supported by
" the testimony of our conscience by our feelings,
" and by the principles we profess, we have here, in
" this capital, almost in the presence of His Ma-
" jesty, expressed our sentiments with the same
" frankness and the same liberty as if we had been
" in the bosom of our families, and without being
" influenced by the interpellation of the sovereign
" authority.

" This reliance, this unlimited confidence in the
" wisdom and in the exalted views of His Majesty
" were certainly no ordinary proofs of our un-
" bounded veneration. At last the Emperor has
" acquired the certainty that the religious laws of
" Moses contained, neither in their precepts nor
" in their practice, any which could justify the
" exclusion of its followers from the enjoyment of
" the civil and political rights of Frenchmen.

" But His Majesty, deeply impressed with the
" principle, that, in religious matters, faith is to be
" left to its own workings, is convinced that our
" answers, however satisfactory to him, were insuf-
" ficient; that it was necessary that all the Syna-
" gogues of France and of Italy should adopt and
" adhere to them, and they should become rules of
" faith for all the Jewish congregations of the wes-
" tern world. It is in consequence of this tender
" caution, which entitles the most powerful Chris-
" tian Prince to our eternal blessings, that he has
" determined, in his wisdom, to call together a
" GREAT SANHEDRIM, as mentioned before, in
" order to give to the decisions of this assembly that
" religious sanction which they ought to have.

" Thus the ruler of the fate of Europe, the
" dispenser of thrones, this Monarch respected
" above every thing, himself respects the liberty
" of religious opinions, and the sacred asylum of
" conscience.

" Thus a new monument is raised to the glory
" of His Royal and Imperial Majesty, more last-
" ing than marble and adamant. His reign will
" be the epocha of the regeneration of our bre-
" thren. Europe will be indebted to him for mil-
" lions of useful citizens; and, what must be still
" more grateful to the heart of His Majesty, he

" will behold the men indebted to him for their
" happiness.

" The more important functions which His Ma-
" jesty now deigns to intrust to our care might
" appal us, by the more arduous duties they im-
" pose, had you not promised, Gentlemen Commisi-
" oners, to assist us with your extensive know-
" ledge, in order to enable us to meet His Majesty's
" views with proportionate exertions. Estranged
" from studies relative to such elevated subjects,
" both by our situation and by the nature of our
" occupations, we should only have brought to our
" discussions the plain light of common sense,
" pure intentions, and an unabated zeal; but these
" dispositions are not sufficient; we have need of
" your indulgence, and we claim it as a boon."

The President, after this discourse, which was
applauded by the assembly, informed the Commissioners, that, wishing to take the sense of the
assembly on the communications they had just
made, he requested they would retire, for an instant, into one of the adjoining rooms, where the
result of the deliberation should be transmitted
to them.

The Commissioners were accompanied by the
deputies, and when these had resumed their seats,
the President proposed the following resolution.

" The Assembly of the Hebrew Deputies of France
" and Italy, having heard the official Communi-
" cations, just made by the Commissioners of
" His Royal and Imperial Majesty,

" Considering that his Majesty the Emperor and
" King, in allowing the formation of a society
" of a fixed number of doctors in the law and of
" the most distinguished laymen, to form a GREAT
" SANHEDRIM, has anticipated the wishes and the
" wants of all those who profess the religion of
" Moses in Europe; that his Imperial benevolence
" towards his Israelitish subjects shews itself every
" day in so unequivocal a manner as to impose
" on them the obligation of exerting all their ef-
" forts to further the execution of his grand de-
" signs, for the welfare of all their brethren of the
" western world,
" This assembly resolves, that the President
" and the officers of the assembly shall wait on
" the Commissioners of His Imperial and Royal
" Majesty, and intreat them to carry to the foot of
" the throne the expression of the deep and un-
" shaken loyalty which animates every member.
" That a proclamation shall be addressed by
" this assembly to all the Synagogues of the French
" Empire of Italy and of Europe, to acquaint
" them, that, on the 20th of October next, the

" GREAT SANHEDRIM will open in Paris, under the
" protection and by the special permission of His
" Majesty.

" That the Rabbies, members of this assembly,
" shall beinvited to become members of this GREAT
" Sanhedrim.

" That five and twenty deputies, members of
" this assembly shall be elected, by ballot, to be
" also members of it.

" That His Imperial and Royal Majesty shall
" be most humbly requested to give the necessary
" orders, that twenty-nine Rabbies, chosen in the
" Synagogues of his French empire, and in the
" kingdom of Italy, may come to Paris to assist
" at the GREAT SANHEDRIM.

" That this assembly shall proceed by ballot,
" and by three different lists, to name a Committee
" of Nine, which committee shall, in concert with
" the Commissioners of His Majesty, prepare such
" matters as are to be submitted to the GREAT
" SANHEDRIM.

" That this assembly shall not separate till the
" GREAT SANHEDRIM has terminated its sittings;
" that it requests the Imperial Commissioners to
" convey to His Imperial and Royal Majesty their
" humble wish of being admitted in a body to his
" presence, to lay at the foot of the throne their
" just tribute of love and respect.

" Resolved also that a copy of these resolutions
" shall be immediately delivered to the Commissi-
" oners before the close of the sitting."

These several resolutions were translated into
Italian, and into German, and adopted unanimously amidst loud acclamations.

Immediately after, the President and the
officers of the assembly went to meet the Commissioners, and delivered them a copy of the
above resolutions, requesting them to lay the
same before His Imperial and Royal Majesty.

On returning into the assembly, the President
proposed immediately to proceed, by ballot, to the
nomination of the new Committee of Nine.

Some members thought, that this might be put
off till the day after; others were for beginning
immediately. The assembly adopted this last proposition, and the ballot commenced.

Out of ninety-nine votes, M. Segre obtained
seventy-eight, M. Cologna sixty-seven, and MM.
Formiggini and Cracovia, thirty-four each.

In consequence, the President declared MM.
Segre and Cologna members of the Committee of
Nine.

The assembly began afterwards a fresh ballot
to name a third member among the Italian deputies.

Out of one hundred votes M. Cracovia having

obtained fifty-three, and M. Formigini forty-seven, the President proclaimed the former a member of the Committee of Nine.

The assembly proceeded afterwards to the election of three members to be chosen from among the deputies of the north.

Out of ninety-eight votes, M. Jacob Gondchaux obtained forty-six; M. Berr-Isaac-Berr, forty-six; M. Zinzheimer, forty; M. J. Lazare, thirty-nine; M. Lyon Marx, twenty-five; M. Worms, twenty; M. Moise Levi, twenty.

None having obtained the absolute (32) majority, the President deferred the election till next sitting, and left the chair.

Sitting of the 19th of September, 1806.

The President took the chair at twelve o'clock; he read the law on the mode of ballotting by scrutiny; it appeared, from its contents, that the nomination of the third Italian member, which

(32) The French, with their usual metaphysical distinctions, have two kinds of majority; the *absolute* majority, requisite in the most important elections, must be composed of more than one half of all the voters. The relative majority, is that majority which is decided by the actual majority of votes among any number of candidates, without reference to the number of voters.

had been made by ballot on the second scrutiny, was not regular. (33)

It was proposed to proceed to the election of the German and Portuguese members, and afterwards to have a new ballot for a third Italian member.

Others demanded that the nomination of the third member should be maintained, and that the law should only apply to the future nomination of German and Portuguese members.

The President observed that as the law was clear on the point, it was impossible to act against it in any case.

Some members insisted on having the nomination confirmed, because it had been made *bona fide*.

Others thought, that the law was applicable only to electoral assemblies, and not to an assembly like this; that M. Cracovia, having been proclaimed a member of the Committee by the President, his nomination was sanctioned, and it could not be annulled; but that, if any doubts were entertained, it was fit to consult the Commissioners of His Imperial Majesty on this subject, before the assembly should come to any determination.

---

(33) The second scrutiny was so far irregular, as the law directs that *all* the members who have obtained votes in the first instance shall be balloted for in the second. Those only who have the majority on that repetition are balloted for the *absolute majority* on the third.

A member maintained, that the law of the electoral assemblies was not applicable to this: he mentioned the letter of His Excellency the Minister of the Interior, by which the assembly was left at liberty to chuse such a mode of election as it might prefer.

Others observed, that the question was to conform to the law, and not to confirm or reject the nomination of the Italian member; and that, even for the honour of that deputy, his nomination ought to be sanctioned by the legal mode.

A member thought that the law alone could confirm or annul the election of M. Cracovia; and, till such time as the case was decided, he proposed to the assembly to proceed to the nomination of the German and Portuguese members.

To remove all doubts, it was proposed to send a deputation of three members to the Commissioners of His Imperial and Royal Majesty, to know, from them, whether the assembly was to begin a new ballot to replace the Italian member, whose nomination did not appear regular.

This proposition was adopted by the assembly, and the President named MM. Cracovia, sen. Oppenheim, and J. Rodrigues, jun. Secretary, to compose that deputation. They immediately left the assembly to wait on the Commissioners of His Imperial and Royal Majesty.

The assembly proceeded afterwards to a second ballot to name the three German deputies. Out of one hundred votes, M. J. Lazare obtained fifty-five; M. Moise Levy, fifty-five; M. Lyon Marx, forty-nine; M. Berr-Isaac-Berr, forty-seven; M. David Zinzheimer, forty-six; M. Cerf Jacob Goncheaux, forty-one. In consequence, MM. J. Lazare and Moise Levy, having obtained the absolute majority of votes, the President proclaimed them members of the Committee of Nine.

The three members deputed to the Commissioners of His Imperial and Royal Majesty entered the hall. They said, that they had brought the answer of M. Portalis, the only one of the Commissioners present; that his idea was, that no opinion could be formed of the legality or illegality of the nomination of the third Italian member till the minutes of the proceedings of the assembly were formally laid before the Commissioners; that a nomination might be annulled in two ways---- either at the request of a party interested, or on the requisition of the civil power intrusted with the care of enforcing the observation of the law.

" The assembly," he said, " may confirm this " nomination, if it thinks it fit; but as the law " has not been attended to, should any interested " parties object to it, the Commissioners would " be obliged to take their objections into consi-

" deration, provided they were signed by the ob-
" jecting parties, and transmitted to the Commis-
" sioners by the assembly." As to the applicati-
of the law to the assembly, he said that, although
it had been made for electoral assemblies, yet it
was general for all nominations made by ballot,
and by an absolute majority. M. Portalis added,
that it appeared to him to be the best way to leave
things as they were, until the Commissioners could
be made officially acquainted with the doubts
which had arisen in the assembly as to the validity of the nomination of the third Italian member
for the Committee of Nine.

The assembly took that advice, and proceeded
to a third scrutiny to ballot MM. Lyon Marx and
Berr-Isaac-Berr, who, in the second scrutiny, had
obtained the greatest number of votes after MM.
Jacob Lazare and Moise Levy, who had an absolute majority. Out of one hundred votes M. Berr
Isaac-Berr obtained fifty, and M. Lyon Marx forty-eight; two votes were null, one of the lists being blank, and another containing the name of an
Italian member. In consequence the President
proclaimed M. Berr-Isaac-Berr a member of the
Committee of Nine.

The assembly continued the ballot for the nomination of the Portuguese members. Out of one
hundred votes M. Furtado the President obtained

seventy; M. Avigdor, Secretary, fifty-one; M. Cremieux, forty-nine ; M. Abraham Andrade, Rabbi, forty-six; M. Sabbaton Constantini, thirty-five; M. Marg Foy, sen. thirty-five, MM. Furtado and Avigdor, having obtained the absolute majority of votes, were proclaimed members of the Committee of Nine.

At the repetition of the ballot for the nomination of the third Portuguese member, out of ninety-four votes M. Cremieux obtained thirty-seven; M. Andrade, Rabbi, thirty-seven; M. Marg Foy, sen. eleven; and M. Sabbaton Constantini, seven. None of these members having obtained the absolute majority of votes, it was proposed to postpone the third ballot for those two members who had the relative majority of votes, to the following sitting. This proposition was adopted by the assembly.

The President quitted the chair at half past four o'clock, and announced that, on Tuesday, the 23d inst. the assembly would resume its sittings.

Sitting of the 23d of September, 1806.

The President took the chair at twelve o'clock. The minutes of the proceedings of the last sitting were read, and adopted with a few slight alterations.

MM. Cadet Carcassonne, Marg Foy, sen. and Lyon Marx, were named Commissioners to maintain order in the assembly. The President announced that the ballot between MM. Cremieux and Andrade, to complete the Committee of Nine, stood for the order of the day. Out of ninety-eight votes M. Andrade obtained fifty-one, and M. Cremieux forty-seven. The former was accordingly proclaimed a member of the Committee.

The President afterwards read the draft of a circular letter to all the Synagogues of France and Italy, as well as to all the Synagogues of the western world, to announce the opening of the Sanhedrim in Paris, and to invite them to send thither doctors of the law, to concur, by their advice, in the benevolent views of His Royal and Imperial Majesty.

The assembly approved the design, but thought that, considering the importance of the measure, a single reading was not sufficient to sanction a resolution on a document which was to be sent all over the world; and thought it prudent to refer the circular letter to a Committee.

After some observations from several members, on the question, Whether it should be referred to a new committee or to the Committee of Nine? the assembly adopted this last proposition; and the

President requested the members of the Committee to meet at his residence, that very evening, to settle the plan of the proposed address, and to this end to add to their number M. Zinzheimer, Rabbi. This measure was approved by the assembly.

A member proposed, that the address should be first written in Hebrew, and afterwards translated into French and German; remarking that it was much more difficult to translate French into Hebrew than Hebrew into French; that, besides, the Chiefs of the Synagogues, to whom the address was directed, understood Hebrew much better than modern languages; that the first had a peculiar turn which made all literal translation excessively difficult; and lastly, that, in every point of view, the Chiefs of foreign Synagogues would place much more confidence in the address if written in Hebrew.

After a slight discussion on the proposition of the last speaker, the assembly resolved, that the address should be translated from the French into Hebrew and into German; and that it trusted to the known talents of the Rabbies to give the translation all the precision and all the correctness of the ideas contained in the original.

A member thought, that this circular address ought not to be sent into the countries now at war with France.

He was answered that, as the object His Majesty had in view, in allowing a GREAT SANHEDRIM to be assembled under his protection, was evidently to attach more particularly the Israelites to the different countries they inhabit, and as it was the interest of every government, whether friendly or hostile, to adopt the principles which occupy the attention of the assembly, there could be no inconveniency in sending the circular letter indiscriminately to all the Synagogues of the western world. This proposition was referred to the Committee, with instructions to confer upon it with the Commissioners of His Imperial Majesty on this subject.

The President thought that no time should be lost in chusing, by ballot, the five and twenty lay members, who were to form a part of the Sanhedrim.

One of the Rabbies thought that, before the assembly should proceed to such nomination, it seemed necessary to ascertain what qualifications were necessary to become a member of that august assembly.

A deputy observed that he, and several other members, had carefully investigated this subject; that he had looked into all the Jewish antiquities without being able to find any rule which prescribed any particular qualifications as indispensable to entitle any man to a seat in that august assembly. Several members supported that opi-

nion, and the assembly passed to the order of the
day.

The assembly began the ballot for the nomination
of the twenty-five members; but after reading the
first four lists, the President, observing that it was
four o'clock, proposed to adjourn to the next day.

A member, considering the tediousness of a ballot, in which the lists contained so many names,
proposed to form several Committees for the registering of the votes.

The assembly adjourned the consideration of this
proposition to the next day. The President quitted the chair.

It is, no doubt, worth while to remark, that the
importance of the functions attributed to the Committee of Nine has made the assembly most particularly scrupulous in the choice of the members
who were to compose it; and it may safely be said,
that the expectations raised in consequence have
been completely fulfilled.

The Italian Rabbies, MM. Segre, Cologna, and
Cracovia, are all three equally distinguished by
their virtues, by their zeal, their talents, and their
learning. The Rabbies of that country have
been the first to give the example of literary and
historical pursuits, connected with theological
learning, and a profound knowledge of the Holy
Writings. The German members are all three

equally commendable for the qualities of the mind and of the heart. M. Berr-Isaac-Berr has been one of the first in France to claim for the Jews the indefeasible rights of citizens, and has strenuously laboured to make them worthy of these rights, by his example and by his writings. The productions of M. Michel Berr, his son, prove that he has rendered his zeal and his talents hereditary in his family, equally distinguished by the learning and polished manners of those who compose it. M. Moise Levy joins to an extensive fund of knowledge, and to various talents, the most ardent zeal for the interest of his Israelitish brethren ; he belongs to one of those Jewish families, equally respectable and respected, which, at all times, have ranked high in public esteem. M. Jacob Lazare joins active zeal to extensive learning: and lastly, the choice of the members taken among the Portuguese, completes the proof of the discerning spirit of the assembly. The talents and the qualities of M. Furtado, the President, the zeal and the learning of M. Avigdor, Secretary, the profound erudition of M. Andrade, Rabbi, fulfil all the expectations which that nomination excited. The choice of such men may well justify the most sanguine hopes entertained by all the Israelites of the happy result of the momentous undertaking which the Committee of Nine has to

commence and to complete under the direction of
the Imperial Commissioners, so worthy themselves
of an unlimited confidence, and so well entitled to
general esteem.

Sitting of September 24, 1806.

The President took the chair at twelve o'clock,
and named as Commissioners to maintain order
in the assembly, MM. Gumpel Levi, Wittersheim,
and J. Benjamin.

One of the Secretaries read the minutes of the
sitting of the 23d, which were adopted.

The ballot for the nomination of the twenty-five
lay members, who are to form a part of the GREAT
SANHEDRIM, was resumed : to proceed with more
dispatch, it was proposed to form three Committees to register the votes, one of the Scrutineers
presiding over each. The assembly adopted this
proposition : and the President named for the first
Committee, MM. Emilie Vitta, Berr-Isaac-Berr,
and May, of Paris; for the second, MM. Theodore Cerf-Berr, Benjamin, and Castro, jun.; for
the third, MM. Olry-Hayem-Worms, Cerf-Jacob
Gondchaux, and Baruch Cerf-Berr : at four o'clock
the registering of the votes was concluded.

A member demanded that, before the result

should be known, the votes should be reckoned, in order to ascertain that the ballot was correct. There were, he said, one hundred deputies, which, at twenty-five votes each, made two thousand five hundred votes. This proposition was adopted, and the number of votes, registered in the three committees, amounted only to two thousand three hundred and eighty two. A member, seeing so great a difference, proposed to annul the scrutiny, which was adopted. It being late, it was proposed to adjourn the new scrutiny for the nomination of the twenty-five lay members of the GREAT SANHEDRIM to Friday, the 26th inst.; this proposition was adopted.

To prevent the recurrence of similar errors, it was proposed to form five Committees instead of three; that each Committee should carefully keep the lists, to compare them when necessary. That one member only should be called at a time to deliver his votes; that his list should be opened before it was put in the box, to ascertain the number of names it contained. The assembly approved these propositions.

A member demanded the reading of the Address to the Synagogues of Europe, which had been referred to the Committee of Nine.

The President read it.

It was as follows:

" Our dear Brethren in Israel,

" The Most High clearly manifests his benevo-
" lent designs in our behalf; a great event is pre-
" paring. What our fathers had not seen for a
" long course of centuries, what we could never
" expect to see ourselves, is now on the point of
" exciting the wonder of the world.

" The 20th of October is the day fixed for
" the opening of the GREAT SANHEDRIM, in the
" capital of one of the most powerful Christian
" empires, under the protection of the immortal
" Prince who governs it.

" Paris is to be the scene of this great event,
" for ever memorable, and which shall be, for the
" scattered remnants of the children of Abraham,
" a new æra of deliverance and of felicity.

" We this day invite you to partake of our joy,
" and to share those sentiments which our com-
" mon origin and our common religion cannot
" fail to excite, and which are deeply impressed in
" our own hearts.

" Who would not admire with us the impene-
" trable designs of that Providence who, by means
" unknown to our weakness, changes the face of
" human affairs, consoles the afflicted, raises the
" humble from the dust, sets a term to those trials
" decreed in his wisdom, and excites the esteem

" and the benevolence of nations towards those
" whose hearts have remained faithful to his law!

" Since our dispersion, numberless changes have
" manifested the vicissitude of human affairs: na-
" tions have been successively overwhelmed by na-
" tions, and all have been afterwards mingled and
" heaped on each other; we alone have withstood
" the torrent of ages and of revolutions.

" Every thing seemed to announce for us, in
" Europe, a happier state, and a less precarious
" existence. But it was only a distant though
" cheering prospect : to see those hopes realized,
" it was necessary that, from the midst of public
" tempests, from the tumultuous fluctuations of
" an immense people, one of those powerful men,
" round whom nations rally from an instinct of
" self-preservation, should, conducted by Provi-
" dence, raise his head above the roaring elements.

" This benevolent and protecting genius wishes
" to do away every humiliating distinction be-
" tween us and his other subjects. His piercing
" eye has discovered, in our Mosaic code, those
" principles of strength and of stability by which
" it has stood the test of ages, and which formerly
" gave our fathers that patriarchal simplicity, still
" an object of veneration in present times, and
" that heroical character so glowingly pourtrayed
" in our history.

" In his wisdom he has thought it consonant to
" his paternal views to allow the convocation of a
" GREAT SANHEDRIM in Paris. The functions of
" this body, and the objects it is to have in view,
" are clearly laid down in the eloquent discourse
" delivered by the Commissioners of His Imperial
" and Royal Majesty. We send it to you, dear
" Brethren, that you may yourselves judge of the
" spirit in which it is written, and see that the sole
" object in view is to bring us back to the prac-
" tice of our ancient virtues, and to preserve our
" holy religion in all its purity.

" We now call upon you to assist your Brethren
" with your knowledge, as the means of giving a
" greater weight to the decisions of the GREAT
" SANHEDRIM, and of happily establishing among
" us uniformity of doctrine, more consonant to
" the civil and political laws of the several states
" which you have adopted as your country.

" Your advice will be useful to us; and we are
" authorized by government to claim your assist-
" ance.

" Be not deaf to our voice, dear Brethren! Se-
" lect among you men known by their wisdom,
" the friends of truth and of justice, and able to
" assist us, in the completion of this great work.
" Send them to take their places among us, that

" their wise and enlightened views, may conduce
" to general advantage.

" It must be a pleasing task for all the Israelites
" of Europe to concur in the regeneration of their
" Brethren, as it must be glorious, for us, in par-
" ticular, to have fixed the attention of an illustri-
" ous sovereign.

" Never had men on earth motives equally pow-
" erful to love and to admire this sovereign, for
" none could ever boast of the effects of so signal a
" justice, so marked a protection. To restore to
" society a people commendable for private virtues,
" to awake men to a sense of their dignity, by in-
" suring to them the enjoyment of their rights,
" such are the favours for which we are indebted
" to NAPOLEON THE GREAT.

" The Sovereign Ruler of kings and nations has
" given him to this empire, to heal its wounds,
" to calm its political commotions, aggrandize its
" destinies, and fix our own, and to be the delight
" of two nations, which shall for ever bless the day
" when they placed their happiness in his hands,
" already intrusted with their defence.

(Signed)   " FURTADO,
                                President.

" RODRIGUES,   AVIGDOR,
                        " Secretaries."

N N

The assembly applauded the sentiments contained in this address, and adopted it unanimously.

The President afterwards proposed to take into
consideration the indemnities to be granted to the
deputies by their brethren in the departments;
the assembly approved the plan almost unanimously, and resolved, that the President should
send it in a circular letter to all the departments
of the French empire, and of the kingdom of Italy, which have deputies in Paris, after having first
obtained the approbation of His Excellency the
Minister of the Interior.

A member proposed, that measures should be
taken to send into the countries at war with France
the proclamation addressed to the Synagogues of
Europe.

Another proposed to consult on this subject the
Commissioners of His Majesty the Emperor and
King, and to conform to their directions. The
assembly approved this proposition, and directed
the Committee of Nine to confer with the Commissioners on this subject.

The President quitted the chair at half past
four, and announced that he should take it on the
26th inst. at eleven o'clock.

Sitting of September 26, 1806.

The President took the chair at eleven o'clock; he named, as Commissioners to maintain order, MM. Auguste Lorrich and Isaac Rodrigues. He announced that the nomination, by ballot, of twenty-five lay members, who are to form a part of the GREAT SANHEDRIM, stood for the order of the day.

A member observed, that, before the assembly should proceed to a new ballot, it was proper to decide whether the first was irregular, as had been stated.

Another maintained that the former ballot was regular, and that the hundred and eighteen votes wanting in the gross calculation, made by multiplying one hundred by twenty-five, could not afford a motive for annulling the nomination of those who had obtained an absolute majority; he therefore demanded that the assembly should annul the resolution adopted at the last sitting, and that the members already named should form a part of the Sanhedrim.

Others observed, that the assembly had already annulled the ballot made at the last sitting; that it found on its results sufficient motives for that resolution, and moved for the order of the day.

It was maintained, on the other side, that a ballot could not be considered as void, because the number of votes was less than that of voters. That nullity followed only in case the number of votes exceeded that of voters.

Other members combatted that opinion, and pretended that any difference, in more or in less, rendered the ballot void. They again called for the order of the day. The President put it to the vote, and it was adopted.

Some deputies objected to the order of the day as it stood, and protested against the decision; they proposed to adjourn the sitting, and to refer the whole of the affair to the wisdom of the Commissioners of His Majesty.

It was answered, that a question already decided required no further examination. The order of the day was again called for; the President put it again to the vote, and it was again adopted by the majority.

One of the Secretaries called over the names of the deputies; they, one by one, went to the table, and put their lists into a box.

The Scrutineers registered the votes in proportion as they were given in: there were ninety-eight voters. The result of the ballot was as follows:

VOTES.

For M. Berr-Isaac-Berr, deputy of La
Meurthe - - -   68
Jacob Benjamin, (34) deputy of
Mont-Tonnerre - -   72
Mayer Nathan, deputy of La Sarre   60
Isaac Samuel Avigdor, deputy of
Les Alpes Maritimes -   76
Lipman erf-Berr, deputy of the
Upper Rhine - - -   72
Israel Cohen, deputy of L'Adige   77
Theodore Cerf-Berr, deputy of La
Seine - - - -   75
Saul Cremieux, deputy of La
Seine - - - -   72
Furtado, deputy of La Gironde   86
Aaron Friedberg, deputy of Mont
Tonnerre - - -   64
Formigini, deputy of L'Olona   74
Cerf Jacob Goudchaux, deputy
of La Moselle - -   75
Aaron Latis, deputy of L'Adria-
tique - - - -   64
Herz Loeb Iorich, deputy of
Mont-Tonnerre - -   67

(34) He was afterwards replaced by M. Abraham Cohen, deputy of
the Lower Rhine——how and why is not stated.

VOTES.

For M. David Levi, deputy of Po   84
Marg Foy, deputy of Lower Py-
renees - - - -   76
Lyon Marx, deputy of Rhin et
Moselle - - -   69
Isaac Rodrigues, deputy of La Gi-
ronde - - - -   74
Rodrigues, jun. deputy of La
Seine - - - -   62
Aaron Schmoll, deputy of La
Seine - - - -   71
S. Wittersheim, deputy of the
Lower Rhine - -   77
Olry Hayem Worms, deputy of
La Seine - - -   69
Benoit Fano, deputy of Mincio   86
Daniel Levi, (35) deputy of the
Lower Rhine - -   74

The President, in consequence, proclaimed them members of the GREAT SANHEDRIM, and requested the assembly to proceed to a fresh ballot, to name a twenty-fifth member. The result of that ballot gave forty-eight votes to M. Constantini, and forty-four to M. Emilie Vitta.

(35) Replaced by M. Baruch Cerf-Berr, deputy of the Lower Rhine.

The President announced that a ballot would take place between these two members. There were only seventy-two voters for this third ballot: M. Constantini obtained forty-eight votes, and M. Vitta twenty-four. The President, in consequence, proclaimed M. Constantini, deputy for the department of Bouche du Rhone, the twenty-fifth member for the GREAT SANHEDRIM, and quitted the chair.

Sitting of the 9th of December, 1806.

The President took the chair at twelve o'clock. He named, as Commissioners to maintain order, MM. Baruch-Cerf-Berr, Felix Levi, and Dreyfoss.

He announced, that a report of the Committee of Nine stood for the order of the day, the object whereof was to propose a series of regulations for the organization of the Mosaic worship, on which the assembly was to deliberate.

The President then requested one of the secretaries, member of the Commission, to read the report.

REPORT.

" Gentlemen,

" Your Committee is about to give you the re-
" port of a plan agreed upon with the Commis-

" sioners of His Imperial Majesty, and which is
" to be submitted to your decision.

" It contains a series of regulations intended to
" organize our religious worship. It is the result of
" communications given by your Committee, and
" of the instructions given by His Majesty to the
" Commissioners intrusted with the management
" of affairs which concern you.

" Before we proceed further, I am directed by
" your Committee to say, that it is an absolute
" duty for every one of its members publicly to
" declare that they have experienced, from the per-
" sons thus invested with His Majesty's confi-
" dence, amenity, good advice, benevolence, and
" a constant and sincere wish to promote the salu-
" tary measures we thought it our duty to pro-
" pose.

" If the Mosaic religion, its dogmas, and its
" practices, had been as perfectly known to go-
" vernment as the other forms of religion, our as-
" sistance would have been altogether useless.
" Much better informed than we are ourselves of
" what may tend to our happiness, government
" might have decided without calling us to Paris.
" The regulations which I am going to submit to
" you formed an essential part of the objects for
" which this assembly was convened.

" Already more than once, Gentlemen, you have

" had opportunities of being convinced, that the
" government, under which we have the happiness
" to live, was far from attempting to act contrari-
" ly to our consciences by attacking, in the least,
" very ancient religious opinions, or by shocking,
" in the smallest degree, that sentiment of predi-
" liction which men in general entertain for things
" they hold sacred from their very infancy.

" And, in consequence, whatever could inter-
" fere with our religious dogmas, or with our reli-
" gious practices, has been carefully avoided. We
" have been consulted on every point connected
" with our faith; and in none of the articles of
" these regulations will you find any point which
" either directly or indirectly militates against it.

" You will, on the contrary, easily perceive that
" now, for the first time, the Mosaic worship
" emerges from the obscurity in which it has been
" involved these two thousand years; that it
" emerges from that almost complete state of dis-
" organization in which it had been ever since the
" revolution; that it now acquires a legal exist-
" ence; that its ministers are acknowledged by
" public authority; their functions are fixed and
" settled; their salary assured, and their influence
" directed to its true destination.

" These regulations, while they preserve the Mosa-
" ic worship in all its purity, are far from encroach-

" ing in the least on your civil and political rights.
" They afford, in general, and in every particu-
" lar, a full confirmation of what you heard in your
" sitting of the 18th of September from the Com-
" missioners of His Majesty---*The free exercise of*
" *your religious worship and the full enjoyment of*
" *your political rights are secured to you.* But, in
" return for his gracious protection, His Majesty
" requires a religious pledge for the strict adhe-
" rence to the principles contained in your an-
" swers.

" You know, Gentlemen, that such a pledge will
" be found, in the doctrinal decisions of the GREAT
" SANHEDRIM, grounded on your answers. In the
" plan of regulations which is about to be sub-
" mitted to you, and which, as I have already ob-
" served, is the result of the instructions given by
" His Majesty to the Commissioners, and of the
" views of your Committee, every thing has been
" calculated with the intention to give and
" strengthen such a pledge.

" The paternal instructions of His Majesty, in
" this respect, clearly evince his magnanimous
" design of raising an ancient and celebrated na-
" tion from the state of abasement in which it was
" unjustly retained by prejudice. Every thing is
" disposed to secure the attainment of this phi-
" lanthropic object.

" The experience of the past made you justly
" apprehend whatever tended to establish distinc-
" tions, either in opinion or in deeds, between you
" and the rest of Frenchmen. You had marked
" with grief that those different shades in man-
" ners greatly widened the breach caused by the
" difference in religion, and had an evident tend-
" ency to keep us farther removed from social in-
" tercourse, and to perpetuate our forlorn state.
" Nothing like it is to be apprehended now. As
" subjects of the French empire or of the king-
" dom of Italy, the laws of both states contain no
" exceptions affecting us. As subjects of a particu-
" lar religion, the public authority places it imme-
" diately under its inspection, and thus gives it a
" legal existence. As objects of the august protec-
" tion of the prince, we find, in his benevolence, a
" sure pledge of experiencing, in future, like sen-
" timents in the breasts of our fellow-citizens. His
" Majesty himself has been pleased to declare,
" through his Commissioners, that, till now, you
" had not been treated with justice. Where could
" we find stronger grounds of reliance than in the
" avowed intentions of so magnanimous a prince?
" Who among us but sees and feels all the ad-
" vantages of our new situation? who but finds in
" it an incitement to emulation, to loyalty, and to
" the most enthusiastic attachment to our country

" and to its illustrious ruler? Who, in short, does
" not wish, most ardently, to prove himself worthy
" of such favours?

" The means are sure and easy; let the Israelit-
" ish youth take up again the profession of arms,
" in which our ancestors shone so conspicuously;
" let them be numbered among the brave who are
" more particularly devoted to the service of a so-
" vereign who has so many rights to our most un-
" limited services.

" It is, then, evident to every one, that the firm
" and avowed intention of His Imperial and Royal
" Majesty, is to restore our Israelitish brethren to
" the dignity of men and of citizens. As the plan
" of regulations I am going to present contains all
" the encouragement which benevolence and jus-
" tice could dictate for our protection, your Com-
" mittee would think it an insult on your wisdom to
" doubt, for an instant, of its being adopted in all
" its parts."

The plan is as follows:

*The Deputies composing the assembly of the Israelites,
convened by the Imperial decree of the 30th of May,
having heard the report of the Committee of Nine,
named to prepare the ground-work of the deliberations of the assembly, considering what plan might
be presented to their brethren of France and of Italy*

(285)

*for the better regulation of their religious worship
and for the internal police of the same, has* **unani-**
mously (36) *adopted the following.*

PLAN.

Art. I. A Synagogue and a Consistory shall be
established in every department which contains
two thousand individuals professing the religion of
Moses.

II. In case a department should not contain two
thousand Israelites, the jurisdiction of the Consistorial Synagogue shall extend over as many of the
adjoining departments as shall make up the said
number. The seat of the Synagogue shall always
be in the most populous city.

III. In no case can there be more than one Consistorial Synagogue for each department.

IV. No particular Synagogue can be established,
but after being proposed by the Consistorial Synagogue, to the competent authority. Each particu-

(36) This anticipation of the *unanimity* of the assembly, which, in fact,
was very far from relishing the plan, must appear rather strange to an
Englishman.

·lar Synagogue shall be superintended by a Rabbi and two elders, who shall be named by the competent authorities.

V. There shall be a Grand Rabbi in each Consistorial Synagogue.

VI. The Consistories shall be composed, as much as possible, of a grand Rabbi, and of three other Israelites, two of whom shall be chosen among the inhabitants of the town which is the Seat of the Consistory.

VII. The oldest member shall be President of the Consistory. He shall take the title of *Elder of the Consistory.*

VIII. In each Consistorial district the competent authority shall name twenty-five *Notables* among the Israelites who pay the largest contributions.

IX. These *Notables* shall name the members of the Consistory, who must be approved by the competent authority.

X. No one can be a member of the Consistory if he is not thirty years of age, if he has been a bankrupt, unless he honourably paid afterwards, or if he is known to be a usurer.

XI. Every Israelite, wishing to settle in France or in the kingdom of Italy, shall give notice of his intention, within three months after his arrival, to the Consistory nearest his place of residence.

XII. The functions of the Consistory shall be—

1st. To see that the Rabbies do not, either in public or in private, give any instructions or explanations of the law, in contradiction to the answers of the assembly confirmed by the decisions of the GREAT SANHEDRIM.

2nd. To maintain order in the interior of Synagogues, to inspect the administration of particular Synagogues, to settle the assessment, and to regulate the use of the sums necessary for the maintenance of the Mosaic worship, and to see that for cause or under the pretence of religion, no praying assembly be formed without being expressly authorized

3d. To encourage, by all possible means, the Israelites of the Consistorial district to follow useful professions, and to report to government the names of those who cannot

render a satisfactory account of their means
of subsistence.

4th. To give annually to government the
number of the Israelitish conscripts within
the district.

XIII. There shall be formed in Paris a Central
Consistory, composed of three Rabbies and two
other Israelites.

XIV. The Rabbies of the Central Consistory
shall be selected from the Grand Rabbies, and the
rules contained in the tenth article shall apply
to all others.

XV. A member of the Central Consistory shall
go out every year, but he may always be re-elected.

XVI. The vacant place shall be filled by the
remaining members. The member elect shall not
take his place till his election is approved by government.

XVII. The functions of the Central Consistory
are,
1st. To correspond with the Consistories.
2nd To watch over the execution of every
article of the present regulations.

3d. To denounce to the competent authority all infractions of these said regulations, either through negligence or through design.

4th. To confirm the nomination of Rabbies, and to propose to the competent authority, when necessary, the removal of Rabbies and of members of Consistories.

XVIII. The Grand Rabbi shall be named by the twenty-five *Notables*, mentioned in the eighth article.

XIX. The new Grand Rabbi elect shall not enter into his functions till he has been approved by the Central Consistory.

XX. No Rabbi can be elected—

1st. If he is not a native of France or of Italy, or if he has not been naturalized.

2d. If he does not produce a certificate of his abilities, signed by three Frenchmen, if he is a Frenchman, and by three Italians, if he is an Italian: and from the year 1820, if he does not understand the French language in France, and the Italian in the kingdom of Italy. The candidate who joins some proficiency in Greek or Latin to the know-

P P

ledge of the Hebrew language, will be
preferred, all things besides being equal.

XXI. The functions of the Rabbies are---
1st. To teach religion.
2d. To inculcate the doctrines contained in
the decisions of the GREAT SANHEDRIM.
3d. To preach obedience to the laws, and
more particularly to those which relate to
the defence of the country; to dwell especially on this point every year, at the epoch
of the conscription, from the moment government shall first call upon the people
till the law is fully executed.
4th. To represent military service to the Israelites as a sacred duty, and to declare to
them, that, while they are engaged in it, the
law exempts them from the practices which
might be found incompatible with it.
5th. To preach in the Synagogues, and to re-
cite the prayers which are publicly made
for the EMPEROR and the *Imperial Family.*
6th. To celebrate marriages and to pronounce
divorces, without, on any pretence, acting
in either case, till the parties who require
their ministry have produced due proofs of
the act having been sanctioned by the civil
authority.

XXII. The salary of the Rabbies, members of the Central Consistory, is fixed at six thousand livres; that of the Grand Rabbies of Consistorial Synagogues at three thousand livres; that of the Rabbies of particular Synagogues shall be fixed by the community of Israelites which shall have required the establishment of such a Synagogue; it cannot be less than a thousand livres. The Israelites of the several districts may vote an augmentation of these salaries.

XXIII. Each Consistory shall present to the competent authority a plan of assessment among the Israelites of the district for the sums necessary to pay the stipends of the Rabbies. The other expences of worship shall be fixed and assessed by the competent authority, on the demands of the Consistories. The salary of the central Rabbies shall be proportionally paid out of the sums levied on the several districts.

XXIV. Each Consistory shall name an Israelite, not a Rabbi, nor member of the Consistory, to receive the sums which shall be levied in the district.

XXV. This Treasurer shall pay quarterly the salary of the Rabbies, and the other expences of worship, upon orders, signed by at least three members of the Consistory. He shall give his account every year, on a fixed day, in a full assembly of the Consistory.

XXVI. Every Rabbi who, after the promulgation of the present regulations, shall be unemployed, and will choose, nevertheless, to remain in France or in Italy, shall be bound to adhere formally, and to sign a declaration of his adherence to, the decisions of the GREAT SANHEDRIM. The copy of this declaration shall be sent to the Central Consistory, by the Consistory which shall have received it.

XXVII. The Rabbies who are members of the GREAT SANHEDRIM shall be, as much as possible, preferred to all others, to fill the places of Grand Rabbies.

PLAN OF AN *Arrêté*.

" The assembly of the Israelites of the French " empire, and of the kingdom of Italy, having " heard the report of its Committee of Nine, and " having adopted altogether the plan of regula- " tions it has proposed ; considering that the close

" of their sitting is not very distant; and that it
" has thought it a duty to call the attention of His
" Majesty on sevĕral measures, which it thinks
" calculated to promote the regeneration of the
" Jews, although these said measures could not
" all be included in the said plan of regulations;
" considering that among these measures, none
" could be more important than that which tends
" to enforce among the Israelites the obligation of
" military service, which the country has a right
" to require from all her children; considering,
" lastly, that it is the duty of all Israelites in the
" French empire and the kingdom of Italy to shed
" their blood in battle for the cause of France,
" with the same zeal and the same bravery which
" formerly animated their ancestors against the
" enemies of the Holy City, and to seek every op-
" portunity of proving worthy of the favours
" which a great prince now deigns to confer on
" them;

" Resolves,

" That the Commissioners of His Imperial and
" Royal Majesty shall be requested to lay at the
" foot of the throne the dutiful expressions of its
" unbounded and eternal gratitude.

" That the Commissioners shall likewise be re-
" quested to acquaint the Emperor with the hum-
" ble wish of the assembly, that His Majesty

" be pleased to crown all his favours by contri-
" buting something to the salary of the Rabbies,
" and by directing the local authorities of the
" French empire, and of the kingdom of Italy, to
" concert measures with the Consistories, that these
" last might, by their interference and their zeal,
" remove the remaining objections which might
" still prevent the Israelitish youth from following
" the noble career of arms, and thus insure an
" exact obedience to the laws of the conscription."

When the reading was concluded, a member made several observations on various articles of the Regulations.

He requested that a clause might be inserted in the second article, enacting, that the Israelites of a department should always belong to the same consistorial district, and that, in no case, the inhabitants of the same department should belong to different districts.

That the assessment of the local expenditure should be made by the individuals belonging to each particular Synagogue, or by the Consistory, in case they could not agree.

That when a Consistory should undertake the assessment of the charges of the district, each department should have a right to send a deputy to assist at that assessment.

That it should be enacted, in the twelfth article, that the maintenance of the Grand Rabbi only should be charged on the district at large, and that all other expences should be paid by those who might think proper to incur them ; that even one third of the salary of the Grand Rabbi should be paid, in the first instance, by the inhabitants of the place where the seat of the Consistory is fixed, and who shall, besides, furnish their share of the remainder. The reason he gave for this was, that, by the residence of the Grand Rabbi, they were dispensed with maintaining an under Rabbi, who would be necessary for each particular Synagogue.

A member said, that the observations of the last speaker were directed to details which might be taken into consideration by the local Consistories, but that they were not sufficiently important to warrant any alteration in the general regulation. He called for the order of the day.

Another member owned, that the observations of the first speaker were mostly directed to details; some, however, were well intitled to the attention of the assembly. He opposed the order of the day.

The President put the order of the day to the vote; it was adopted; and a member of the Committee of Nine obtained leave to speak.

This member declared that he thought himself
bound to renew in this assembly the objections he
had already made in the Committee to several
clauses of the Regulations, as unbecoming, inefficient, and inadmissible. That the word *usurer*,
which concludes the tenth article, tended, in a
manner, to confirm the prevalent prejudice, that
usury was an inherent vice of men of the Jewish
persuasion, altho' it was to be solely attributed to
individuals, and not to the religion, which strongly
condemned it, as had been proved in the answers
of the assembly. That, because *usurers* were to
be found in some departments, a phrase so vague
and so unbecoming ought not to find a place in a
series of Regulations which were to be common to
all the Israelites of the French empire and of the
kingdom of Italy. He thought that nothing could
justify the clause of the twelfth article, which enacted that the Consistories should report to government the names of those who could not render a
satisfactory account of their means of subsistence,
He thought this the duty of a police officer, and
that it could not, ought not, to form a part of the
functions of Consistories. That those assemblies,
whose seat would be, in many cases, far removed
from several members of the district, could not,
without excessive difficulty, obey the injunction

alluded to. And lastly, that Consistories could not be burthened with police functions, foreign to religion, and which, besides, it would be impossible for them to fulfil; and that, under that three-fold point of view, the clause was inadmissible. He spoke afterwards against the clause of the same article which enacts that Consistories shall, every year, report the number of Israelites within their district liable to the conscription. " Shall the ". Consistories," he said, " keep a register of the " birth of every Jew in their district?" He observed that the law of conscription called equally upon all Frenchmen, whatever religion they professed; that, from the information conveyed by several deputies, it appeared that the young Israelites, liable to that common duty, fulfilled it as well as others; that this clause would tend to establish a supposition that they were less devoted to their country than other Frenchmen; that such a supposition was unfounded; that, besides, if some were refractory, the law could enforce obedience; that it must not be believed that Consistories have more powerful means to induce the youth to follow the career of arms than the local authorities themselves, which have the immediate inspection of the inhabitants of their particular districts; that, to fix the attention of government more particularly on a class of men following any given religion, was, in fact, establishing a *civil* difference on account of a *religious* one ; and, in this point of view, he thought the clause inadmissible, as it was inefficient in every other. Lastly, he observed, that, as two-fifths of the members of Consistories were Rabbies, to direct them to watch that Rabbies should fulfil their duties, was, in fact, giving the power of inspection to those whose conduct was to be inspected. He also expressed a wish that the twenty-second, twenty-third, twenty-fourth, and twenty-fifth articles should be replaced by a single one in these words: *The expences of worship shall be provided for.* He concluded by moving the amendments alluded to in his observations.

Another member thought that the Regulations contained many equivocal clauses; he demanded that the necessary amendments at least should be adopted, and a new plan of resolutions proposed.

One of the members of the Committee of Nine defended the proposed Regulations in the whole and in their details. He maintained that none of the clauses were injurious to civil liberty.

He observed that the members who argued against separate clauses took a wrong view of the question, because they considered their Israelitish brethren, in general, to be, not such as they really were, but such as they ought to be, which was far from being the case in many parts of France. He thought that, while the benevolent views of government were so clearly ascertained---while no doubt could be entertained of its wisdom, it was unreasonable to suppose that it wanted our assistance to know the means which might complete our regeneration; that the word which concluded the tenth article reflected no more on the Israelites than the law of the republic of Geneva, which excluded from the magistracy the children of insolvent debtors, unless they paid the debts of their fathers, reflected on the Genevese; that the eleventh article had neither the importance nor was likely to produce the effects which had been attributed to it. " Government," said he, " knows now the " amount of the Jewish population in both coun- " tries; its intention may be to ascertain, at some " future period, whether it has increased or dimi- " nished. How could it be known, with certain " ty, whether any emigrations have taken place, " from foreign countries, if the means are not ta- " ken to distinguish the exterior causes which may " have influenced the state of population from the " natural ones? Who, in short, has informed us " that government is not seeking the solution of a " statistical question?" He observed, besides, that a measure which should tend to prevent or to lessen the too great influx of a foreign population, driven into France by the oppression of the laws under which the Jews live in foreign countries, could certainly not be considered as useless; that the alarms excited by the twelfth article were equally groundless; for surely, honest fathers of families, who have no known means of subsistence, will not be driven from a country they have inhabited this great while solely on account of their misery.

Another member observed that the objections which had been made on account of the police regulations which the plan was said to contain, were altogether groundless; that if, in the eyes of those who profess a religion, the Regulations relative to its mode of worship appeared only in that plain point of view, the case was different with a government which connected those regulations with the political system: that, in this point of view, it was not to be wondered if there were in the Regulations clauses relating to the internal administration, necessary for the maintainance of social order.

A member said that he would vote for the Regulations, provided the word *usurer* was expunged. He observed that a bankrupt was a thing notorious and ascertained by a variety of facts, but that the accusation of usury was vague and unsupported; that such an expression would tend to confirm a prejudice which we should, on the contrary, endeavour to do away ; he thought that the eleventh article was liable to be misunderstood, and he proposed to alter the wording of it. He also stated his apprehensions lest the twelfth article should revive that *spirit of community*, which formerly kept the Israelites isolated from the great national family. He demanded that whatever, in that article, related to civil matters, should be omitted, and that Consistories should have no other functions but those immediately connected with religion.

Another spoke on the same side of the question; he presented the observations of the last speaker in a fuller point of view, protested against every clause which tended to establish distinctions, and demanded the adoption of the amendments already proposed.

A third proposed to adopt the Regulations, omitting the tenth, eleventh, and twelfth articles.

A fourth proposed to add to the Regulations an article concerning charitable institutions, which he supposed connected with religious worship.

A fifth wished for a clause allowing legacies or rents in the public funds, to be devised for pious purposes, as in other religions.

Many members loudly called for the question, others wished to continue the debate.

Others were for the Regulations with the amendments.

A member proposed to adopt the whole of the

Regulations as they stood, and that, influenced by the entire reliance which the assembly had in the wisdom and in the magnanimous views of the sovereign, it should only insert in its minutes an abstract of the objections made by several members principally against the tenth article, that such objections might be known as they deserved by Government.

The President put the Regulations to the vote, by shew of hands, and they were adopted by the majority.

He gave afterwards in the following words, an abstract of the several objections against that part of the tenth article which states that no man shall be a member of the Consistory if he is known as a usurer.

" If the evident intention of His Majesty is to " put an end to the abasement of the Jews, to in- " corporate them more intimately with the rest of " Frenchmen, and to make them worthy of the " dignity of man and of citizen, can it be doubt- " ed that one of the readiest means to effect that " purpose, is to do away as much as possible, all " the shades which might, in public opinion, af- " ford some pretence to contempt, and thus im- " pede the progress of that happy conformity in " manners and in habits which make but one " family of a numerous nation ?

(303)

" If in an act, sanctioned by public authority, an
" exception is made as to the Israelites only, which
" impeaches their probity and their morality, in
" matters of loans with interest, without any dis-
" tinction as to places, times, or persons, is it not
" throwing on the whole nation the blame deserved
" by a few individuals?

" Will it not be said that the prejudice is in full
" force, and that the qualification of usurer, being
" almost synonimous to that of Jew, the assimila-
" tion will be made, whether the article contains
" that clause or no?

" But if this qualification is acknowledged as
" unjust, when applied to all indiscriminately, will
" not the insertion of that allusion in a law, sanc-
" tion, as it were, an injurious prejudice against a
" worthy class of men, and extend its duration to
" an unlimited period?

" If this law was not intended to be public, if
" it was not common to all, if it was only transi-
" tory, it would not be attended with the same in-
" conveniences, and would, on the contrary, be pro-
" ductive of some advantages. But this law is for
" all, and for ever; for those against whom it is
" thought necessary, and for those who stand in no
" need of it, and who consider the clause as an
" unmerited insult offered to them; but the truth
" is, that it is useless for every description of men;

" for it cannot be rationally supposed that the five
" and twenty electors should chuse for members
" of the Consistory men known as usurers; and
" if they should, by chance, so far forget them-
" selves, could not the competent authority which
" approves or rejects their choice, easily exclude
" the usurer?

" Those, who are so hardened to contempt as to
" follow that vile profession, will not leave it off,
" to become members of the Consistory. To such
" men honour is nothing; they see no shame, where
" they can see profit. The clause will then hurt
" the honest, without changing the manners of
" the dishonest: towards these last, restrictive
" measures of quite another nature must be adopt-
" ed.

" Will it be said that this clause ought to be a
" matter of indifference to those who do not deserve
" to be excluded, since it does not concern them?
" Surely it would be a very wrong opinion to sup-
" pose that those members who strongly object to
" that article are apprehensive of its being ap-
" plied to them ; and it is precisely because they
" have no such apprehension that it gives them
" more pain.

" They are included in that general expression
" of jealousy, which the law attaches to all the
" followers of their religion, and which thus

" stamps for ever an indelible mark of shame on
" every one of them. Those who are charged with
" usury may renounce the practice, but the stain,
" thrown on all indiscriminately, will last for ever.

" And besides, who is to fix the nature of usury,
" since the laws are silent on the subject? where
" is the line of separation between legal and illegal
" interest? Shall public opinion and general cha-
" racter direct our judgment? But then how can
" we believe that the five and twenty *Notables*, that
" the competent authority which shall inspect their
" proceedings, can be so far led astray as to honour
" by their choice a man held in public contempt?

" If the Consistories of the departments in
" which usury is practised, or even of those where
" it is unknown, were to adopt particular regula-
" tions, in order to exclude from all honourable
" functions men degraded by that nefarious traf-
" fic, nothing could be more conducive to good
" manners, more congenial to social spirit, or more
" worthy of the approbation of a government
" bent upon reform: this falls, besides, within the
" compass of the jurisdiction of the GREAT
" SANHEDRIM. But to have such a degrading
" expression sanctioned in an act of the supreme
" authority, would be again to debase, in their
" own eyes, and in those of their fellow citizens,
" men whom it is meant to raise in the public es-

" teem ; it would act in direct contradiction to
" the benevolent intentions of the Prince, and as
" an impediment to the regeneration he wishes to
" effect.

" Consequently, to adopt the clause of the
" tenth article, inasmuch as it affects those Israel-
" ites of the two countries who form an immense
" majority, would amount to this declaration in
" other words, that none can be a member of a
" Consistory if he is known to have been guilty of
" robbery. Would not the supposition that it is
" necessary to inforce such a motive of exclusion,
" throw a slur over one hundred thousand indivi-
" duals, and represent them as capable of giving
" their votes to a few wretches, who follow that
" nefarious profession in a corner of the empire?"

Such is the abstract of the objections made in
the assembly against the last clause of the tenth
article.

The President afterwards opened the discussion
on the plan of the *Arrêté;* but, foreseeing that it
would be impossible to decide the question in that
sitting, he proposed to adjourn, which was adopted.

The President then quitted the chair, and announced that he would take it again on the 11th.
at twelve o'clock.

Sitting of December 11, 1806.

The President took the chair precisely at twelve o'clock, and named, as Commissioners to maintain order, MM. Castro, jun, Hirch, and Lorich.

One of the Secretaries read the minutes of the sitting of the 5th, which were adopted with a few alterations.

The President announced that the plan of the *Arrété*, already read to the assembly, stood for the order of the day.

It was read again, and a member obtained leave to speak. He said that he came to protest against the resolution adopted in the last sitting, which went to approve the regulations of the Mosaic worship. This resolution he maintained had not been adopted with the calmness it deserved. He observed, that as many amendments had been proposed and seconded, they should have been disposed of, before the whole of the Regulations could have been put to the vote. He complained of the mode adopted of voting by shew of hands, which had left doubts as to the state of the votes, and that no second trial had been made to a certain on which side the majority was. He maintained, lastly, that the deliberation had been irregular, that a division had been called for ; and upon these several grounds, he moved that the Resolution should be annulled.

Other members answered successively, that the deliberation had been perfectly regular; that the real irregularity consisted in the attempt of a minority to dictate to the majority; that, in the shew of hands, the number of votes had been reckoned, and the majority ascertained; that the Scrutineers, when called upon for their opinion, had formally declared that there was a majority; and, in consequence, they demanded the order of the day.

A member opposed that motion, and maintained that the deliberation had been irregular: two others supported his opinion, which was combatted by a fourth.

It was proposed that the assembly should divide on the question of the irregularity of the last deliberation: this proposition was carried. Out of sixty one members present, forty-five voted for the deliberation, twelve against it, and four refused to vote.

The President then opened the discussion on the plan of the *Arrete*. A member made several observations on this plan; he thought that to call in the assistance of the Consistories to induce the Israelish youth to follow the profession of arms, was to appear to doubt its readiness to serve the country. He thought that this was an unfavourable and un-

warranted judgment passed upon their children.
He observed that many Israelitish conscripts were
now in the armies ; that others had joined before
the age which made them liable to be called upon;
that he knew personally seventeen Israelitish
officers of the-northern departments; that what
had induced a notion that so few Jews were among
the conscripts was the repugnance they felt at
owning themselves as such in their respective
corps, where they took a *nom de guerre*, under which
they were generally known afterwards; that, in
short, he did not believe, that, in proportion to the
population, the Israelites were in fewer numbers in
the army than any other class of men.

Another member spoke on the same side, and
considered the interference of the Consistories, in
a case where the law admits of no exception, as
a humiliating distinction.

Several articles were proposed to replace that
which was objected to, but the assembly maintained the original article as it stood in the
minutes of the last sitting.

A member observed that this plan of an *Arrete*
contained no grounds, on which the request of the
assembly, that His Majesty would be pleased to
contribute to the salary of the Rabbies, could
possibly be established.

A discussion arose on this; the President, seeing

that it could not be closed in that sitting, adjourned the debate to the next.

The President took the chair at twelve o'clock. One of the Secretaries read the minutes of the last sitting which were adopted *nem. diss.*

The President announced afterwards that the continuation of the debate on the plan of the *Arrete* stood for the order of the day.

A member proposed to close the debate and to put the question to the vote.

Another proposed to insert in the *Arrété* a humble prayer to His Imperial and Royal Majesty, that he might be pleased to modify his decree of the 31st of May, in such a manner as he might, in his wisdom, think proper, to prevent the too great extension usually given to its meaning, which extension was against the real design of the legislator, and was productive of the greatest hardships to almost the whole of the inhabitants of the departments named in the aforesaid decree.

Another observed that such a petition ought to form a distinct object; he proposed to put first to the vote the plan of the *Arrété* as it stood, and afterwards to take into consideration the complaints of the Jews of the eight departments alluded to. This proprosition was carried; the plan of the *Arrété* was put to the vote, and adopted by a majority. The President announced that the discussion was opened on the decree of the 31st of May. A member proposed to name a Committee which should examine into this affair, and make its report to the assembly. Another proposed to intrust the Committee of Nine with the investigation of this delicate point. Another was of the same opinion, and proposed, by way of amendment, that a member of each of these departments should be added to the Committee of Nine, in order to afford such information as was necessary to guide it in its researches. This proposition was adopted, and the President named

M. Cerf-Jacob Gondchaux for the department of La Moselle

Hertz-Loeb Lorich, for Mount Terrible.

Abraham Cohen, for the Lower Rhine.

Calman, for the Upper Rhine.

Lyon Marx, for Rhin et Moselle.

Salomon Oppenheimer, for La Roer.

Jacob Hirch, for La Sarre.

Jacob-Louis May, for Le Vosges.

The President requested these members to arrange, among themselves, the day on which they could attend the Commission.

The assembly proceeded afterwards to name six lay vice-deputies for the GREAT SANHEDRIM. It was agreed that this election should be made by the *relative* majority of votes. M. Ottolenghi obtained forty-seven; M. Ghedeglia, forty-seven; M. Emilie Vitta, thirty-eight; M. Dreyfoss, twenty-seven; M. Hirch, twenty; and M. Felix Levy, sixteen: as they had the relative majority of votes, the President proclaimed them vice deputies to the GREAT SANHEDRIM.

One of the Secretaries read an address from the Israelites of Frankfort on the Maine, signed by two-hundred and fifty individuals ; it was applauded by the assembly. A member demanded that it should be inserted in the minutes, and that the President should be requested to return an answer, and to express, to the brethren who have signed this address, the sincere wishes of the assembly that all the powers might adopt, towards all Israelites, those principles of justice and of humanity, of which France gives them an example this day.

This proposition was adopted unanimously, and the President quitted the chair.

Address of the Israelites of Frankfort on the Maine, *to the President and to the Assembly of the Deputies of those of* France *and of* Italy.

" M. President,

" We could no longer remain silent without " belying our sentiments, and our wishes. The " convocation of the assembly, over which you " preside, had at first filled us with joy, and with " the most flattering hopes; our admiration has " been excited by the answers you have returned " to the questions proposed by the Great Monarch. " Such answers could come only from men equally " and deeply impressed with the true spirit of their " religion and with a just sense of the duties of " virtuous citizens. We have perceived in them " the rectitude of upright negotiators, blended " with those conciliating manners so well calcu- " lated to remove difficulties.

" The Israelites, scattered in the immensity of " the French empire, were already happily rein- " stated in the indefeasable rights of nature.

" The Great Nation had already broke the fetters " of a people held too long in slavery, and had " overthrown the fatal barrier which separated the " Hebrews from their brethren. It had already " restored to the country useful citizens and de-

" fenders too long neglected. Obstacles still im-
" peded the full enjoyment of those inestimable
" blessings, and the immortal NAPOLEON was the
" man destined to complete our happiness.

" His vast genius clearly perceived that abuses
" had crept into our religion, which made reform
" necessary: but, wishing to remove all apprehen-
" sions of his intending to attack, in any degree,
" our ancient religious principles, he has called
" you as a father would call his children, to deli-
" berate with him on your dearest interests. May
" the glorious example of France extend beyond
" the limits of its empire! May the humanity of
" its sovereign gain ground over the whole earth,
" and produce a noble sentiment of emulation, by
" which we shall be admitted to share the happi-
" ness of our brethren, instead of a barren senti-
" ment of admiration! May the Rulers of man-
" kind lend an attentive ear to the mournful voice
" of an insulted nation! O Divine Goodness!
" deign to cast a look of mercy on a people for-
" merly the object of thy complacency? Inspire
" the masters of the world! Move their hearts in
" favour of Israel!"

" As to you, Gentlemen, who are called together
" to prepare the happiness of your brethren, let
" not your zeal abate, and assist, with all your
" power, the benevolent intentions of your sove-

" reign. If the wicked scorn your labours, you
" have the blessings of the wise. Complete the
" glorious work for which you have been called
" together: immortal glory awaits you at the end
" of your career.

" We could wish, M. President and Gentlemen
" Deputies, that our sentiments and our sincere
" good wishes for the success of your enterprize
" were better expressed."

The President quitted the chair.

_____

Sitting of the 23d of December, 1806.

The President took the chair at twelve o'clock.
One of the Secretaries read the minutes of the
13th; they were adopted *nem. diss.*

He read afterwards a letter of the 2d. inst. from
M. Belluomini, Minister of their Imperial and Serene Highnesses the Prince and Princess of Lucca
and Piombino, at the court of His Majesty the
Emperor of the French and King of Italy, in which
that Minister informed the President, that, from
the new maxims adopted by his government, every individual, following the religion of Moses,
would be at liberty to settle and acquire landed

property in the principalities of Lucca and Piombino ; where they would enjoy the same protection
and the same facilities which are granted to the
other subjects of their Imperial and Serene Highnesses. This Minister concluded by requesting
the President to impart this information to the
assembly, to the GREAT SANHEDRIM, and to all
Israelites with whom he was in the habit of cor-
responding.

The assembly received this communication with
applauses, and resolved that the President, in answering the Minister of their Imperial and Serene
Highnesses, should express the dutiful gratitude of
the deputies of the assembly for the new maxims
of justice and humanity adopted by them.

The same Secretary read also a letter from the
Unive si y of Leghorn, signed by M. Pellegrin
Isaac Worms, dignitary of that respectable acade-
my, and by M. Delvecchio, its Chancellor.

This letter, being written in Hebrew and Italian,
several members demanded that it should be translated into French, and inserted in the minutes.

This proposition was adopted unanimously.

M. Felix Levi, member of a Commission, named
in the last General Committee of the Assembly, to
wait on His Excellency the Minister of the Interi-
or, and to deliver a letter from the President relative to the salary of the members of the assembly,

acquainted the President that His Excellency wished to know the names of the departments which had refused to pay their deputies, and that he would suspend his judgment till then.

A member proposed that the President should name a Commission which would collect all the necessary documents to fulfil the intentions of His Excellency the Minister for the Interior.

Another presented a plan of a general assessment for the payment of the deputies. The assembly spontaneously manifested its unwillingness to form a general assessment, which would include in one mass all the Israelites of France and of Italy. Several members took this occasion to declare that they were perfectly satisfied with the departments which had sent them, and demanded that those deputies who had claims to make, should acquaint the President with it, that he might acquaint His Excellency the Minister for the Interior therewith. This proposition was adopted.

The President read afterwards to the assembly the answer he had prepared to the address of their brethren at Frankfort on the Maine; it was as follows:

" Gentlemen,

" I have communicated the letter you did me
" the honour of writing to me, on the 25th of last

" month, and the address which accompanied it,
" to the assembly of which I am President.

" The assembly heard it with the liveliest inte-
" rest, and justly applauded the sentiments and
" wishes expressed in it with such a peculiar ele-
" vation of sentiment.

" It has done justice to your communication by
" unanimously voting its insertion in its minutes,
" and by directing me, as President, to thank you
" for the honourable approbation you express of
" our efforts.

" We have done what circumstances allowed;
" we should have done more and better, if part of
" what happens to day had taken place twenty-
" five years ago.

" Providence, Gentlemen, has been particularly
" favourable to us; it inspires the great man who
" governs us with the idea of putting an end to
" our state of humiliation and abasement. Among
" all the triumphal monuments raised every where
" to his glory, our restoration to all the rights of
" nature will not be the least durable.

" The impulse given by France, the influence
" of its opinions on the European continent, in-
" dulge a hope that many states will be proud to
" follow its example.

" The time will come when people shall no
" longer give vent to those odious and ridiculous
" passions which were gratified by our humiliation.

"The career of esteem and of consideration is "open for us; let us enter it with a bold step; let "us divest ourselves of the rust of prejudices.----- "Thus shall we conquer the prejudices of others.

"Among the followers of our religion we have "too many merchants and bankers, and too few "land-owners and artificers; above all, too few "husbandmen and soldiers.

"We must all wish that sovereigns would adopt "legislative measures to direct your exertions to "these two professions.

"You share, no doubt, Gentlemen, our opinion "on this subject; the good sense which pervades "your address is a sure pledge of your sentiments, "as it entitles you to the profound esteem of every "member of this assembly, and in particular to "that of

"FURTADO.
"*President.*"

This letter was applauded and approved unani-mously. On the proposition of a member, the assembly resolved that it should be inserted in the minutes. The President quitted the chair at three o'clock.

Sitting of the 5th of February, 1807.

When the reading of the minutes of the last sitting was concluded M. Avigdor asked leave to speak, and read the following discourse, and the plan of *Arrete* which follows it.

" Gentlemen,

" The day of the opening of the GREAT SANHE-
" DRIM approaches; that day will not be one of
" least memorable in the history of that hero, at
" whose orders you were here assembled.

" The idea of a GREAT SANHEDRIM could be con-
" ceived only by the GREAT NAPOLEON. He has
" seen in the new formation of this Senate, so cele-
" brated in antiquity, the means of removing our
" own prejudices and those which the world may
" have entertained, or still entertains, against us.

" This philanthropic conception is truly worthy
" of that man, who cannot be said to belong ex-
" clusively to any class of men, to any religion, or
" to any nation; of that sublime genius who is a
" gift of Providence to mankind, and whose bene-
" volent influence must be felt by all men.

" Deeply impressed with his wishes and with
" your duties, Gentlemen, you will, no doubt, fulfil
" his expectations and those of your brethren.

"Israel has been persecuted for many centuries;
" for many centuries he has been held in a state of
" humiliation and abasement; you must assume
" sufficient courage to probe the causes of his de-
" plorable situation; and, in going back to the most
" ancient times, you must not be deterred from in-
" quiring into the motives which have induced na-
" tions to hate, to despise, and to persecute a peo-
" ple, whose origin is lost in the obscurity of cen-
" turies, and whose laws have been a faithful source
" of information to all its persecutors.

" Egyptians, Greeks, and Romans have all taken
" many things from the law of Moses; modern
" nations have made it the basis of their religion;
" and yet all these different people have successive-
" ly and equally hated, despised, and persecuted
" the Israelites.

" From whence can proceed this almost unani-
" mous conceit of all nations against us?

" Are we to seek the cause of it in our religion
" or in ourselves?

" But, from general consent, our religion is con-
" sidered as of divine origin; and, as to us, what-
" ever may be said, we are not of a nature different
" from that of other men.

" Where, then, can we find the cause of such con-
" stant, such deep-rooted aversion?

T T

" Do not seek for it, Gentlemen, either in your
" origin, nor in your laws, nor in your manners.

" Your origin ascends to the first antiquity, you
" are the only people who can trace its pedigree
" to the cradle of mankind; your laws bear the
" stamp of the justice of that great God to whom
" you are indebted for them, and your private
" virtues, even after many centuries of sufferings
" and misfortunes, attest the purity of your manners.

" It is, then, neither to your origin, to your laws,
" nor to your manners, that you must attribute this
" common hatred of nations against you; it must
" be attributed first, to the ignorance of the first
" centuries; to jealousy, that vice of all times; and
" to the too natural force of prejudices on men in
" general.

" To be convinced of this truth, it is enough
" rapidly to recur to the most remarkable æras of
" our history, and to examine your own situation,
" in respect to the nations among which you have
" lived.

" You see, first, that Abraham has been the first
" to proclaim the existence and the unity of a God
" who created all things by his sole will.

" Some years afterwards, Joseph, fourth des-
" cendant of Abraham, became, by his talents, the
" arbiter of Egypt and of the neighbouring coun-
" tries.

" This sudden elevation of Joseph may, in a
" political point of view, be considered as the root
" of that astonishing hatred which has lasted to
" our very days, and which has been constantly
" continued by the difference of religion.

" Every one is acquainted with the expressions
" of Pharaoh to Joseph, to the great and the learn-
" ed of his court—*Can we find such a one as this is,*
" *a man in whom the spirit of God is?*

" Then turning to Joseph :

" *Forasmuch as God hath shewed thee all things,*
" *there is none so discreet and wise as thou art. Thou*
" *shalt be over my house ; and according unto thy*
" *word shall all my people be ruled: only in the*
" *throne will I be greater than thou.*"

" These words, pronounced with great dignity,
" must have been keenly felt by all the courtiers
" of that prince.

" Fallen all at once in the opinion of so power-
" ful a monarch, obliged to bend before a stranger,
" their sole sentiment must have been an unjust
" desire of revenging themselves for so many humili-
" ations; and as they could not wreak their re-
" sentment on Joseph, it fell with redoubled
" violence on his posterity.

" Thus ignorance and jealousy were the first
" causes of the persecution which the Israelites ex-
" perienced from the Egyptians.

" Moses delivered them from the yoke of these
" oppressors, and conducted his people to the
" frontiers of that land promised to Israel, but
" of which he was to possess himself by conquest.

" It was there that God's elect, admonished
" that his death was at hand, intrusted to Joshua
" the fate of the Hebrews. It was under the com-
" mand of that worthy successor of Moses, that
" Israel entered the land of Canaan. There he
" fixed his dwelling; and the world beheld, for the
" first time, a regular code of civil, political, and
" religious laws put into practice ; it was there,
" too, that, after long vicissitudes, Israel acknow-
" ledged that a monarchical form of government
" was the only one which could suit a nation com-
" posed at the same time of husbandmen, soldiers,
" and merchants.

" As, however, this conquest had been necessari-
" ly attended with a vast effusion of blood, the
" vanquished, driven from their country, must
" have naturally hated a people who abominated
" idolatry, and who had conquered their country
" by force of arms.

" Nevertheless, Solomon, third King of Israel,
" by his wisdom succeeded in procuring peace from
" his external enemies, and in inspiring his subjects
" with the love of sciences, arts, and commerce.

" The description of the temple, raised by that

(325)

" great king to the true God, and the details of the
" magnificent decorations which adorned it, are so
" many proofs that Solomon had already carried
" commerce, arts, and sciences to a very high
" pitch, such as probably no nation had yet at-
" tained.

" The people of Israel, thus become, by its civili-
" zation, the centre of intercourse between the east-
" ern and the western world, soon arrived to that
" degree of splendour, the natural consequence of
" such an advantageous situation. The wish of des-
" poiling it, which jealous neighbouring nations
" must have continually cherished, was evidently
" the second cause of that active animosity which
" incessantly broke out in repeated hostilities, and
" which lasted to that epocha of horrid memory
" when the Holy City fell under the arms of the
" Romans.

" From that period Israel ceased to be a nation;
" it is now only a particular race of men, scattered
" over the whole world.

" It may be believed that Providence wished
" to punish this people, led astray from the ways
" of the Lord by the pride of prosperity; but
" at least his intention was not to destroy it utterly.
" Had it been collected on a single point of the
" globe, it would have been annihilated at once:

" but its dispersion over the four parts of the world
" has for ever secured it from total destruction.

" After eighteen centuries of persecution, a small
" fraction of Israel is incorporated with the great
" nation. It was the destiny of the greatest of
" monarchs to confirm that law, one of the most
" noble monuments of the justice of the Constitu-
" ent Assembly. It was the destiny of a Christian
" Prince to inforce that spirit of toleration, so care-
" fully recommended by Christian morality.

" And indeed, in considering the usual projects
" of human passions, nothing will appear more
" natural than that deep-rooted hatred of ancient
" nations against the Israelites.

" The Egyptians, at first, subjugated by Joseph
" ---the Egyptians who worshiped an ox, a dog, a
" crocodile, could not love a people who acknow-
" ledged only the true God.

" Neither could the idolatrous Canaaneans, con-
" quered and driven out of their country by the
" Hebrews, love them; they must, on the contrary,
" have hated them, as political foes, and have ab-
" horred them as religious enemies.

" The Greeks, who coolly and judicially murdered
" Socrates, because he taught the existence of one
" only God, must have detested a people who pro-
" fessed publicly to worship one only living God.

" Lastly, nor could the Romans who believed in

" oracles, in soothsayers, in augurs, in auspices,
" love the Jews who had opposed them with more
" obstinacy than any other nation, who abhorred
" idolatry, and worshipped only one God, Creator
" of the universe.

" It is, then, no difficult matter to account for
" the hatred of those nations against the Jews.
" All, equally attached to their idols, to their gods,
" to their demigods, in short, to all the supersti-
" tions of the blindest ignorance, must have de-
" tested, hated, and persecuted the Jews, the avow-
" ed enemies of all these superstitions. But what
" is really inconceivable, is to see that the Chris-
" tians, who have the same origin with us, the
" Christians, our fellow-sufferers under Nero, Ves-
" pasian, Titus, Domitian, Adrian, and several
" others, could, contrary to their duty, have inherit-
" ed, from those irreligious nations, that hatred and
" that contempt which we at first shared together.
" It is really difficult to find the solution of that
" problem.

" This conduct is the more incomprehensible, as
" the most celebrated Christian moralists have for-
" bidden persecution, professed toleration, and
" preached Christian charity.

" St. Athanasius (book i.) says,

" *It is an abominable heresy to attempt to convert*

" *by force, by blows, by imprisonment, those whom*
" *reason has not been able to convince.*

" *Nothing is more contrary to religion than con-*
" *straint,* says Justin Martyr (book v).

" *Shall we persecute those whom God tolerates?*
" says St. Augustine.

" Lactantius (book iii.) says, on this subject,
" *Compulsory religion is no longer religion: we must*
" *persuade, not constrain. Religion is above the*
" *reach of power.*

" *Advise,* says St. Bernard, *but do not compel.*

" Since, therefore, Christian morality teaches
" every one the love of his neighbour and of his
" brother, the causes of the vexations and of the
" persecutions which we have so frequently expe-
" rienced must be sought for in ignorance and in-
" veterate prejudice. This is so true, that those
" sublime virtues of justice and humanity have
" been frequently put into practice by Christians
" truly learned, and especially by worthy minis-
" ters of that pure morality which calms the ef-
" fervescence of passion and instils the love of vir-
" tue into the mind.

" It is in conformity to these sacred principles
" of morality that, at different times, Roman pon-
" tiffs have protected and received into their do-
" nions the Jews, persecuted and driven from
" various parts of Europe, and that clergymen, of

" every country, have often raised their voice in their
" defence in several states in that part of the world.

" Towards the middle of the seventh century,
" St. Gregory defended the Jews, and protected
" them in the Christian world.

" In the tenth century, the bishops of Spain re-
" sisted, with the greatest energy, the violence of
" a furious multitude, bent on their destruction.

" The pontiff Alexander II. wrote to those bi-
" shops a letter full of congratulations on their be-
" haviour on that occasion.

" In the eleventh century, the Jews, then very
" numerous in the diocesses of Uzes and of Cler-
" mont, were powerfully protected by the bishops.

" St. Bernard defended them in the twelfth cen-
" tury from the rage of the Crusaders.

" They were protected likewise by Innocent II.
" and Alexander III.

" In the thirteenth century, Gregory IX. shel-
" tered them in France, in England, and in Spain,
" from the imminent danger which threatened
" them ; he forbad, under pain of excommunica-
" tion, to force their consciences, or to disturb their
" religious ceremonies.

" Clement V. went farther; he not only pro-
" tected them, but also afforded them the means
" of instruction.

" Clement VI. gave them an asylum in Avig-

" non, when they were persecuted over the rest of
" Europe.

" Towards the middle of the same century, the
" bishop of Spires prevented the general libera-
" tion which the debtors of the Jews claimed by
" main force, under the everlasting pretence of
" usury.

" In the following centuries, Nicholas II. wrote
" to the Inquisition, to prevent it from forcing the
" Jews to embrace Christianity.

" Clement XIII. calmed the uneasiness of pa-
" rents for the fate of their children, torn very
" often from the bosom of their mothers.

" Lastly, in our own times, the bishop Gregoire,
" Member of the august French Senate, publish-
" ed, in 1788 a work replete with erudition, crown-
" ed by the Academy of Metz, in which he victo-
" riously refuted the absurd calumnies laid, at dif-
" ferent times, to the charge of the Jews.

" He pointed out the eventual cause of the vices
" with which they are reproached; and proved that
" they were qualified for the pursuits of every
" profession and of every science.

" It was also on the report of that respectable
" prelate, that the National Assembly passed the
" decree which put the Jews on a level with the
" rest of citizens.

" It would be an easy matter to quote several

" other instances of charity, manifested, at dif-
" ferent times, towards the Jews, by clergymen,
" fully impressed with a sense of their duties as
" men and as ministers of their religion.

" An exalted sense of humanity could alone, in
" the early dark ages of ignorance and barba.
" rism, inspire a courage sufficient to protect un-
" fortunate men, left defenceless at the mercy of
" direful hypocrisy and ferocious superstition.

" Those virtuous men could expect, from their
" philanthropic courage, no other reward than
" the grateful heartfelt satisfaction which deeds of
" charity excite in unpolluted hearts.

" The people of Israel, always unfortunate, al-
" ways oppressed, had neither the means nor the
" opportunity of expressing its gratitude for so
" many favours; it would have been the more gra-
" tifying to us to have acquitted our hearts of that
" debt, as we were thus indebted to men perfect-
" ly disinterested, and therefore doubly praise-
" worthy.

" This great and happy circumstance, for
" which we are indebted to our august and im-
" mortal Emperor, is the most proper as it is the
" most glorious for us, to manifest, to the philan-
" thropic of every country, and especially to the
" clergy, our gratitude to them and to their pre-
" decessors.

" Let us hasten, then, Gentlemen, to avail our-
" selves of this memorable circumstance, to shew
" them that gratitude they have a right to expect
" from us. Let this hall resound with grateful ac-
" clamations. Let us return them our solemn and
" sincere thanks for the favours they have succes-
" sively heaped on the generations which have pre-
" ceded us.

" Let us prove to the universe that we have for-
" gotten our past misfortunes, and that the remem-
" brance of favours only is engraved on our hearts.
" Let us hope that the clergy, our cotemporaries,
" will, by their influence over their flocks, instil
" those mild sentiments of fraternity which na-
" ture has placed in the heart of every man, and
" which is inculated still more forcibly by the
" tendency of every religion.

" The prejudices of the world have already been
" lessened by the progress of instruction : its in-
" creasing influence will complete their extirpa-
" pation. Those dark ages, the shame of huma-
" nity, are happily far removed from us. Let us
" hope that they never will return : let us indulge
" in the pleasing expectation that the principles of
" justice, of humanity, and of public morality,
" first adopted in France, will also find their way
" into the other countries of Europe.

" Israel will be indebted to our august Emperor

" for the termination of its misfortunes; from him
" mankind will receive that lesson of fraternal
" charity which forms the basis of every religion
" and of every society.

" I have the honour to propose, Gentlemen, the
" following resolution for your deliberation——

" *The Hebrew deputies of the French empire and of*
" *the kingdom of Italy to the Jewish assembly con-*
" *vened by the decree of the 30th of May, deeply*
" *impressed with gratitude for the manifold favours*
" *conferred on the Israelites, in former centuries,*
" *by the Christian clergy in various parts of Eu-*
" *rope; no less grateful for the kind reception gi-*
" *ven by several pontiffs and many other clergy-*
" *men at various epochas to the Israelites of all*
" *countries, when barbarism, ignorance, and pre-*
" *judice, leagued together, chased the Jews from*
" *the bosom of society*;

" Resolve,
" That the expression of these sentiments shall
" be registered in the minutes of the proceedings
" of this day, to remain for ever a lasting monu-
" ment of the gratitude of the Israelites who com-
" pose this assembly, for the favours received by

_"the generations which preceded them from cler-
" gymen of various parts of Europe.

" Resolve, also, that a copy of these minutes
" shall be sent to His Excellency the Minister of
" Public Worship."

The assembly applauded the discourse of M.
Avigdor: it was inserted in the minutes, and ordered to be printed.

The resolutions were also adopted.

The President quitted the chair.

AFTER SUMMER

A SUMMER BOYS NOVEL

Also by Hailey Abbott

SUMMER BOYS
NEXT SUMMER

AFTER SUMMER

A SUMMER BOYS NOVEL

HAILEY ABBOTT

SCHOLASTIC INC.

New York Toronto London Auckland Sydney
Mexico City New Delhi Hong Kong Buenos Aires

ISBN 0-439-86367-8

Copyright © 2006 by Alloy Entertainment
All rights reserved. Published by Scholastic Inc.

Produced by Alloy Entertainment
151 West 26th Street
New York, NY 10001

SCHOLASTIC and associated logos are trademarks and/or registered trademarks of Scholastic Inc.

Text design by Steve Scott.
The text type was set in Bulmer.

12 11 10 9 8 7 6 5 4 3 2 1   6 7 8 9 10 11/ 0

Printed in the U.S.A.
First printing, September 2006

AFTER SUMMER

A SUMMER BOYS NOVEL

1

Beth lined up her bare toes along the edge of the platform and arched her body forward, extending her arms over the still, blue water. After a deep breath, she sprang into the air so gracefully, she felt as if she might actually take flight.

But a second later, she sliced through the surface of the cool water. It felt smooth and clean. And for that first, breathless moment, Beth almost believed she was out in the ocean, swimming beyond the moorings in the bay at Pebble Beach, instead of in the over-chlorinated YMCA pool back home in Martin, Massachusetts.

She almost believed it was still summer.

She pulled long, effective strokes down the lane, racing to the far edge of the pool. Beth heaved her body against the water and imagined herself lengthening with every stroke. *Faster,* she thought. *I have to be faster.*

She smacked her hand at the end of the lane and popped up to the surface, gasping for air. She stood, the water coursing from her, and peeled her goggles back from her face.

"Best time yet!" her boyfriend, George, cheered, glancing at the stopwatch he held in his hands. He sat on a stack of kickboards, basking in the greenish glow of the fluorescent lights. "I'm pretty sure next time you may break the sound barrier."

Looking up at George, Beth took in the full impact of his hotness, from his curly black hair, to the snug navy polo that showed off his biceps, to his perfectly torn Abercrombie jeans, to his bare feet, which sported the fading tan lines of flip-flops.

"I don't know, sweetie. I bet I could shave off another few seconds . . ." Beth managed, swimming toward the steps.

"Bethy, as your trainer, I give you my personal assurance that you are guaranteed to make the swim team."

Although George had sacrificed every free afternoon to help Beth prepare for tryouts, he was, first-and-foremost, her boyfriend. So she couldn't put much stock in any of his assurances, no matter how sincere he was.

"All bets are off this year," she argued, rubbing her arms to ward off the chill from the water. "Maddy Echolls told me that her sister's best friend goes to Boston College with our new coaches. She said they coached at this other high school last year and cut the varsity team in half because they have such high standards."

Earning a spot on the swim team was Beth's number one priority. Beth had always been athletic in the general sense — she loved running and volleyball best — but the addition of these new coaches made the swim team an attractive prospect for her free time. After all, swimming was a close cousin to surfing, one of Beth's favorite summer activities. At least the way Beth surfed. She could tread the dark blue ocean for hours, fighting through the burn in her muscles as she waited for the next big wave. The adrenaline rush from riding at the top of the crest was so intense that, as soon as she rode back to shore, she'd flip her board around and paddle back out to do it all over again.

God, she missed summer.

When it came to swimming, Beth knew her natural stamina would work in her favor, but she was anything but an expert in the finer mechanics of the competitive strokes. Hopefully her heart would make up for any technical slack.

George had been listening to her stress out about swimming and coaches, with daily doses of new and unsubstantiated gossip, since their senior year began two weeks earlier. Even though Beth knew she was being annoying, George grinned down at her crookedly.

"Maddy Echoll's sister — who no one has ever met, by the way, which I think supports my theory that Maddy made her up — seems to have a lot of information on the swim team for someone who doesn't actually, you know, swim." He reached over and tapped his stopwatch against Beth's swim cap affectionately. "Chill, baby."

"Okay, okay, you're right." Beth yanked off her swim cap and shook out her straight blonde hair. "Let's get out of here. If you get the car, I'll change and meet you out in front."

George leaned over and kissed her, his mouth hot. "Remember, the quicker you change, the more time we'll have . . . *in the car*." He waggled his eyebrows at her until she laughed.

As George left, Beth quickly swam another length of the pool to get back to her towel. Once inside the dressing room, she dressed quickly, pulling on her jeans and a Martin High School sweatshirt. She toweled her hair to remove the excess water and then twisted it back into a casual ponytail. A junior girl stood in front of the mirrors, yanking each strand of her long red hair with an enormous cylindrical brush while her other hand worked a blow-dryer. Though Beth had seen her fashion-conscious cousin, Ella, use a blow-dryer, Beth still suspected it doubled as a torture device. She felt thankful for about the eight millionth time that she had George. He wasn't the type of guy who cared about stupid things like perfect hair.

All he cared about was Beth, if the wide smile he sent her from behind the wheel of his car when she emerged from the building was any clue. Beth ran around to the passenger seat and climbed inside.

"You should come over for dinner tonight," Beth told him. "My mom made your favorite."

"How can you think of lasagna at a time like this?" George said in a fake-tortured voice. "We're teenagers with a free half hour before dinnertime." He put his beat-up VW into gear, but instead of turning toward town when he exited the YMCA parking lot, he headed the other way. Out toward the woods.

"Just enough time for some backseat wrestling?" Beth asked with a grin. She shot a glance at the tiny bench seat over her shoulder and laughed. "Remember the time you almost knocked yourself out because you sat up too fast?"

She and George had spent a lot of time in that backseat, even before they'd finally gone all the way that past summer. Back before they'd actually done it, they'd planned how The Moment would be. Yet all their elaborate plans had faded when the simple perfection of the right time came upon them. Beth felt a thrill sneak down her spine just remembering that delicious, starry night in Maine. It had been a little bit more than a month ago.

George parked the car in a small clearing just off a winding dirt road. A familiar trail headed deep into the woods, where sometimes, on the weekends, Beth and George would hike out and have a picnic near the river. Tonight was a Tuesday, however, and the place was deserted. There were only trees just starting to boast their rust and gold fall colors, the September moon beginning to rise between them.

"I'm not going to knock myself out tonight," George said, turning to face Beth and lowering his voice. "At least, not in the sense of banging my head into the roof." He squeezed her leg. "I've got a plan."

Beth smiled as George reached over and pulled her on to his lap. It was a tight, cozy fit, but they moved into place with the ease of practice. He trailed kisses slowly along her jaw and finally settled on her mouth. His kiss was warm and deep.

Beth sighed happily. It was hard to believe that she'd almost let this go. Last summer, she'd done something incredibly stupid, and was so grateful that George had still returned to her, despite the hurt she'd caused him.

She said her thanks in each of the kisses they shared, mouth to mouth and pressed against each other. One kiss because he'd forgiven her. Another because they'd gotten so close, so much closer than she'd believed it was possible to be with someone else. Another long, intense one because they'd been together a little longer than a year now and she felt like she loved him more than when they'd started.

The crazy, messy summer was behind them, where it belonged. Beth wasn't going to get confused again.

Beth, as always, had spent the summer on the Maine seashore with her cousins, supersmart Kelsi and wild, beautiful Ella (who were sisters, and lived in Connecticut — though Kelsi had just started her freshman year at Smith), while the fourth part of the tight Tuttle girl team, Jamie, had been at a writing course at Amherst College. Over the summer, each of the girls had experienced her own romantic crisis. But now — after summer — for possibly the first time ever, Beth, Kelsi, and Ella were each involved in real, intense relationships. Jamie had just transferred to an elite New Jersey prep school for her senior year, so she was too busy to fall in love. But Beth and her other cousins were each experiencing the agonies and ecstasies of just that — being in love.

It was going to be an interesting year.

"I'm glad to be home," Beth whispered, pulling away so she could look at George. He had that blissed-out, dazed look on his face, but he blinked.

"Wait," he said, peering out the windshield at the woods. "Did your family relocate to a log cabin?"

"I'm talking about the summer being over, idiot," Beth said, poking him in the ribs.

He grunted. "Careful with the G-Man. I'm very fragile."

"Usually I wish summer would last forever," Beth said,

ignoring his ridiculousness. "I hate leaving Ella and Kelsi and all the cousins. But this year it's so much better being back home with you." She felt emotion swell inside her. "I love you," she whispered.

"I love you, too, Bethy," George said in the same tone, and framed her face in his hands. His curly hair flopped across his forehead as he leaned in to kiss her eyelids. Beth felt a wave of tenderness sweep through her as she reached over to push his hair back.

"You know," George announced, drawing back so Beth could see his grin. "I think we should celebrate that love." His hands moved down from Beth's back to her backside, which he gave a fast squeeze. "Meet me outside."

Laughing, Beth climbed off of his lap and George dove over the headrest and landed facedown into the cramped backseat, kicking his legs.

"That was graceful," Beth said wryly, knowing his goofy moves were deliberate.

"Come on," he said when he sat up again, holding a large fleece blanket. "It's time to answer the call of the wild!"

Fall chill had just started to invade the air, and Beth's skin prickled with goose bumps as she and George got out of the car. She curled into his open arms, and George enveloped them both in a blanket cocoon.

"This is pretty romantic," Beth smiled, leaning against his chest.

"And it's a school night!" George replied proudly. "This level of romance is usually reserved for the weekend."

His knees suddenly buckled, sending them onto the mossy ground with a thud.

"Careful, George!"

"Oh, yeah," he teased. "I threw down. Threw *us* down, actually. What are you going to do about it?"

"You're dead," Beth vowed. She shrugged out of her hoodie and flung it into his face.

"As long as it involves full nudity," George replied, with a mouthful of sweatshirt. "I'm okay with it."

A dry twig snapped in the distance, and Beth gave a start.

"Who was that?" she whispered, her eyes scanning the dark woods. "George! Someone's out there!"

"Tick tock, Beth," George said, laughing at her as he drew her close. "That was the wind, and you're obviously stalling. Concentrate on me for a second or two here and I'll even force myself to eat your mother's lasagna —"

"You love my mother's lasagna!"

"— and help you out with your English essay because I know how you hate those things —"

"You're the one who has an English essay, genius, which I *was* going to help you with, but now? Forget it!"

"Genius?" George repeated. "Thanks. I'm flattered."

He was silly. Silly, sweet, and all hers. How could she possibly resist? Beth stuck her tongue out at him.

George immediately leaned in for a sweet, hot kiss. Beth giggled into his mouth but then began kissing him back, letting their tongues meet in that easy, sensual way they had. George, as with everything in his life, sometimes got a little overeager when it came to fooling around, so Beth wasn't surprised when he flung his arms around her, sending them rolling back onto the blanket. They wrapped their arms around each other.

"I've got the goods in my back pocket," George whispered, kissing Beth's neck as his free hand dug around in the pocket of his jeans for the condom packet.

"George, hang on," Beth whispered, taking hold of his other hand, which was zooming in straight for the top button on her Levi's. "I'm not sure this is the best —"

"Oh, no, but it *will* be the best," George promised, a sly grin on his face, and Beth found herself laughing again and tightening her arms around him.

Ever since they'd lost their virginity to each other, over the summer in Pebble Beach, George had — like any red-blooded boy — assumed that sex was now on the menu every time they fooled around. Which Beth was fine with most of the time, but there were moments — when she was beat from swimming, for instance — that she wished they could go back to the way things had been, when she and George could just make out for making out's sake. Factoring sex into the equation had changed everything, as subtly but surely as summer had changed into fall.

But as she and George began kissing again, and touching, and undoing each other's buttons, Beth didn't want to stop. She felt as if the black night were shielding them, embracing them as they were embracing each other. This was right, this was now, this was what she wanted to be doing, with this boy, for always.

Beth had never been so sure about anything in her life.

2

Ella waded through the hordes of girls on her way to the bathroom mirror. The first coed assembly of the year began in a few short minutes, and the girls of St. Augustine's were in a tizzy. They clustered around the mirrors in the bathroom, talking excitedly and trying desperately to adapt the St. Augustine's uniform from frumpy disaster into Catholic schoolgirl–chic. A few girls sat huddled around the open window, passing around a lit cigarette and fanning the errant smoke away. Though Ella had officially quit smoking last month, at her boyfriend Jeremy's request, a knot of craving blossomed inside her chest. She held her breath as she passed them and fought the urge to sneak a quick drag.

Then Ella bobbed and weaved through a pack of wide-eyed freshmen, nodding at a few sophomore girls she recognized. She laughed softly at the look of intense concentration the girls all wore as they smoothed blouses and fluffed hair.

Once a week, the guys' and girls' sections of St. Augustine's gathered as one in the big auditorium in the center of the private school campus. Most girls spent *hours* agonizing over these all-too-brief moments of coeducation. They worked hard to shine and sparkle every time there was the possibility of seeing the boys.

A goal Ella knew about personally, since she'd once been the queen of primping to impress.

Thank God I have Jeremy now, she thought, rolling her eyes at a frenzied-looking senior girl who was completely overapplying her mascara.

With a happy little sigh, Ella performed a strategic dodge and claimed a position at the farthest mirror from the door. She smiled at her reflection.

She'd rolled the waistline of her plaid kilt up exactly twice, the better to show off her long legs, which were still nicely tan from her summer at the beach in Maine. Her wavy, sun-kissed blonde hair had that almost-tousled look that made the boys drool, while not being *quite* messy enough to incur the wrath of Sister Margaret Alice.

But Ella didn't believe in working too hard for boys' attention. She merely sauntered about and let the *boys* worry about impressing *her*. In the past, Ella had taken great pride in being unable to choose between the numerous hot boys who vied for her attention. Ella had always loved the all-school assemblies. Because — and she'd be the first to admit it — Ella Tuttle loved boys.

St. Augustine's boys were particularly delicious, with their navy blazers and ties. Ella thought so every September, when a summer at the beach had ended and she was back in New Canaan, Connecticut. They might not be summer boys —which meant that Ella had to be *slightly* more careful with them, since they didn't conveniently disappear after a few months —but they had their own kind of appeal.

But this year, Ella couldn't care less who checked her out. And her primping wasn't for anyone at St. Augustine's.

Ella Tuttle was actually involved in a long-distance relationship for the first time in her life. Jeremy had made the leap from Summer Boy to Official Boyfriend.

Ella thought of the IMs she'd exchanged with her cousins Beth and Jamie that morning before school, and smiled to herself. Her cousins, it seemed, knew her better than anyone — well, except for her older sister, Kelsi, who was busy settling into college life.

Beth had written: Is it true, El? Are you still WITH Jeremy? You haven't shed him like you did your Steve Madden platforms at the end of August?

And Jamie had chimed in: Bethy, give El the benefit

of the doubt. She SO has it in her to be an awesome girlfriend.

And they both were right, Ella thought with a toss of her luxurious blonde curls. Snarkiness aside, Beth's comment *had* hit the nail on the head, and Jamie's typically sweet, hopeful tone confirmed what Ella had always suspected about herself: that she WAS capable of being true to one boy and one boy only.

And that boy happened to be Jeremy.

Things with Jeremy had been completely different from the start, Ella thought, smiling as she pictured her brown-haired, brown-eyed, Seth Cohen-y boyfriend. And it totally didn't matter that he was a thousand miles away. Okay, not actually a thousand miles. However many miles there were between her mom's house in New Canaan and his parents' house outside Philadelphia, it was way too many. Over the summer they'd been able to walk in flip-flops to see each other.

It was funny to think how hard Ella had fallen for a boy who was relatively indifferent to her looks. Obviously, he thought she was gorgeous, and told her that on a regular basis, but Jeremy wasn't the type of guy who wanted a girl to look like the airbrushed cover of a magazine 24-7. In fact, he even seemed to like the less glamorous side of her better.

At the tail end of last summer, she'd randomly come

15

down with a bad cold, and Jeremy had surprised her with a bag of Hershey's Kisses and a bottle of Tylenol Cold & Sinus. Unfortunately, Ella was sneezing in front of the television in bleach-stained sweatpants and one of Kelsi's formless and boxy T-shirts, her hair up in a greasy bun and her face without a stitch of makeup. She'd tried to run upstairs to change, but Jeremy had grabbed her and, ignoring the threat of germs, kissed her more passionately than ever before. He insisted that she stay just how she was and they cuddled on the couch together all afternoon.

Still, Ella knew Jeremy would fully appreciate the way she tucked her white oxford shirt tight into her waistband, the better to invite a closer inspection of her curves. She assured herself with a quick pat that her Body by Victoria bra kept the lushest of those curves luscious and high. And Jeremy would also be a big fan of the way her clear MAC lip gloss accentuated her lips, while not in outright — or any way visible — defiance of St. Augustine's no makeup rules. She rubbed her lips together, and made a kissing face at herself. After all, he was still a boy.

Next, Ella slipped into the nearest stall for some privacy, pulled out her cell, and took a few pictures of herself.

When Ella was satisfied with her impromptu photo shoot, she fired off the results to Jeremy with a quick text: BET U MISS ME!

And then, the warning bell rang. The bathroom erupted into squeals and curses, and Ella joined the crowd of her classmates as they all raced outside and onto the quad. The autumn sunshine was bright, though there was a slight snap in the air.

Ella slowed down to enjoy the crispness of the morning. Everything felt and smelled new. She liked that she felt that way, too. It was going to be a great year, after an even better summer. She just knew it.

Ella ran across the quad and into the auditorium slightly ahead of a few other stragglers, making sure not to be dead last — which would definitely get her in trouble with the nuns. Ella could expect to be in enough trouble with the sisters simply because she was Ella Tuttle and a disappointment next to saintly, studious Kelsi Tuttle, which made Ella want to puke. But that was how it was. So she knew better than to invite extra attention.

Once inside, Ella slowed to her natural saunter and headed down the aisle. Ella couldn't help smiling at all the girls licking their lips and tossing their hair, desperately trying to win some male attention. A number of male eyes skipped over some of her classmates and landed on her, and she wasn't even trying.

Stifling her laughter, Ella slid into the place her friend Marilee had saved for her at the end of the senior girls' row.

"Check out Eric Polski," Marilee said at once. "Looks like he spent his summer channeling his inner hottie. Who knew?"

Marilee and Ella had shared a basic philosophy since they'd met in the fifth grade, which was: Most things in New Canaan, and particularly at St. Augustine's, were very, very boring. If it was up to them to liven it all up . . . well, they were both okay with rising to that challenge. Kelsi had called them Double Trouble, which Ella used to think was so incredibly stupid and annoying. Now that Kelsi had gone away to college, though, Ella kind of missed the nickname.

When she slid a look across the aisle to check out the sudden hotness of Eric Polski, her attention was caught instead by Jake, the captain of the lacrosse team. He was a square-jawed blond who'd been after Ella since middle school, and he was grinning in her direction.

"Gross. As if Jake isn't totally with Cheryl Anderson," Ella said in a murmur, rolling her eyes at Marilee.

"I heard he wants to dump her because she refuses to go past second base," Marilee replied in a whisper.

"I heard that *she* doesn't know it, though," Ella replied. It was only the first week of school and already the gossip was at a fever pitch.

Cheryl Anderson's not-for-long boyfriend gave Ella another smile. Ella turned her head.

"Too bad for him you're totally in love with that boy from Philly." Marilee elbowed Ella in the ribs. "Is it really true that no one at St. Augustine's can hold a candle to this guy?"

Ella surreptitiously slid her cell phone out of her bag and checked her in-box. Sure enough, she had two new texts from Jeremy.

YOU'RE KILLING ME WITH THOSE PICTURES, said the first.

SERIOUSLY. I THINK I DIED, said the second.

She smiled at Marilee as she put her phone back in her bag quickly — because heaven would definitely have to intervene if Sister Margaret Alice caught her with a cell phone.

"No one even comes close," she told Marilee.

"Then you can be my wingman!" Marilee whispered, delighted. "You may not be single, but I am. And I have big plans for this year, El."

"You *always* have big plans," Ella reminded her friend.

Marilee leaned close and jerked her chin across the aisle. "Yeah, well, my plan starts right there."

Ella followed Marilee's gaze. There was a new face sitting among the other senior boys, most of whom Ella had known for years. This guy was lounging on the wooden pew, all smoldering brown eyes and a mouth to die for. His collar was flipped high up, his striped tie knotted loose and askew, and his chocolate-brown hair was the very definition of bed-head. Anyone could look like a rebel in a leather jacket and blue jeans, but it took a special guy to look badass in a school blazer and tie. Ella inched forward and squinted, picking out a set of tiny colorful band pins that the new boy used as cuff links.

"*That*," Marilee murmured in Ella's ear, "is Ryan Eastley. Completely drool-worthy. His parents weren't psyched about his grades and excessive partying, so boom! St. Augustine's. It could have been military school, right?"

"It wouldn't suck to see him in a military uniform," Ella observed. Not that she was *personally* interested.

"He plays lacrosse and doesn't have a girlfriend," Marilee continued. She shrugged. "Or anyway, not one he admits to."

"I'll bet," Ella murmured.

Sister Anne pressed her wrinkled fingers on the organ keys, indicating that the assembly was about to begin. Everyone stood and tried to look angelic as the school choir struggled with the high notes of the hymn.

Ella glanced across the aisle again at Ryan, and instantly recognized the way he stood in the midst of his new classmates, like he expected them all to pay attention to him. Because Ella was good at it herself, she knew that if he kept up that easy, confident vibe, they all *would* pay attention to him. More than that, she liked his messy hair and the sexy smirk he wore when he looked up and caught her staring at him.

Other girls might have blushed or giggled. Which was why they weren't Ella.

She just held his gaze.

His smirk kicked up a few notches, and only if Ella were dead would she not notice the heat he was sending her across the aisle. She had to respect that kind of bravado.

"Too bad you have a boyfriend," Marilee whispered in her ear.

"Too bad for *him*, you mean," Ella said with a wicked smile.

Marilee laughed. "It's good news for *me*," Marilee continued. "You can consider Ryan your first wingman test."

Ella settled back against her seat and relished the fact that Marilee wanted her advice.

"A guy like Ryan is easy," she whispered, knowing that she was right. "To get his attention, you have to act like you don't want it. But not in an obnoxious way. In a totally confident, you're-doing-your-own-thing way. Believe me, he'll eat it up."

"I feel like I should be taking notes," Marilee said with a laugh.

Ella glanced across the aisle again, to find Ryan still watching her with a challenging expression on his face.

Ella knew that look. She'd given and received that look a million times. There were times when looks like that had made her burn right up.

But everything was different now.

Jeremy was different from every boy Ella had known before. Jeremy never bored her. He e-mailed her silly little surveys to fill out — ones he made up especially so the right answers spelled out JEREMY, and texted her whenever he had a free moment — walking to class, sitting at a red light, whenever. He liked hearing the details about the things she did — even if all she'd done that day was lounge around watching DVDs — as if the things she did were interesting simply because *she* did them.

Ella planned to hold on to Jeremy as long as she could.

Across the aisle, Ryan was ignoring Sister Bernadette and her welcoming remarks. He just kept staring at Ella with that same daring look.

The look Ella recognized. And could, therefore, use against him.

"Trust me," Ella whispered to Marilee. "We'll have this guy eating from the palm of your hand in no time."

"Kelsi, seriously, enough with the e-mail!"

Kelsi closed the screen of her iBook and smiled up at her roommate, Taryn Gilmour.

Taryn danced in the middle of their prison-cell-sized dorm room to a techno song with French lyrics. She shimmied up and down the length of their full-length mirror, testing out her current outfit with what she called "simulated party action." A pile of colorful wardrobe rejects covered most of the hardwood floor.

"It's one of my cousins," Kelsi explained. "Jamie started a new school and she's feeling kind of weird, I think."

"Jamie's the fearless one?" Taryn asked, cocking her head to one side as if visualizing every branch of the Tuttle family tree.

"The fearless one is my sister, Ella," Kelsi corrected her, smiling. "Jamie's the creative one."

In the month Kelsi and Taryn had been at school, during cafeteria snack runs, long walks across the quad, or marathon study sessions, they'd told each other every single detail of their previous lives. Taryn knew all about the Tuttle girls, although she was still connecting the names to different stories. In turn, Kelsi knew all about Taryn's older brother, Bennett, who was a year older and went to Amherst. Kelsi hadn't met him yet, but she knew he was a hipster — obsessed with Iron & Wine, screen-printed rock posters from boutique design studios, and early Death Cab for Cutie songs (before they sold out, an important distinction).

It was obvious that Taryn adored her brother. One of the ways Kelsi had known she and her new roommate were going to get along was the fact that Taryn understood what it was like to be close to family members. Some people didn't get that.

"Unless your cousin is going to drive us over to U Mass tonight, she can wait. We've got a frat party to attend!" Taryn twirled again in front of the mirror, considering her reflection. After a moment, she peeled off her bleach-splattered tank and let out a frustrated sigh. "Ugh. I hate all my clothes."

Clad in her black bra, denim mini, and fishnets, Taryn

walked over and helped herself to one of Kelsi's cardigans. But instead of buttoning it closed, she wrapped it across her tiny frame and secured it with a vintage brooch.

"Go right ahead," Kelsi said drily, but she was just teasing. Taryn was already like family.

"You know you want me to borrow your clothes," Taryn said, making a face at Kelsi. "See? I'm immediately cuter. Your Anthropologie obsession helps both of us!"

"You were cute already," Kelsi assured her, although the blue Anthropologie sweater Taryn had put on did suit her.

Taryn was one of those girls with the cheekbones to pull off short hair, which made Kelsi incredibly jealous. On Taryn, a pixie cut wasn't harsh, because she left the top a little shaggy and playfully messy, twisting the longest pieces back with an arsenal of glitter-covered bobby pins. It was punky, feminine, and adventurous, all in one.

Next to her roommate, Kelsi looked the very definition of "Playing It Safe." Her hair was a rich, nutty brown these days, falling just past her shoulders. She liked a casual bohemian look when she dressed — opting tonight for a pair of green cargo pants, a cocoa-brown camisole, a dark denim jacket, and a fuzzy angora scarf to ward off the bite in the air.

She might not be as funky as Taryn and her brother, but

that kind of thing didn't bother Kelsi. She'd grown up in the same house as Ella, for God's sake. If that hadn't taught her how to be comfortable in her own skin, nothing would.

"We might as well go," Taryn said. "I look like an anime character tonight and there's nothing to be done about it. Oh, well — right? It's only frat boys." She put up a hand when she saw Kelsi's expression. "Nice frat boys, yes. But still frat boys."

It was a crucial difference, Kelsi mused as she locked their door behind them, and headed outside into the September night. They climbed into the car Taryn shared with her brother, and Kelsi gazed out the window as Taryn drove north along Route 9 toward the town of Amherst. Outside the window, dark and stormy-looking clouds raced by an oversized moon. It made the night seem epic.

Kelsi pointed that out to her roommate.

Taryn laughed. "More epic than a party with frat boys is likely to be, anyway," she said.

"Here we go again," Kelsi said with an exasperated sigh that was almost entirely for show. "You don't have to go, you know."

"I want to go!" Taryn cried. "What could be better than keggers and dumb jocks?"

"Ha-ha," Kelsi said. "I used to agree with you, you know. But Tim is different."

Before Tim, Kelsi had had a lot of preconceived notions

about guys who looked the way Tim looked. Good-looking jocks with easy smiles and their polo shirt collars flipped up had made her gag. Tim had changed all that, though, with his Heath Ledger-ish cuteness and that confident swagger of his. Not to mention his knee-weakening kisses.

"If you say so." Taryn's voice was noncommittal. "I just think you deserve a guy who you can hang out with in an intellectual sense, you know?"

"Tim *is* that guy," Kelsi assured her. "You'll see when you get to know him better." Taryn had only met Tim briefly, during the few times he'd stopped by their room to pick up Kelsi.

Kelsi wasn't surprised that Taryn was concerned with her intellectual health — they were both amazed daily by how exciting college was in that sense. The classes were awesome, and the other women totally smart and inspiring. Kelsi loved being a part of Smith's history. She liked imagining all the women who had walked the campus paths before her, possibly thinking about the same poems or theories as she was, in the same crisp fall weather. Some of the girls in her high school class — and Ella, of course — had made fun of Kelsi for choosing one of the few all-female colleges left, but Kelsi had known since visiting Smith in her junior year that it was the place for her. The lack of boys at Smith was hardly noticeable, anyway, since Kelsi spent so much of her time ten miles away at U Mass with her gorgeous, wonderful boyfriend, who made Kelsi's head spin a little bit whenever she thought about him.

"Oh. My. God." Taryn gasped. "Is this for real?"

Kelsi jolted back into reality and realized they had just pulled up to the frat house.

The blue-and-white building, emblazoned with three Greek letters, sat elevated on the side of a steep hill. A winding staircase leading up to the house was clogged with students trying to enter a foam pit, erected on the front lawn using various tarps and an enormous machine that expelled an endless river of sudsy bubbles. A DJ on the porch scratched a Beastie Boys record, while girls in mini-togas shook their stuff on top of the oversize speakers.

"I guess," Kelsi said slowly. This was certainly a very typical-looking frat party for someone she believed was a very atypical pledge. "It's their first party of the year," Kelsi explained. "Tim said they have to prove themselves to all the other fraternities, or something." As Taryn's cell buzzed and she answered, Kelsi watched as a posse of frat boys, naked except for bathrobes and boxer shorts, handed out Jell-O shots and sprayed whipped cream into a line of open mouths.

"Shit!" Taryn said, flipping her cell phone closed. "I have to go pick up Bennett at Amherst. A local gallery had some extra space for their opening tomorrow, so they've agreed to show a few of his huge-ass paintings. But he's got to get them over there and hung up tonight."

"That's great!" Kelsi said, trying to muster up some genuine excitement. But she secretly wanted an ally with whom to navigate this extremely foreign locale.

"Please, I wish I was staying with you," Taryn said with a laugh. "Look at this party. It's like the real live version of *Animal House!*"

"Next time," Kelsi promised. "Good luck with your brother." She leaned over to kiss Taryn on the cheek, and then climbed out of the car.

"Give me a buzz if you can't get a ride back to campus!" Taryn shouted as she drove off. "And take plenty of pictures!"

Once Taryn pulled away, and Kelsi was alone, her smile slipped a little bit. It was one thing to talk up the frat scene to Taryn. On her own, Kelsi could admit to herself that shouting, drunken foolishness wasn't at all on her list of preferred activities. Kelsi headed across the lawn toward the front door, trying to ignore the worst of the mayhem. When she was shoved by a particularly rowdy group chanting fight songs, she almost called Taryn to come rescue her.

But she took a deep breath and reminded herself not to judge anyone. Everyone around her was having fun. And why shouldn't they?

She might not know why all these people seemed to think being so loud and drunk was delightful. What she did know was that she'd never felt anything as good as the heat that flashed over her when she made it up the front steps and found Tim standing there, waiting for her.

He was so hot, it amazed Kelsi that he was actually hers. Those hazel eyes and his dirty-blond hair all worked together to give him that J. Crew model look that Kelsi adored. Except that he traded in his trademark oxford shirt for a ripped Hanes tee sloppily marked PLEDGE with a black sharpie.

He smiled when he saw her. "Finally," he said.

He reached out and pulled Kelsi close by hooking his hand around the nape of her neck. He kissed her long and hard, and was grinning wider when he pulled away.

"Hi," Kelsi whispered. It had been two days since she'd last seen him, and they'd talked about fifty times in the interim. Even so, it had felt too long. He leaned close to kiss her again, and the chanting of a frat song faded far into the background.

"Isn't this insane? The brothers said this isn't even half the people who'll show up here tonight. We have more than forty kegs!"

"Wow! That's amazing!" Kelsi said, trying her best to sound genuinely impressed.

Tim led her away from the crowd to the side of the house. Her ears were already ringing from all the noise and she wasn't even inside yet.

"Weren't you gonna come with Taryn?"

"She had to bail. You might need to give me a ride back to school tonight."

"My roommate took off for the weekend," Tim said, high-fiving a bouncer who was guarding a quiet back staircase. "I'm telling you that with full and total respect for your feelings on the sex subject," he added, flashing a grin at Kelsi. "But I thought you should know that Matt won't be busting in if we want to have a nice, quiet sleepover. Or a loud, passionate sleepless sleepover."

Kelsi couldn't help but laugh. She loved fooling around with Tim, because, unlike guys she'd dated in the past, he never pressured her. While he made no secret of the fact he would love to have sex, he also never made her feel weird or awkward about saying no.

Whenever you're ready is cool, he always said with a kiss and that sweet smile that made her melt.

"But we can talk about that later." Tim ran his hands through her dark hair. "Right now, there's a ton of people I want you to meet."

Kelsi cuddled underneath Tim's arm, and followed him through the thick heat of the overcrowded rooms. While it wasn't at all her scene, Kelsi still felt like she belonged.

Because she belonged with Tim.

"You're not even listening to me!" George gasped, pretending to be outraged. He stopped dead in the middle of the high school corridor, and Beth had to haul him out of oncoming traffic before he was trampled.

"I just came up with the most fantastic idea for a new television series *ever*," George continued, not seeming to notice that Beth had just saved him from certain death by student stampede. "You were *pretending* to listen, but you weren't at all. You didn't even *laugh*. If I didn't know such a thing was impossible, I might think you were bored with the G-Man."

"I *was* listening, George," Beth insisted, shifting her heavy pile of textbooks from one sore arm to the other. Her daily swim practices made her muscles ache. All her hard work had paid off; Beth had made the swim team. She and George had celebrated over chili dogs and Cokes in town, and now Beth was knee-deep in her regular practices. "But if I don't get these into my locker like right now, my arms might fall off."

"And now you're changing the subject." George trailed after Beth as she hurried along the hall. "Evasive tactics won't work. You're busted."

"I heard every word you said," Beth told him, over her shoulder and without slowing her stride. "And I think you're crazy."

"Because I could tell you weren't paying attention to my amazing idea that will make us a trillion dollars?"

"Because no one is going to pay you anything, much less a trillion dollars, to make *George: The Televised Years*." Beth grinned at him as they approached her locker, and propped her books up with her knee while she wrestled to open the metal door. "Trust me on this."

"I think there's market demand," George said, leaning back against the next locker over and shoving his hands in his pockets.

Beth felt herself weaken when she looked at him. His curly hair went every which way, and he'd acknowledged the cold snap outside with a long-sleeved T-shirt beneath the short-sleeved political one, with a donkey wrestling an elephant, which was his current favorite. He felt Beth's eyes on him and smiled.

"What?" he asked.

"You're pretty much looking at the market for George," Beth replied. "In its entirety. I hate to break it to you."

"You say that now," George retorted, unfazed. "But I bet you'll change your tune when I come up with a screenplay of such genius that I'll have every director in Hollywood on the phone."

"When that happens, I'll definitely change my tune," Beth agreed. She zipped her books into her backpack and slammed her locker shut. "In fact, I solemnly swear that the day Hollywood directors start calling you, I'll *serenade* you from the highest building in Martin. I'll even climb up there myself."

George's dark eyes fastened on hers, and Beth felt a shiver trail along her skin. She knew they were both thinking of last summer, when Beth had proven her love to George by climbing up to a rooftop in Pebble Beach and shouting her true feelings into the night sky, in complete defiance of her paralyzing fear of heights.

George moved closer and pulled Beth to him, his warm lips teasing her neck.

"That ended up being the best night of the summer," he said, holding her tight.

Beth felt guilt wash over her. Because she knew that night hadn't started off as "the best" or even close. The truth was, Beth wouldn't have had to prove her love to George if she hadn't risked it all — with a lifeguard named Adam.

Here in the hallway of their high school, in George's arms, Beth couldn't believe any of that had ever happened.

"That was definitely the best night of the summer," she agreed, squeezing him.

"Almost worth the crap that came before," George said. His tone was light, but there was a distance in his eyes that Beth hated. She didn't know what to say so she kissed him, apologizing once more with the touch of her mouth against his.

"I was thinking I would get right to work on my Oscar-winning screenplay," George murmured, running his hands along her arms. "But before I get down to the writing, I think I need food. Want to grab a burger?"

"I can't," Beth replied with a sigh. "I have swim practice." She knew the little shiver of joy that still coursed through her when she thought about the fact she'd made the team would fade, but it hadn't happened yet.

"What do you mean?" George asked, knitting his brow. "It's not even three o'clock yet. You don't have to be at practice until six. You have three entire hours."

He was right, but that meant Beth only had those three hours to go for a run, do her homework, eat dinner, appease her mother with some long-overdue chores, and drive the forty-five minutes into Boston to make it to practice on time. And sometimes the drive took more than an hour and a half at that time of day. There was no way she could hang out with George.

She looked over at him to tell him so.

"I can hear what you're thinking," George said, his expression bright. "But you have to eat, don't you? And we both know that if I don't make you eat with me, you'll do something else instead and you'll forget. And nobody likes an Olsen twin."

Beth felt herself waver. Lately, she hadn't been seeing George as much as she'd like, not with the new swim team coaches taking over her life. That was how they'd introduced themselves: *"We're here to take over your lives,"* they'd said that first day. *"If you have a problem with that, don't waste our time — just go."*

Beth had stayed, of course. And she'd learned pretty quickly that the coaches weren't kidding.

Their names were Katy and Lance. As the rumors had indicated, they were students at Boston College and the hardest coaches Beth had ever encountered in all her years of athletics. She thought on many occasions that she hated them, and yet had the perverse desire to please them — which was how she knew they were doing the coaching thing right.

But none of that has to do with George or being in love,

she thought then as they stared at each other next to her locker. She'd nearly let their relationship slip away over the summer, and she wasn't about to do it again.

She would run six miles tomorrow, she vowed, to make up for not running her three miles today. She might have to start getting up even earlier if she was going to get a daily run in, the way Katy had recommended. And her mom could wait a little bit longer for Beth to help put away the summer clothes. Finally, it wouldn't be the first time she'd stayed up past midnight to finish her homework, or cut her first-period health class to get it done the next morning.

And she'd be getting a burger and George in the deal, which outweighed all the rest.

"Okay," she told George, loving the way he looked so delighted at her answer, in that fully happy way only he could get, from his sparkling eyes down to the way his legs practically vibrated with excitement.

"*Exx-cellent*," he said, drawling out the word. "I think I speak for myself and the beef industry when I say you made the right choice."

Beth hurried across the wet pool deck, tucking the last strands of her blonde hair up under her swim cap. She was late. She and George had gotten burgers and fries and then spent way too long making out in the parking lot. Beth felt herself flush, almost as if his mouth was still on hers, his hands on her skin. Her heart was still pounding. Beth laughed to herself and adjusted the stiff Lycra cap.

If there was anything uglier than a swim cap, Beth didn't know what it was. Except possibly a Speedo racer-back one piece. Her cousin Ella would keel over and die if she ever saw Beth wearing both at once.

Thinking about Ella made Beth grin. She couldn't believe she had to wait until Thanksgiving to see all her cousins in one place.

"Tuttle." Coach Katy held a clipboard and was wearing an incredulous expression as Beth approached. "You're fifteen minutes late."

"Um." Beth felt herself flush again. With embarrassment this time. "I'm sorry."

She was normally self-assured around other athletic types, but something about Katy made Beth feel like an idiot. Maybe she was a little intimidated. Beth let Ella do the worrying about which girls were cute and which girls wore the right clothes. Beth was the only Tuttle who could look at another girl and see that her sleek muscles and powerful legs meant she could — and probably would — completely kick Beth's ass.

Okay, maybe she was a *lot* intimidated.

"I'm sorry," Beth said again, her voice soft.

"Don't be sorry," Katy snapped. "Just don't be late. We

have a huge meet coming up. You should be in the water working your butt off, or you shouldn't be on the team."

"I understand," Beth said, feeling chastened, and kind of furious. More specifically, with George.

"Then *get in the water!*" Katy retorted, pointing at the pool. She shook her head in amazement.

Beth threw her towel on the bleachers, and got into a lane as fast as she could. Once she'd slipped into the rhythm of her warm-up strokes, her embarrassment faded. She began to breathe evenly, stretching farther with each arm.

Katy probably thought she was a moron. Great.

Beth hated being yelled at — but even more than that, she hated giving her coaches a reason to yell at her in the first place. Lance and Katy had been perfectly clear about how unacceptable they thought being late to practice was. No tardiness. End of discussion.

"Swim team is either a priority or it's not," Lance told them at almost every practice. *"If you're late, you're sending us a message about your commitment level. We'll send one back. Trust me."*

I shouldn't have gone out with George. The words, heavy with regret echoed in Beth's head. And as hard as she swam, she couldn't get them out.

"What are you having for lunch?" Jeremy asked over the phone. His voice was low and sounded like he was smiling. If Ella closed her eyes, she could imagine the crook of his mouth and the light in his big dark eyes.

She could pretend he was there.

Until she opened her eyes again and found herself walking across the quad in Connecticut, surrounded by falling leaves, talking to her boyfriend on the phone. Alone.

"Diner food," she said, adjusting her book bag. "Why?"

"I wish we were having lobster rolls together down at Red's in Wiscasset," Jeremy replied. "I mean, how awesome would it be to hop in the car and take a drive there together right now?"

Ella sighed wistfully. "That *would* be awesome." Last

summer, she and Jeremy had taken that road trip a few times together. Red's had the fattest, most delicious lobster rolls in the whole state of Maine. They'd order two (his with mayo, hers with melted butter) and a side of fries to split. Then, they'd find an open table on the back deck and eat in the sunshine while the boats passed through the harbor, their knees touching under the rickety table.

At the end of summer, they'd driven down one last time and got the very last rolls of the season, right before Red's boarded up for the fall. It was a bittersweet moment, and with all the tables packed away, they'd had to find seats out on the weathered wooden planks of the pier. It was a quiet meal, save for the times Jeremy kissed away a trickle of melted butter from the corner of her mouth. Ella would giggle uncontrollably and push him away. But then things got quiet again, both of them heavy with the notion that they'd be parting ways for the next few months.

The memory of Red's reminded Ella that Jeremy was worth doing the long-distance thing for.

He was worth waiting for. Wasn't that what she'd learned over the summer?

"I also ask because *I'm* having a hoagie and I have to tell you, it's very disappointing," Jeremy continued in that casual way he had. "The bread-to-cheese ratio is way off, and I won't even get into the meat."

Ella could hear Jeremy's high school cafeteria noise in

the background, and wrinkled her nose. Thank God she was an upperclassman, and could avoid the revolting industrial food altogether.

"In the history of hoagies," Jeremy continued, "this one might be the worst. Like, ever."

"I get to go off campus for lunch," she bragged. "If you were here, I could pick you up something tasty."

Today, Ella couldn't get off St. Augustine's grounds fast enough. Sister Margaret Alice had jumped all over her in study hall (like Ella could be expected *not* to apply Stila lip gloss when she had a free moment), and Ella was in dire need of a break from school.

"You're cruel," Jeremy told her, affection in his voice.

Ella held her cell phone to her ear with one hand, and looked for oncoming traffic as she ran across the street. Deciding to risk it, she completely misjudged the distance, bringing traffic to a halt. She wiggled her fingers and sent a naughty smile to the driver of the first car, an older guy in a sedan. He waved back at her, obviously dazzled.

Yes. Ella Tuttle was the kind of girl who regularly stopped traffic.

"Can't help it." Ella laughed, popping a piece of Dentyne Ice gum in her mouth. She'd always been a chain-chewer, but had gotten more addicted since quitting smoking.

Outside the diner, Ella paused as Jeremy's voice became more intimate.

"I miss you," he said. "We haven't talked in so long." There was a longing in his voice that Ella instantly recognized from the night they'd said a special goodbye to each other. The most special goodbye a girl and boy could share.

It had been the next-to-last night of the summer, humid and still. They had walked hand in hand down Peachtree Road toward the beach. The moon was a sliver in the clear sky. Jeremy had a beach blanket tucked under his arm, and he spread it out on the still-warm sand.

She took his hand and let him pull her down. They started kissing, their lips hot, their hands warm. They tangled themselves in each other's arms and legs, holding on so tight Ella could barely breathe. She knew he wanted her, and she wanted him more than anything. Had wanted him all summer. It was the perfect moment for Ella to shine, brighter than even the stars overhead, and Jeremy let her take control. She pulled his soft shirt up over his head, undid the button on his jeans. Just the thought of his taut stomach in the moonlight gave her the chills. Everything had happened so quickly, so perfectly.

"I miss you, too." She transferred the phone from one ear to the other and looked through the glass window of the diner. If only they didn't live so far apart, nights like that first one could happen all the time. If only.

In the diner, Marilee was seated in one of the booths,

surrounded by a pack of boys from St. Augustine's. One of whom was the sexy new guy, Ryan.

Through the window, Ella watched as Marilee shot a straw wrapper across the table, making sure she leaned forward and exposed a flash of cleavage. Ella could see the effect it had on Ryan. He grinned and said something that made Marilee toss her hair and laugh.

It was such a patented Ella move that Ella was a little bit surprised no one was calling Marilee on it. Not that Ella thought her friend shouldn't be just as flirtatious as she wanted to be, it was just . . . Ella was used to being the flirtatious one.

Something weird washed over Ella then. Some emotion she couldn't exactly place, but it made her stomach hurt a little bit.

"Are you okay?" Jeremy asked.

For a moment, Ella didn't know what to say.

"I'm fabulous," she assured Jeremy.

"I know you're fabulous," Jeremy was saying. "It's eighty-seven percent of what I think about all day. Call me later this afternoon, you promise?"

"Okay, baby," Ella purred. She snapped the phone shut and immediately felt guilty. She had Jeremy. What did she need a bunch of Catholic schoolboys for when she had the real thing?

Ella slid her phone into her bag and threw open the door

to the diner, because standing around outside was making her feel like a huge loser.

She paused in the doorway, letting the rush of air mess up her hair a little bit, knowing perfectly well that she made quite the pretty picture as she stood there. She knew the light made her blonde hair shine, and her legs were still tan and supple. Her usual uniform modifications, she was also well aware, drew even more attention to her assets.

Satisfied, Ella ambled over to Marilee's booth. She leaned her hip up against the table and waited for everyone to stop fawning all over Marilee and look up at her instead. It didn't take long.

"Hi Ella," Marilee said, sounding both amused and resigned.

"Is there room for me?" Ella asked, in a teasing voice, because she expected them to make room for her — and they did.

Marilee rolled her eyes.

"There's always room for you, Ella," Ryan told her and patted his lap.

"I'm good over here," she told him, flouncing a little bit as she sat down.

"That," Ryan said with a smile, "I can see."

Ella lounged across the table from him, and watched him as he lounged in the same careless fashion.

"I hear you were one step away from military school," she said.

Ryan's mouth kicked up into a smile. "You, too, from what I hear," he said.

They smiled at each other, acknowledging their similarities.

"Hey, Ella?" Marilee interrupted in a sugary voice that got Ella's attention at once. Ella turned to look at her and saw a flash of resentment in her friend's eyes. "Is your boyfriend coming up this weekend or next?"

"I don't know, Marilee," Ella replied, shooting her friend a look that should have incinerated her on the spot. Couldn't Ella even *talk* to Ryan?

"I can't wait to meet him," Marilee went on with a sigh. "The guy who finally got the legendary Ella Tuttle to settle down. He must be something."

Ella clenched her fists. But then she wondered why she was getting so angry. After all, Jeremy really *was* something. And Ella shared something with him that Marilee couldn't begin to understand.

"It's true," she said, smiling and settling back in her seat as she thought of their earlier conversation. "He's pretty amazing."

Marilee bit her lip, clearly not expecting that response. As Marilee turned to answer another boy's question, Ryan cleared his throat and leaned toward Ella.

"A boyfriend, huh?" Ryan smiled thoughtfully. "Too bad."

Ella shrugged nonchalantly. "Not for me."

"I would have to disagree," he said.

Ella found herself watching him as he played with the napkin in front of him, folding it into some sort of origami shape with his long fingers.

"Thanks for caring," she said. She tried to keep the flirtatious lilt out of her voice but, whatever, it was the only voice she had.

"That's what friends are for," Ryan said

Then he slid the origami creation across the table, and continued to watch her with those fiery eyes. Ella looked at the little bird for a moment and then reached over to scoop it up.

She saw Ryan smile triumphantly, and wondered what she'd gotten herself into.

But then she relaxed.

It was just a napkin. Ryan was just a flirt.

Ella could handle it.

There were a lot of things that Kelsi liked about college, but the drunken morons who comprised the bulk of Tim's frat buddies weren't among them.

It had been a few weeks since the start of the Greek Pledge, but the number of parties hadn't tapered off. In fact, they'd increased. There were parties for football games, themed parties celebrating different brothers' nicknames (Moose, Itch, Belcher, and Tango), and a 48-hour weekend bash called the Beer Olympics.

Kelsi tried to be a good sport about it. After all, it was nice to spend time with Tim. But the time they actually got to spend together at these frat functions became less and less quality. It was usually Kelsi with her back to the wall, dodging beer spills or impromptu Fallout Boy mosh pits, and

Tim off laughing with his buddies. And while she still clung to the belief that her boyfriend was an amazing, intelligent, and incredibly hot, his frat brothers were definitely of the idiot variety.

It wasn't just that they were idiots. It was that they were frigging *loud*. Kelsi was slightly concerned she'd end up deaf. And that while becoming so, she would also lose about sixty IQ points.

For some reason, these things didn't seem to concern Tim.

Tonight, for example, she and her boy were standing in a hallway, watching one of Tim's pledge buddies do a kegstand. Kelsi, holding a sweaty cup of beer in one hand, felt slightly ill, but Tim was cracking up, his hazel eyes gleaming. Tim never seemed to have any problem fitting in wherever he happened to be. Kelsi had watched him interact with the same brand of confident ease back at parties at Smith, too, where things were significantly more chill. Usually, she found his ability to have fun wherever he was endearing. Even hot.

But tonight she was just tired.

Maybe it had something to do with the fact that she'd even see her boyfriend doing kegstands. So far, the brothers had made the pledges sing, perform kegstands, and keep their beers permanently full, which required a whole lot of racing around the crowded fraternity hall.

"We'll go soon," Tim promised her, as Kenny staggered away from the keg, looking green. Tim leaned over and kissed her. "Just let me finish my beer."

"Because the other eight hundred beers weren't enough?" Kelsi asked with a slight edge in her voice that even she could hear. She hated being a downer.

Tim just smiled at Kelsi's disgruntled expression. "What can I tell you? It's Miller family tradition. No dead soldiers."

"We have traditions in the Tuttle family, too, you know," Kelsi said. She made a face at Tim. "It's just that none of them involve drunk, smelly boys."

"Are you sure about that?" Tim asked and laughed when Kelsi swatted at him. "Okay, okay." He looked across the room. "I'll go say good-bye. Wait here."

Kelsi leaned back against the wall, set down her unfinished beer, and surveyed the crowd as Tim wove a path through it. She didn't feel *too* bad about making Tim leave — he'd been out until five A.M. the night before and had told Kelsi he'd felt like a zombie all day.

She watched Tim approach the upperclassmen in charge of the frat. The way they started ragging at him, maybe she'd been too hasty. She didn't want to get him in trouble with his soon-to-be brothers.

"I don't mind," Kenny slurred, hitting the wall next to her with a loud, reverberating thud.

Kelsi jumped, half expecting the wall to come tumbling down. Kenny was a big guy. At least he wasn't chugging anything at the moment.

"Hi, Kenny," Kelsi said. He could barely keep his eyes open. It took her a moment to retrieve what he'd said from her memory. "What don't you mind?"

"I'd let you drag me off early, too," Kenny said, or at least that's what Kelsi *thought* he said.

"Oh, yeah?" Kelsi wished Tim would come back, if only because she was slightly afraid Kenny might pass out and take her down with him. She'd seen Kenny crash to the floor at a previous party. Everyone had yelled, "TIMBER!" and then gone about their business.

"Tim says you're amazing in bed," Kenny slurred on. "I don't mean to be disrespectful, you know? But I can totally see it. I can fully envision the way you tore that dorm room up when Matt was away!"

Kenny chuckled, said something else that was totally incomprehensible, and then mumbled some kind of good-bye and staggered away. He didn't wait for a response.

Which was good, because Kelsi was speechless. She felt frozen solid in her place against the wall, unable to comprehend what she'd just heard.

Don't fly off the handle, she cautioned herself. *Kenny is a moron even when he's* not *too drunk to stand. And every time you've ever gotten mad at Tim in the past you've been wrong about him.*

Which was why she kept her cool until Tim came to collect her. She smiled and said her good-byes to the people Tim cared about, because she could be perfectly polite even when she was screaming on the inside. She waited until they were outside, in the cold, still night air. She tucked her hands deep into the pockets of her coat and bit her lip for a moment, not knowing what to say. Or how to even begin saying it.

"Is something wrong?" Tim asked with his usual perceptiveness.

Kelsi held on to that. He *was* perceptive. He was also kind and sweet and not at all the kind of guy who would do something as disgusting as lie to his friends about her.

She looked at him and opened her mouth. Very carefully and quietly, she repeated what Kenny had said. She was proud of herself for not getting upset while she said it.

"Jackass," Tim spat, with a shake of his head. "I don't know what he was thinking. He needs to stop drinking so much."

Kelsi felt a wave of relief.

"I knew you would never say anything like that," she said, breaking into a small smile. A smile that faded when Tim stayed quiet. Suspiciously quiet.

She couldn't believe what that silence had to mean.

"Tell me you would never say anything like that!" she demanded, stopping short in the middle of the quad.

Tim hunched his shoulders against the October chill. "I didn't actually *say* anything," he hedged.

Kelsi no longer felt the cold. Or cared that other students were walking by, eyeing them with obvious interest.

"This is unreal," she said. "Why would you talk about our sex life in the first place? Much less *lie* about it!"

"I didn't lie about anything!" Tim said, his hands up like he was trying to ward her off.

"So why would Kenny even know about the night I spent in your room while your roommate was away?" Kelsi demanded. A night which they'd spent making out, and talking, and then making out some more. But they hadn't gone all the way. Now, Kelsi was glad she'd held back.

"You're blowing this way out of proportion," Tim said, and it made Kelsi furious that he obviously thought she was getting too emotional. "I didn't tell anyone anything. I just didn't *correct* them when they jumped to their own conclusions."

"Oh, that's much better." Kelsi hugged herself and swallowed back the threat of tears. "Because heaven forbid your drunk frat buddies know the hideous truth about your virgin girlfriend!"

"It's not like that!" Tim retorted, and Kelsi saw his

temper flash a little bit in his eyes. Perversely, it made her feel better. Like he should be hurting — or angry — too.

"Then how *is it*?" Kelsi demanded. "If you're as supportive of me as you claim to be, why not admit to your friends that you're not having sex with me? Or are you too afraid that they'll think you're *less of a man*?"

"Do me a favor, Kels," Tim snapped. "Spare me your Smith College knee-jerk reaction feminist crap, okay?"

"You're the one who has to pretend to be someone he's not so a group of Neanderthals will think he's cool!" Kelsi shouted.

"That's not what happened at all," Tim said, lowering his voice. "It was a stupid conversation that got even stupider. Someone said you were hot and a couple of people made some assumptions. I didn't think you'd want me announcing your sexual status to a roomful of guys you don't know, so I didn't correct them. Why Kenny the Wonder Lush decided to share that with you, I don't know. But none of this has anything to do with our *actual* relationship."

He sounded so rational and his eyes searched hers, but Kelsi shook her head.

"I don't know," she said. Now she felt less like crying and more like socking Tim in the gut. "I mean, what happens if I do have sex with you? Will you, like, send out a mass e-mail?"

"Jesus Christ, Kelsi. Obviously not!" Tim snapped.

Kelsi was quiet for a long moment, looking down at the leaf-strewn grass.

Tim swore and looked away, his breath coming out in clouds against the dark night.

"You know what?" Kelsi spoke, still looking down. "I should probably go home. To *my* dorm." Her message was clear.

"Fine," Tim said tersely.

"Fine," Kelsi snapped back in the same tone.

They walked in silence across campus, back to Tim's dorm, and they sat in silence waiting for Kelsi's taxi to arrive. When it honked downstairs, she waited in his doorway for a moment, thinking he would say something — anything — to fix things, but he looked as miserable as she felt.

The whole cab ride back, she swallowed back the hot tears building in her throat. Then when the car got to her dorm, she got out of the car, slammed the door, and ran up to her room, which was, thankfully, empty.

There, finally, she threw herself onto her bed, burst into tears, and cried herself to sleep.

When she woke up the next morning, Kelsi immediately remembered the events of the night before, and the humiliation and regret made her stomach drop. She rolled over and saw, with a small pang of relief, that Taryn's bed was still empty. She hadn't come home last night.

Probably having sex with someone, Kelsi thought, and tears sprang to her eyes again.

Okay. She'd admit it. The whole mess last night had forced her to admit it to herself. She was ashamed. Ashamed that she was eighteen years old and had less experience than her little sister. Ashamed that her own boyfriend was so embarrassed by her lameness that he lied about it to his friends.

Blinking away her tears, Kelsi lay with her comforter pulled up to her chin, and wished, as hard as she could, that her virginity meant to her what it had meant to Ella. For Ella it had been something insubstantial — an inconvenience to be gotten rid of as quickly as possible.

If only Kelsi believed that.

Kelsi's first two boyfriends had broken up with her for refusing to sleep with them. One right after the other. Kelsi could make all kinds of excuses for how each one of them was a jerk in his own right, but the fact remained — they had each wanted to have sex with her. And she'd refused. And now, once again, she was back to the same issue. *What is* wrong *with me?*

Ella always said that Kelsi made it a bigger deal than it was. *Just get it over with,* her sister would say with an exaggerated roll of her brown eyes, and part of Kelsi thought she should. But another part of her, for no reason she could tell, just said no. In that quiet, sure voice deep inside. She didn't know why. She just knew she wasn't ready.

"Good morning!" Taryn singsonged, pushing into the room. "You know why you love me? Because I picked up a special Starbucks chai latte, just for you."

She came over and plopped onto Kelsi's bed, tucking her legs beneath her.

"You got chais?" Kelsi couldn't process such luxury (or industry on Taryn's part) so early on a Sunday morning. But she still took the cup Taryn held out to her.

Taryn blew on her chai and took a sip. "Yup. I can't believe you didn't come to the Italian movie festival last night. It was amazing! *Totally* worth staying up all night for." She leaned closer to study Kelsi's expression. "Oh, my God, Kels. Have you been crying? What's wrong?"

Kelsi hadn't intended to tell Taryn anything about last night, but she was undone by her roommate's kindness.

She opened her mouth, gave into her tears, and let the whole story flood out.

When she was finished, her eyes were puffy, the chais were drained, and Taryn was shaking her head.

"Guys," she said with a resigned sigh. "That Tim is yummy, but when push comes to shove, just as much of a dimwit as the rest." She paused, squeezing Kelsi's hand. "What are you going to do?"

"I have no idea," Kelsi said with a hitch in her voice. "I mean, I feel like I'm this — embarrassment to him."

"First of all," Taryn said briskly, "that's totally ridiculous. No one should make you feel bad about anything you do — or *don't* do — when it comes to sex."

"I just think there's something wrong with me," Kelsi confessed in a near-whisper, afraid to look at Taryn. It felt kind of good to finally be so honest. She felt her hands ball into fists beneath her comforter. "I mean, everyone else has this overwhelming urge to do it and I just don't. I mean, I love fooling around with Tim, and sometimes it's really hard *not* to go all the way with him, but I just don't . . ."

"You don't have to justify feeling how you feel," Taryn said matter-of-factly. "Not to Tim. Not to yourself. Not to anyone."

Kelsi just shook her head. How did Taryn get so sane? She was so calm, never particularly fazed. Everything Kelsi felt she wasn't.

"My philosophy? Sex is supposed to be *fun*," Taryn said after a moment. "Not weird or dramatic or whatever. Definitely not something to get upset about, or you're missing the whole point."

"I'm not sure other people agree with you," Kelsi mumbled. Meaning herself.

"I'm also not big on other people's expectations," Taryn said, grinning. "I guess I'm a kind of a nonconformist."

Kelsi sniffed back tears. "Let me guess. So you're not a weird, dramatic virgin like me?"

"Well, I'm not a virgin," Taryn said, drawing her knees up to her chin. "And I'm not even sure I'm straight. But I try not to be weird or dramatic about anything."

"Oh." Kelsi blinked.

"It's okay, though," Taryn went on. "Only you know what's good for you, and you should run with that."

Kelsi was still stuck on the *not even sure I'm straight* part.

"But . . . but I thought you said something about your last *boyfriend*?" Kelsi asked, confused.

"My last relationship was with a guy, yes," Taryn said with a shrug. She looked as indifferent as if she'd announced a preference for humid weather as opposed to dry. "But I've kissed girls. I don't really rule anything out."

"Huh." Kelsi tried to process this new information.

The fact that Kelsi was so flummoxed by Taryn's blasé announcement made her feel like an even *bigger* prude. Even Ella, as far as she knew, restricted her wildness to boys. How had she managed to find someone even more experienced than Ella?

Or was it just that nobody alive was as *inexperienced* as Kelsi?

7

AOL INSTANT MESSENGER

JAMIE_TUTTLE: LADIES! It has been too friggin'
long. What is UP? Did all of you get engaged to your
respective boy-toys without telling me?

QUEENTUT18: I don't know about the rest of you but
I am mostly definitely NOT engaged to Tim. In fact,
we're kind of in a fight right now. Things are . . . weird.

PRINCESSELLA: Tell us more Kels. We need
details in order to help. Every time I call u to talk
u say ur studying and blow me off. Not very sisterly
u know.

QUEENTUT18: That's because I AM always studying.
Argh.

JAMIE_TUTTLE: Ditto. Why did nobody warn me how much prep school would kick my ass? Kelsi, what's this about T?

QUEENTUT18: It's a long, sordid story. Maybe I'll save it for Thanksgiving.

SWIMFAN: Thanksgiving! Can't wait. Food! Girls! Gossip!

PRINCESSELLA: Bethy, there you are! I saw ur name but totally thought u'd fallen asleep on us.

SWIMFAN: Almost. 2 much swimming. No rest.

JAMIE_TUTTLE: Whoa. You're in bad shape. How's George?

SWIMFAN: Energetic. Any boys in prep school?

JAMIE_TUTTLE: Kinda. But not in a good way.

PRINCESSELLA: Ooh!! ☺

JAMIE_TUTTLE: No, there's this pompous I-was-born-with-a-trust-fund guy, Dex (think slicked-back brown hair, blue blazer, the works). He's in EVERY. SINGLE. ONE. OF. MY. CLASSES and is always acting like he's in competition with me. Yes, he's smart — he was top of his class — but I've been getting better grades than him on some stuff, so he's totally out to get me. Every time I raise my hand in class, he does, too, and then shoots me this LOOK. All grinning and twinkly eyed. And he's always sneaking by me in the library and

peeking over my shoulder to see what I'm reading.
UGH!

QUEENTUT18: Are you guys thinking what I'm thinking?

PRINCESSELLA: Most def.

SWIMFAN: Huh? What happened?

JAMIE_TUTTLE: What?! What are you guys talking
about?

PRINCESSELLA: Hel-LO Jamie! The guy OBVIOUSLY
has a crush on u. Boys don't pay that much attention
to girls unless they're out to get them in OTHER ways!!
☺

QUEENTUT18: And I'm just going to go out on a limb
here and say that maybe you have a crush back. . . .

JAMIE_TUTTLE: You guys, that is SO not true!! He
DOESN'T like me, and I find him repulsive!! So arrogant. Totally not my type.

PRINCESSELLA: Mmm-huh.

QUEENTUT18: Did you know there's a river in Egypt
called DENIAL? (LOL to myself — lame, I know).

JAMIE_TUTTLE: Not speaking to any of you until
Thanksgiving.

SWIMFAN: Wait, what are you guys talking about? I
think I dozed off for a minute.

QUEENTUT18: Oh, Bethy. We love you.

The next day, Beth sat in public speaking, the only class she had with George. But she wasn't looking at George today. Her chin was in her hands, and her eyelids were drooping shut. She'd stayed up extra-late last night, just so she could IM with her cousins. She'd missed them so much, and it was great to catch up. But she'd kept drifting off, mid-IM. Things in her life were so busy. She hated that her personal relationships were starting to suffer for it. There was too much to catch up on! Senior year — and especially swimming — was taking a serious toll.

One of the other students was standing in the front of the room, droning on about the last presidential election. It would have been controversial if it weren't so boring, Beth thought idly. Beth sighed and wondered — not for the first time — if you really *could* use toothpicks to keep your eyes open.

George had his desk flush against Beth's, so he could also have his thigh flush against hers beneath it. Beth knew he'd be upset if she moved away, so she stayed there, even though the last thing she felt like doing was anything George might construe as "action." Every single inch of her body ached from swim practice. Even a game of footsie could be potentially crippling.

Beth knew she'd better learn to suck it up, because things were only going to get more hectic. The team had had an undefeated season so far, a record everyone was committed to keeping. They would swim against their archrivals in the last meet during Thanksgiving week, and Beth was prepared to give it 110 percent. If she could just keep herself awake.

George leaned in even closer, his eyes squarely on the student standing in front of them, and surreptiously reached over to lightly brush his hand against Beth's breast. Right there in class!

Beth stiffened and snuck a glance around to see if anyone else had noticed. Luckily, everyone else looked as sleepy and bored as she felt, including Ms. Baransky, who was teaching.

"Sign me up for the Red Sox!" George whispered, chortling a little when she glared at him. "I just stole second base!"

Beth gritted her teeth. "I'm punishing you," she told him in a whisper, scooting her chair away. "Don't touch me again for the rest of class. I'm serious!" she hissed when he reached out anyway.

Beth spent the rest of the period ignoring George, which was harder than it sounded, because George prided himself on being un-ignorable. He drew elaborate comic strips (very badly, Beth thought, but the art wasn't really the point) that illustrated the ways Beth should forgive him, and then pushed his notebook at her. He fidgeted, because he knew that drove Beth crazy. He cleared his throat repeatedly and sneezed while saying words like "sorry" — even though they had just watched *Bring It On* for about the eight-zillionth time last weekend and both agreed that the "Loser Sneeze" was completely lame.

When the bell rang, Beth turned to give George a cold glare — which she had to struggle to keep in place, because she wanted to laugh — and wasn't at all surprised when he grinned back at her.

"You're the most annoying person who ever lived," Beth told him, stacking her books.

"I think you mean 'quirky.' " George waggled his brows at her. "Or maybe 'eccentric.' "

"Annoying," Beth retorted.

"Thank God it's finally a free period," George said with a sigh as they headed for the door. "All this school is inhuman. That time I went to work in my dad's office one summer, I discovered that adults waste *whole hours*. They wander around the office, they go to the bathroom every half hour, they have long lunches in between several short coffee breaks. Yet we have to be here, working, from eight to two forty-five every day. It's completely unfair."

Beth couldn't help but laugh. He sounded so *personally* injured.

"My parents are always telling me these are the best years of my life," she said, glancing at him. "God, I hope *that's* not true."

She had completely forgotten how annoying George had

been in class, because this was what she loved. The way they talked to each other. The teasing and silliness. They'd had that long before they'd even kissed for the first time.

Beth was remembering that first kiss, on the beach in the moonlight, when George slung his arm around her neck and pulled her in tight to kiss her in the here and now. It was a sweet, warm kiss, and made Beth smile when he pulled away.

"I have a plan," George said. "I think we should take off right this minute for lunch. I'm wounded to the core that you forgot this, Bethy, but today's our anniversary."

Beth blinked at him. "No, it isn't. Our anniversary was in August."

George heaved a fake-dramatic sigh.

"Um, no," he said. "Not *that* anniversary. The third anniversary of the first time you let me call you *Bethy* instead of Beth. I can't believe you don't remember."

Beth smiled. "I don't know *how* I could overlook such an important milestone."

"I thought we could maybe head out to the woods, hang out in the backseat, see what happens . . . ," he continued. He let the words trail off suggestively.

Beth pulled away from him, her earlier annoyance returning tenfold. Along with her exhaustion.

"I told you I have to do all my math homework at lunch," she said.

"I hate to point this out," George replied with a grin. "But it's right there in the name. It's called *homework*. You're supposed to do it at *home*."

"And if I was ever home for more than five seconds, I would." Beth sighed. "Please don't argue with me, okay? I'm beat already."

"I know you are," George said. "It's just —"

Beth knew she needed the whole lunch period to fight her way through the calculus problems, but George looked so sad, standing there against the lockers. She couldn't bear it.

"It's just what?" she asked in a softer voice.

"You're always beat," George said, ducking his head. She saw his mouth tighten. "Last night you kept falling asleep in the car — while we were in the middle of a conversation!"

"I know," Beth said, trying to placate him with a hand on his arm. She shrugged when he didn't respond. "My schedule's crazy right now."

"And everything's a schedule!" George looked up again. "It's like you only want to hang out in between the things that are *actually* important to you, but then you're so tired out I'm basically just your chauffeur."

"George, that's complete bullshit and you know it!" Beth was stung.

"Well, that's how it feels," George said stubbornly. "You complain that you're so exhausted that you can't hang out or even, you know, fool around, but you manage to get peppy enough for your *swimming practices*."

"I have math homework," she snapped at him after a minute, when she was sure she could speak without yelling, and stalked off toward the cafeteria, too pissed to look back and see how he'd reacted.

Beth fumed for the rest of the day.

Just a few weeks ago, George had been Mr. Supportive. He'd *helped* Beth out when she was stressed instead of going out of his way to *add* to it.

It occurred to Beth — in a flash of guilt — that maybe George was pulling away because of *her*. After all, he'd been supportive during the summer and what had she done? She'd hooked up with Adam.

But she'd apologized. Again and again. What else she was supposed to do?

Beth sat in her last class of the day, mulling it all over. It wasn't George's fault that the swim coaches were so demanding, and that Beth felt this overwhelming urge to somehow impress them by not buckling under their demands. George didn't do athletics, so sometimes it was hard to explain to him that sports teams were like these weird, aggressive families that Beth felt deeply loyal to.

She wished she could explain these things to George, but lately he'd been even more hyper than usual. Especially about sex. Every time they started to have a normal conversation, George would start groping her. It was like he kept trying to squeeze in all this extra sex time because they didn't see each other as much. And Beth and George had been each other's first times, so Beth figured that, like most boys who made the leap from virgin to non-virgin, George was all about celebrating his new status. She could understand that — she even loved it —most of the time.

She was thinking about that as she headed for her locker after the final bell. She wasn't surprised to see George already there, waiting for her. He leaned back against the locker door and fiddled with his cell phone. Beth watched him as she walked closer. She loved him so much. She'd loved him for so long. Beth swallowed hard.

"I'm a jerk," George said when she came to a stop in front of him. The look on his face was almost bashful. "My picture's in the dictionary. You can look it up, if you want. George is spelled J-E-R-K, in case you didn't know."

Beth laughed, despite everything. He could always make her laugh.

"I have an idea," she said, before she could second-guess herself. "I think we should take advantage of your parents being at a dinner party tonight. To celebrate our very important anniversary. What do you think?"

"I think you have swim practice," George said, but his eyes were suddenly a lot brighter.

Beth forced out a few fake sneezes. "What would you say if I told you I was too sick for practice, and the doctor prescribed some quality time with my boyfriend?" Beth asked, tugging at his sleeve.

"I would say that you won't believe the quality time we're about to have," George said, wrapping his arms tight around her waist and grinning. "So much quality they might have to redefine the term."

So much for redefining the term "quality time," Beth thought later that night.

She didn't know what was wrong with her, except that she felt something small, hard, and mad, right in the center of her chest. She'd thought that skipping practice would mean she and George would have hours and hours to cuddle and talk about the things they never seemed to talk about these days. Where they wanted to go to college next year, for example. Who they wanted to be. These were the things Beth thought about all the time, and used to be the things she talked about with George.

But not tonight.

Tonight she'd barely had time to finish the Spaghetti-Os George had prepared for them before he had dragged her up to his bedroom. They'd stretched across his bed and started kissing and touching and moving against each other.

Beth had felt all flushed with pleasure — it was so nice,

just messing around for a change — but then of course George had undone his zipper and reached for the condoms, and everything else had taken its due course.

Afterward, George fell asleep immediately (as was his custom), and Beth lay there, staring up at the ceiling, wondering why she felt so alone. She knew she loved George, knew he knew her better than anyone. He had always been, and still was, her best friend. But if that was the case, why had he never *once* noticed tonight that Beth was feeling different, and that something was wrong?

Ella pretended she was far too engrossed in her copy of *Us Weekly* to notice that Ryan had just walked through the door of the boys' building and out into the sharp sun of the quad. She subtly adjusted the way she was sitting on her bench, and began, ever-so-gently, to wind a strand of her hair around and around her finger.

It was a little flirtatious, sure.

But *flirting* wasn't *doing*, as she had explained to Jeremy last week on the phone. She had pretended that she was talking about the latest episode of *The Hills*, which was partly true. Jeremy had agreed. They hadn't caught up in a lo-ong time — Ella felt guilty about not calling him back often enough — and she had been so wanting to hear his voice. But Ella knew they'd more than make up for their lack of correspondence that weekend.

"Hey, Ella," Ryan drawled, coming to a stop in front of her.

Ella looked up slowly, as if it was hard to tear her eyes away from the latest Lindsay Lohan Goes Wild story.

The wind brought the smell of winter with it, and kicked up color in Ryan's cheeks. Today he'd managed to mess around with his uniform a little bit, so everything sat just outside school guidelines, right down to the mussed-up hair and loosely knotted tie. Even though Ella *knew* he probably did it himself — deliberately — she couldn't help but admire the careless sort of vibe it gave him.

"Hey," she said after a moment, as if she was thinking of other things. He smiled.

"What are you doing out here?" he asked. "Waiting for me?"

Ella gave him her patented *you wish* look. "I had to get outside," she said. "Sometimes school feels like it's suffocating me."

"I hear you," Ryan said, dropping down next to her on the bench, so they could both look out across the autumn-colored quad, trees losing leaves every time the wind picked up.

"So, friend," he said, raising his eyebows and looking at

her. "I think it's time that I cement my reputation as the coolest kid at St. Augustine's."

"I didn't know that was your reputation," Ella murmured teasingly. "I thought you were just the *new* kid."

"At the moment, yeah." He gave her a sly look, indicating that he knew exactly how cool everyone thought he was. It was that kind of confidence that made Ella feel like purring. "Which, obviously, needs to change."

"Aw, poor baby." Ella laughed. She reached over and patted his hand. "Not getting enough attention?"

Ryan shot her a look as if to say that no amount of attention would be enough.

It was moments like this that made Ella think she and Ryan were two halves of the same whole. Or something else lame and vaguely poetic. She just knew that she *got* him.

"So I've decided to throw the Halloween party to end all Halloween parties this weekend." Ryan leaned forward and fastened his gaze on Ella's. "I'm thinking you should come over early on Saturday and help me dress."

"You don't know how to dress yourself?" Ella asked, feeling her cheeks — what the hell?— flush. Ella *never* blushed.

"I think you could do a better job," Ryan replied with a smirk. "And who knows? We might have fun."

His tone was completely suggestive, and he made absolutely no attempt to hide it.

He was just so naughty. And Ella wanted to lap it up.

It was almost too bad that she couldn't go to his house. Almost.

"My boyfriend's coming up for the weekend," she said, letting her lashes sweep closed, as if she was regretful. In truth, her whole body hummed with excitement every time she thought about *finally* seeing Jeremy again. "We have our own private Halloween party planned. Otherwise, I'd swing by. *After* you were dressed, of course."

"You should bring him," Ryan said, his eyes steady on hers when she looked at him again. "Let him check out the scene around here." He sounded unabashedly like he planned to take Jeremy down. Ella was a sucker for teenage boys' competitive urges. She thought they were just adorable.

"Here's the thing about Jeremy," she said, leaning forward herself, so they were in the same position. Like a mirror image. "He's not really into the scene here." She gave Ryan a smile. "He's into me."

"Who could blame him?" Ryan's grin was wide. "But this party is going to be epic. I guarantee it. We're talking DJ, light show —"

As he continued, Ella felt a swell of regret. She really didn't want to miss out on anything, truth be told.

"It might be a great party," she said. "But since I'm not going, it obviously can't be *that* epic. By, like, definition."

"You make a good point." Ryan looked at her, slowly, carefully, and it was like he could read her. "You know you want to come, Ella."

"What I know," she told him with a dazzling smile, "is that I can't wait to see my boyfriend."

Because as bummed as she might be to miss a party, Ella knew she wanted to see Jeremy more.

When her cell rang Friday evening, Ella was already nearly dizzy with excitement. Her mom was, mercifully, away for the weekend (Ella's parents were divorced). She'd rented a selection of slasher flicks, decorated the den with jack-o-lanterns, and bought bags of Halloween candy. The only challenge would be to keep herself from slipping into her costume before Saturday night. The costume she'd prepared especially to wow Jeremy.

No matter what Ella told Marilee or Ryan, being in a long-distance relationship was a challenge. Ella wasn't as good on the phone as she was in real life. She always had the best intentions of blocking out time for her and Jeremy's daily scheduled phone call, but other things always seemed to pop up and interrupt those plans. Whether it was an impromptu shopping trip for Halloween costumes with Marilee, forgetting to put her cell phone on the charger after a long conversation with Jamie, or just zoning out while updating her MySpace profile, poor Jeremy sometimes got the shaft.

She wasn't happy about it. It frustrated her, especially when he complained about their recent lack of phone time. It wasn't that she didn't care — she obviously did. But she knew no amount of phone calls or texted-photos could ever achieve what the real-life sight of her in something clingy could.

Ella grabbed her phone, seeing it was Jeremy. "Where are you?" she cried. By her calculations, Jeremy should have left his home around 3:30 or 4:00 at the latest, which meant he should be rolling into her driveway anytime after 7:00. It was 6:45.

There was a pause. "Ella, I don't know how to say this," Jeremy spoke quietly. "I'm not coming."

The words didn't make sense.

"What do you mean?" Ella asked.

"I mean, I'm not coming," he said. "I'm still in Philadelphia. I've been sitting here with the car keys in my hand. For hours."

"What?" Ella felt stupid. Her tongue felt clumsy in her mouth. "Is something wrong with your car?"

"It's not the car." His voice sounded heavy, and Ella felt something freeze in her belly.

"Then what is it?" she demanded. "Jer, you could have been here by now!"

"And then what?" he asked. "I know that if I see you, I'm just going to overlook the fact that you always forget to call me, and when you do, it's like you're concentrating on everything but our conversation. And for all the quizzes and stuff I e-mail, you've never once sent me one."

"I know," she said hastily. "I'm not very good at all the communication stuff, but I can be —"

"I don't think you can," Jeremy said sadly. "I don't think that's who you are, Ella. Maybe we should have left things the way they were in the summer. We work better when we can *see* each other."

Ella had the strangest flashback then. She remembered that night in Maine when she'd pulled out her biggest power move on a date with Jeremy, and he hadn't reacted at all the way she'd expected. This moment felt similar. Like he was playing some game she'd never even heard of before.

"What are you saying?" she asked then, even though she was pretty sure she didn't want to hear his answer.

"I'm really sorry, Ella," Jeremy said, and it didn't make Ella feel any better that he sounded legitimately upset. "I think we should just . . . end things."

For a moment, Ella felt frozen in place. She could hear Jeremy's voice saying her name, but it seemed to come from very far away. She had to struggle for a moment to breathe.

And then a tiny voice inside her whispered that maybe Jeremy was right. Maybe she'd been kidding herself.

Because she was Ella Tuttle. And just maybe *she* was the one who'd had enough — enough of pretending to be satisfied with silly e-mail quizzes, late-night phone calls, and an absentee boyfriend. She had lost her head in this Jeremy situation, she realized. She didn't need this long-distance shit. She needed someone right in front of her. Someone real, and fun, and exciting.

Someone more like her.

"Ella?" Jeremy sounded worried. "Are you okay?"

"I'm fine," she said. She took a breath and then let it out. "You know, I'm glad you said something. This long-distance thing doesn't really work for me, either."

"Well, maybe we should talk more —"

"I don't think there's anything to talk about," Ella said smoothly.

She didn't feel frozen anymore. She knew how to do this part. She was excellent at breaking up, actually. All her cousins said so. It was a skill, like anything else. She knew it was best to hit them with it quick and then get out of the conversation even quicker.

"Ella —"

"I'll never forget last summer," she said, and then she clicked off, because she'd never seen the point of hanging around talking things out when someone (usually her, of course) had decided to go. There was nothing left to say.

9

"Okay," Taryn announced on Friday night. She marched over to the closet, took out Kelsi's peacoat, and tossed it at her. "Let's go. I told Bennett that this time you would absolutely be there. He's beginning to think you're my imaginary friend."

"I don't know," Kelsi said, folding her hands in her lap as she sat on her bed. "Tim said the pledges might get out of their secret thing on the early side —"

"Which means anywhere between midnight and two A.M.," Taryn cut in. "Come on, Kels, you have time to come over and watch the movie. Bennett and his friend from high school spent all summer filming it. Even if it sucks, we'll have fun, which" — she gave Kelsi a significant look — "you could use."

She was right. The truth was, Kesli thought as she got up, put on her coat, and followed Taryn out the door, she was glad to have the diversion. She and Tim hadn't really talked things out after their fight outside his frat's party. They'd just sort of . . . kept going. Pretending everything was the same. But a coldness had grown between them. They hadn't even fooled around once since The Fight.

Sneaking a glance at Taryn as she climbed into the car, Kelsi knew what her roommate would say: that Kelsi and Tim needed to hash it out. Taryn was a big fan of hashing things out. She was as free and forthcoming with her emotions as she was with her sexuality. Kelsi both admired and feared that.

Kelsi knew she should talk to Tim, but that felt so heavy, like some object she had to roll out of the way before she got to what she really wanted — which was simply to kiss and curl up beside him again. To be easy with him again, the way it had been before.

Half an hour later, Kelsi was sitting in Bennett's dorm room with him, while Taryn parked the car. His room was as small and cramped as the room her cousin Jamie had stayed in over the summer while taking a writing course at Amherst, but it was decorated with amazing, brightly colored artwork and band posters.

Kelsi thought of bringing that up to Bennett — about

Jamie having gone to Amherst. Anything to break the awkward stillness in the room. Bennett, sitting in a chair across from her, was simply studying Kelsi's face.

"It's really nice of you to share your movie with me," Kelsi finally said nervously. She thought maybe she'd said that before, but she couldn't stand another moment of the oppressive silence. "I'm really impressed that you have a movie to show in the first place, to be honest."

Bennett, Kelsi couldn't help noticing, didn't appear to notice the quiet. He had that same compelling ease about him that Taryn did, although he didn't look much like her. Kelsi had expected someone small and skinny like Taryn. But Bennett was taller and lankier than Kelsi had been imagining. He was every inch the hipster, in a frayed corduroy jacket and Buddy Holly glasses that seemed custom-made for his intelligent face and shaggy coppery-red hair.

"Taryn says that I got all the creative genes in the family," Bennett said, leaning back in his creaky desk chair. He grinned, showing a dimple in his cheek. "It's cute, especially coming from Taryn. Her whole life is creative."

Also cute, Kelsi couldn't help thinking, was Bennett's raspy, Kiefer Sutherland-y voice.

"So how are you liking freshman year so far?" Bennett asked, still smiling. "Taryn's pretty psyched that she got such a cool roommate."

"Taryn's great," Kelsi said truthfully. "But you know that."

"Yeah, she's okay." But he was laughing.

"She, and so many of the girls at Smith, are so smart — it's amazing." Kelsi forgot to feel awkward as she began speaking. In fact, she was excited to have an actual discussion with a guy that didn't involve keg-pumping strategies. "In one of my classes the other day, we got into this huge debate over which female mythological figures were male constructs and which were more clearly feminine, and then it turned into a whole *different* discussion about how to read pop culture today for the same messages."

"Like how the Brad-Angelina-Jennifer triangle taps into social concerns about women?" Bennett asked, grinning.

"Exactly!" Kelsi said, laughing. "I mean, believe me, nobody thought about stuff like this at St. Augustine's."

"Don't tell me you went to Catholic school," Bennett said with a chuckle.

Kelsi laughed, too, rolling her eyes. "My whole life. The sisters might have been interested in intellectual discussions, but none of the other girls were." Kelsi sighed.

"College is cool," Bennett said simply.

Kelsi nodded. "I guess I like that I'm finally in a place where nobody thinks I'm a freak for *wanting* to study," she said, and paused. "Taryn said you guys went to a much more creative kind of high school."

"Well, sure," Bennett said. "But then it became a whole competition about *how* creative you were. How many ironic references you could put into your film, how many inter-textual asides in your poetry — if you see what I mean." He grinned. "So I, obviously, had to be the *most* creative."

"Of course." Kelsi waved a hand at the wall over his desk, which was covered with abstract paintings in different sizes. Wild, moody colors, purples and browns. "I like those," she said. "Did you do them?"

"I'm experimenting," he said, swiveling to look at them. "Did you see that exhibit in the college art center?"

"Yeah, Taryn took me," Kelsi said, sitting forward. "My favorite was the huge seascape in all those random colors."

"That's exactly what I'm trying to play with," Bennett said, leaning forward, too. "I'm not much of a painter, but I like to mess around with ways of seeing."

"Like that seascape," Kelsi agreed. "Somehow, making the colors nothing like the ocean at all made me miss the ocean more than any photograph would have." She thought of Pebble Beach with a pang of longing.

"Right!" Bennett said with obvious delight, and then they both gave a start when the door swung open and Taryn bounded in.

"Oh, my God," she cried. "Did you guys even notice I was gone for about a hundred years? Thanks for answering your cell phones, losers!"

Under the guise of pulling out her phone to check the missed calls list, Kelsi took a deep breath and put aside the surprising disappointment she felt. Was this just another cool conversation, like ones she'd had with different girls at Smith? Was Bennett just another smart, interesting person?

If so, why were her cheeks so hot and flushed?

She was being ridiculous.

First of all, she was in love with Tim. She knew that, despite the recent turmoil.

And besides, Bennett was Taryn's brother. Observing them talking to each other, gesturing in the same way and so obviously easy in their skin, Kelsi figured that Bennett had just been sweet-talking her. If he was as similar to Taryn as he seemed, he probably spent a lot of time getting impressionable girls out of their pants by talking about *art* and whatever.

And Kelsi would sure as hell not be one of them.

"Okay," Bennett said. "Crisis averted. Can we watch the movie now?"

"Let's do it," Kelsi said, and smiled.

Ella didn't answer her cell all day Saturday. Calls from Jeremy, leaving no voice messages. Calls from Kelsi, wanting to know what Ella was doing for Halloween. Ella ignored them all. She had other things to do.

Namely get dressed — in the skimpiest little cat costume she could pull together. It involved a low-cut bustier top and fishnet stockings, both of which enhanced her curvy figure. She slipped on her highest, blackest heels. She fluffed up her blonde hair into a sexy tousled mess, attached little kitten ears because that was what made it a costume rather than just slutty. And then, finally, after a quick nip of her mother's vodka, she walked out the front door.

Outside, the moon was high in the cold October night, and the wind buffeted the windows. Ella felt hurt wrap around her without warning, which threatened to suck her in, but she hurried down the block. *Forget Jeremy.* She didn't have time for emotion. She had to get to Ryan's party. Suddenly it was like everything would make sense if she could just see his face, and those bright eyes of his that seemed to know her through and through.

Ryan's house was a sprawling prefab mansion transformed into a Hollywood-worthy haunted house. The lawn was lit by eerie flickering floodlights that cast spooky shadows on a front deck swathed with spiderwebs. Ella strutted past unmarked gravestones, disembodied mannequin limbs, and fake blood spatters on the slate walkway. Noise and hip-hop and laughter blared from the house. She smiled. As she had suspected, Ryan certainly knew how to throw a party.

The front door creaked open, leading Ella into a big foyer and an even bigger living room beyond. It was hard to tell exactly how big, since it seemed as if every teenager in New Caanan was packed in there, all of them dressed in elaborate costumes.

Ella made her way through the throbbing crowd. She dodged a beefy boy in an old lady's house dress and wig, who practically drooled all over her. She waggled her fingers at a football player who was now dressed as a classic 1920s mobster in a pinstripe suit. She nodded hellos to the St. Augustine girls who greeted her, most of them dressed as girls scouts or ghosts or brides of Frankenstein. Ella enjoyed the faces they made when they got a closer look at how little she had on. Though her uniform restricted her during the schoolday, she was delighted to remind them that, during off hours, she did, in fact, still have it.

Ella stopped steps away from the hoagie table, where a long sandwich was dressed to look like an undulating centipede. She saw a familiar figure, in a French maid costume Ella had personally picked out, straddling a guy dressed as a horse jockey on a nearby couch. They were going at it like crazy. It took her breath away. Ella had been beaten to a guy. Marilee had made Ryan hers.

But just then, Marilee lifted her head and revealed that she was actually making out with the captain of the lacrosse team, Cheryl Anderson's former boyfriend. Ella grinned and breathed a sign of relief. She loved a good scandal almost as much as she loved getting what she wanted.

Then she was back on the hunt, dodging and weaving though Darth Vader costumes and lip-locked couples in her search for the master of ceremonies. A fog machine purred out smoke, making it hard to see through the crowd. Animatronic spiders dropped down from the ceiling only to climb back up their silk webs. The DJ, wrapped in Ace bandages like a proper mummy, worked a crowd of gyrating dancers, dropping one amazing record after another. The party boy himself, however, was nowhere to be seen.

She finally found him over by the keg (marked appropriately as poison), dressed like Johnny Depp in *Pirates of the Caribbean*, all braids and stubble and dirty pirate swagger. Yummy.

He flipped up his eye patch when he saw her coming. A slow smile stretched across his mouth.

"You are the hottest girl at my party. Without. A. Doubt."

Ella smiled and gave a little twirl. "A beer for the lady?" She giggled.

Ryan growled, stepped closer, and nuzzled his face into her neck. The prickles of his facial hair ignited in friction on her skin.

"I thought you said you were hanging out with the boyfriend tonight," he said, stepping back passing her a foaming plastic cup. "Not that I'm complaining. This pirate feels like he's just found his treasure. Arrrrgh!"

"Plans change," Ella said carelessly, and smiled back at him. "I decided to make this party epic after all."

"Lucky me," Ryan said. He nodded toward Marilee, who was now practically giving the guy a lap dance. "I knew she liked me, you know."

"Really," Ella said, tilting her head to one side and smiling.

"I had to blow her off," Ryan said, moving closer. "I'm interested in someone else."

"Oh, yeah?" Ella teased him. "Who's that?"

"Someone I consider a friend." Ryan replied. "Someone like me. I could tell we were alike since the moment we met."

"Happy Halloween," Ella said with a grin, and tilted her face up to his.

Ryan grinned back, and didn't wait one more second. He took Ella's chin in his hand and kissed her — hard. And hot. His lips were demanding, and his arms that slowly snaked around her waist felt wildly possessive. Ella pressed right up against him, delighting in the feel of his muscular frame. She kissed him right back, her tongue teasing his, her lips tempting him with everything she had. And he tempted her right back.

When they both drew back to catch their breath, they were smiling at each other in the same knowing, devious way. Ella was flushed with pleasure, but she wanted more.

"Come on," Ryan said in a husky voice, pulling Ella right up against him. "I want more." And they started kissing again, hotter and hotter, oblivious to the party around them.

Finally, Ella thought, things made sense again.

Beth had never seen George look so excited. And she found
that the tired feeling she seemed to carry around these days
was no match for George being excited about something. In
fact, it was breaking right through the fatigue and kicking
her into high spirits, too.

It was Saturday, late afternoon. The annual big Halloween
party, thrown that night at the summerhouse of one of their
Martin friends, was out on Cape Cod. George had decided
that they should book a hotel with some of the money he'd
saved up working construction over the summer.

This was an exciting prospect, considering the sleeping
arrangements at this particular party were first come, first
served. Beth remembered last year sleeping on top of the

pool table when all the floor space was occupied. Still, she had been better off than the kid who had slept on top of the washing machine. But nothing could beat their own private hotel room.

It was to be, as he'd told Beth a zillion times, the Weekend of Beth and George.

"This is going to be legendary," he told her again, navigating his way through the traffic. His eyes were on the road but he was grinning nonstop. "Seriously, Bethy. You might have to take drastic measures on Monday morning and, like, contact the media to brag about this weekend."

"Assuming we make it," Beth said, looking out at the sea of taillights. "Have you ever noticed that the amount of traffic is in direct proportion to how badly you want to get somewhere?"

"Oh, we'll *make it!*" George promised her, cocking an eyebrow at her in a naughty way. "Don't you worry."

Beth leaned her head back, and instructed herself to relax into the moment. She'd been so tense lately, and the last thing she wanted for this weekend was to be tense. This was like a mini-vacation. With George. What could be better?

George loved Halloween. He always had, as long as Beth had known him. And the Cape Cod party was the kind where everyone got *very serious* about their costumes, and even awarded prizes at midnight for creativity. Last year

Beth and George had gone as Homer and Marge Simpson — and it had been one of Beth's favorite nights all year. Something about being caked in yellow makeup and wearing blue hair, she guessed. This year, in what had started out as a kind of a fight about Beth's swimming commitments, Beth had told George that if he wanted to go to Cape Cod, *he* needed to plan everything.

And I mean actually *making a plan instead of* planning *to make a plan,* she'd told him, because she had this vision of ending up sleeping in the backseat of the car, which George would claim was romantic.

To her surprise, George had been all over it. There'd been no fighting at all as he started to talk about how cool it would be to go away together, which they usually did during the summer. They hadn't spent the whole summer together this year and maybe that was why things were weird between them. Neither one of them actually said that, but Beth wondered if they were both thinking it.

Every time she'd asked about Halloween weekend since, George seemed to buzz with more and more excitement. He had even taken on responsibility for their costumes, which he said would be a surprise. And his eyes had danced when he said it.

As Beth gazed out the car window at the traffic, which had begun to speed up, she let her belief in George wash over her. This weekend would be exactly what they needed. Maybe they could finally talk — not just have sex and/or argue.

Everything was going to be great.

Several hours later, Beth stood in the bathroom of their hotel room and stared at herself in the mirror.

She wanted to cry.

She also wanted to burst out through the door and pummel George with whatever heavy object was close at hand.

The chair, the minibar, whatever worked.

She couldn't believe he'd done this to her.

Everything had seemed fine at first. The traffic had been bad the whole way down to the Cape, so they arrived much later than planned. They'd giggled about how adult and formal it seemed to check into a hotel together, and then they'd each had to shower and quickly start getting ready.

Beth fully expected George to come up with a brilliant costume for the both of them. Something kitschy but cool, like Tom Cruise and Katie Holmes. He was good at things like that. He *lived* for things like that.

Apparently, not anymore.

"I was going to get some Bonnie and Clyde thing," George called from the other side of the door while Beth was drying off after her shower. "But I saw this one and *knew* you had to wear it."

She'd known it was bad when George opened the door partway and handed her the tiny, flimsy little package. The sort of Halloween costumes Beth normally wore did not come in teensy packages.

But she hadn't known *how* bad it was until she put it on.

And it was really, *really* bad.

She was wearing a devil costume, made up of a red bikinilike top festooned with sequins and a pair of skintight, practically nonexistent red silk hot pants. A wide swath of skin was exposed between the bottom of the bikini and the top of the hot pants. The long lengths of Beth's legs were completely exposed, and finished off with the red, spangly heels George had also handed to her.

I look like a complete ho, Beth thought. A ho with a swishy, pointed tail and a pitchfork she'd like to ram into her boyfriend's eye, that was.

Taking a deep breath, Beth opened the bathroom door.

George was at the sink in the little vestibule, dressed in a long white robe with tiny gold wings and a halo attached to a headband. His eyes lit up when he saw her.

"You look *amazing!*" he said.

"What," Beth asked in the calmest voice she could manage, which wasn't all that calm, "were you thinking? I can't wear this *outside.* I show less skin at swim practice!"

"But you look so hot!" George argued. "I wanted to dress you so you can finally see yourself like I do!"

Um, *what?* This was how George saw Beth in his mind's eye — in red silk hotpants?

"I feel ridiculous," she said. But even as she said it she felt guilty, because maybe this was George's stupid boy way of complimenting her.

"I think you look so hot," George said in a husky voice, moving closer and running his hands along her sides. "Maybe we should stay right here."

"Oh, no," Beth said, pushing him away. "I've been looking forward to this party all week. We're going." She eyed his robes. "But maybe *you* can be the devil, and I'll hang out in those robes."

George made a face at her. "Nice try, but the shoes are way too small. You'll have to stay the devil."

Beth rolled her eyes, and marched over the bed to scoop up her school sweatshirt, which she tied around her waist.

"Okay," she said. "Let's go."

"You can't wear that sweatshirt!" George cried.

"Well, too bad. I am."

"You *can't.*" George's face got very serious. "This is a costume party, Bethy. People aren't going to care that you're maybe showing a little skin. But they're definitely going to notice if you have a sweatshirt over your costume!"

"I'm wearing it anyway," she told him.

"Fine," he said. "But you know that will only call more attention to what you're wearing, right?"

Which was, of course, the one thing he could say to make her leave the sweatshirt behind.

But she seethed about it all the way to the party.

"Wow," Taryn said, and not in a good way. "What are you doing?"

It was Saturday night — Halloween — and Kelsi was wiggling into her fishnets. She then smoothed her white miniskirt down.

"What?" she asked, glancing up. "I'm getting dressed."

"Barely," Taryn said.

"Hello," Kelsi retorted. "You're wearing cling wrap!"

"Ahem. *I* am a sea goddess!" Taryn said, twirling around. "I guess I'm just not used to seeing *you* in fishnets and minis. Or low-cut bustier tops."

"I had an epiphany," Kelsi told her and placed a tiny white hat atop her head. "A sexy nurse epiphany."

It had been coming for a while, really.

In high school, Kelsi had always been the concept-costume sort of a girl. Sophomore year she'd dressed as a wedding cake — complete with cardboard layers and a miniature plastic groom sticking up out of her white head-dress. It was one of the benefits of attending an all-girls' school — Kelsi had never dressed with boys in mind. Ella, meanwhile, took Halloween as her personal opportunity to dress as sluttily as possible. The more skin on display, the better. This year, Kelsi had begun to wonder if Ella had it right. Something about spending the evening with Taryn and the laid-back louse Bennett had inspired her. So, first thing Saturday morning, she'd called Ella to discuss sexy costume ideas. Her sister hadn't answered, so Kelsi had gone to the giant Party Warehouse near Northampton. She passed up the lab coats, the space suits, and the farmer-in-overalls. She knew she needed something different, more dramatic, something to catch Tim's eye. But none of the costumes around her seemed to be the thing.

What Would Ella Do?

She wandered around for more than an hour, searching every aisle up and down. Then, at the very back of the store, through a sparkly red-beaded curtain, she found what could only be described as the Ella Tuttle Costume Section.

Everything was tiny. And see-though. And lacy. And

frilly. And pleather. The selection of stockings alone was astounding. Varying weaves of fishnets, from striped thigh-highs, to schoolgirl kneesocks. It was daunting.

And then Kelsi spotted it. The tiny white nurse's cap dotted with a little red cross. It was a metaphor for what her relationship with Tim needed. A little emergency attention. And though she second-guessed herself all the way up to the register, she told herself that she was doing the right thing.

"I don't know," Taryn said after Kelsi had explained all this to her. "This isn't really you, is it?"

Which was Kelsi's point exactly.

When Kelsi first walked into the supercrowded, noisy party, packed with kids in wild costumes who were jumping up and down to old hip-hop, her natural shyness took over. What was she *doing,* wearing a slutty nurse costume in public? She started to cross her arms over her chest, but then someone passed her a cup of beer, and after gulping it down in record time, Kelsi began to feel warm, fuzzy, and a lot less shy.

"Kelsi? Is that you?"

She turned at the sound of Tim's voice, and walked slowly over to him. He wasn't in costume, and his curly blond hair fell into his eyes. She wasn't very good at doing the sexy walk (which Ella, of course, had mastered at, like, age two), but she felt she did a decent imitation. After all, she'd gone to all this trouble *for* Tim. To remind him that she wasn't some chaste little flower. To show him she could be the girlfriend he might want after all.

She tried not to think about all the venerable Smith feminists who were rolling over in their graves right about now. "What?" she purred, because Tim was staring at her with a blank expression on his face. Wasn't he supposed to be all lust-crazed and pawing her?

"You look different," he finally said, his tone blank.

"Um, in case you haven't noticed, it's Halloween," Kelsi said, laughing, and then she pressed her stethoscope to Tim's chest.

Tim only shook his head and glanced down, frowning.

Kelsi felt a funny little tug in her stomach, but then decided not to let Tim's weirdness ruin her fun. She turned to rejoin Taryn and the rest of the party.

After a couple more beers, Kelsi was feeling looser than she ever had. She danced around the room, wiggling her hips, flushed and sweaty, and she could feel guys looking at her approvingly. Whenever she felt a little self-conscious, Kelsi just closed her eyes and pretended she was Ella. But when Kelsi was reaching for another beer, she felt Taryn take her elbow.

"I think you've had enough," Taryn said quietly, removing the can of beer from Kelsi's hand.

"I disagree with that diagnosis," Kelsi retorted, and took it back.

"Kelsi, seriously," Taryn pleaded. "What is this?"

"The new me," Kelsi told her.

She turned her back on Taryn and made her way through the party. Around her, frat guys in costume jumped and shouted, and if she almost closed her eyes she felt like she belonged. Here a guy in a *Scream* mask, there two brothers dressed as dead presidents, and all kinds of happy, screaming, half-dressed girls. Kelsi decided she was pleased that finally, she fit right in.

She shimmied her way through the crowd and zeroed in on Tim, still standing by the wall and still clenching that beer in his hand.

"Here," she said, trying for a sexy sort of drawl. She leaned into the wall next to him and held out her beer can. "Take your medicine."

Tim just looked at her with the strangest expression on his face, like he didn't know who she was. Kelsi sighed when he didn't reach out and take the beer. Then she took a hearty swig.

"Want to dance?" she asked. She moved her hips in a circle and ran her hand down his arm. "Come dance with me."

"I don't want to dance," Tim said in a hard voice. He

grabbed her wandering fingers and squeezed them, not hard, but enough to make her look at him.

"What?" she asked.

"What are you doing?" he demanded. "What is this?"

"It's Halloween," she said.

"And what, exactly, are you supposed to be?" he asked.

Kelsi stared at him. It slowly dawned on her that if anything, Tim looked miserable. She didn't understand.

"I thought this is what you wanted," she said.

"My girlfriend drunk and acting crazy in the middle of my frat house?" he asked incredulously. "Not really, no."

Kelsi felt a wave of emotion crest in her, and she shook her head.

"Then I really don't get it," she said. "Why did you lie to all your friends? I thought you wanted me to be more sexy."

Tim stared at her.

"You're sexy the way you are," he said. "I never said I wanted you to change. I just . . ."

"Wish I was sexier," Kelsi finished for him.

Tim looked at her. Kelsi watched his face change from confused, to annoyed, to an emotion she couldn't quite identify, and then to that grudging good humor she'd hoped he'd eventually display. He squeezed her hand again, and then started shouting.

"I lied!" he yelled, in the voice he used during football games, the voice that could carry across stadiums. "My girlfriend and I have never, ever had sex!"

Kelsi was mortified. And also kind of pleased. She watched as Tim's brothers and fellow pledges — including the mountainous Kenny — stared. Across the room, Taryn's mouth dropped open in surprise.

"See?" Tim asked, looking down at Kelsi. "Are you satisfied? I hope so, because while it might look like they're ignoring that statement, they're going to give me shit about it for weeks. Trust me."

"Thanks," Kelsi said.

He studied her face, touching her cheek with his fingers. "I don't want you to do anything you don't want to, Kelsi."

"Okay," Kelsi whispered.

"But you need to understand that it's really hard for me," he continued. "You're gorgeous and smart and sexy. Of course I want to have sex with you. I work really hard to respect your boundaries, and I'm not sure you get how tough that is."

"I understand," Kelsi promised him.

But later that night, when Taryn had gone home with one of the football players, and Kelsi shared Tim's bed with him, she found she couldn't sleep.

Tim snored lightly on his side, and Kelsi lay there in a

tank top and a pair of his boxers, staring up at the lights from outside as they played on his ceiling and across his face.

She studied him.

He looked cute lying there, and okay, a little bit drunk. Less Heath Ledger-ish when in a drunken stupor, and more like . . . Heath's oafish brother.

She thought she should feel better than she did. She thought she should feel victorious. Satisfied. Happy.

And it wasn't that she *didn't* feel those things, necessarily.

It was just that she didn't feel them *enough*.

The rest of the night had been fun. Tim took the predicted ribbing of his friends well, which was one of the reasons Kelsi loved him. He was always able to see the joke, even if it was on him.

But as she lay there, she kept going over their conversation. He'd said that he respected her, but she wasn't sure that was true. Because if he respected her, surely she shouldn't have to be the guardian of her virginity, right? Surely it would be just as important to him. Or was that just a pipe dream?

Was this just the way guys were? Or was it just that Tim was more the traditional jock guy that Kelsi had thought him originally?

He'd seemed so different in Maine, when it had been just the two of them on their excursions. He'd been so smart and sweet, all wrapped up in one package. But now their world wasn't secret Maine islands any longer. It was frat houses and pledge commitments, and Kelsi wasn't sure where she fit in all of it. Where *they* fit in.

She didn't like to even think it, but the thought caught hold and bloomed inside her head: *What if Tim and I aren't meant for each other after all?*

Beth stalked into the party a mile ahead of George, still feel-ing like a freak in her costume. She couldn't *believe* it. She felt like smoke might start pouring out of her ears, which actually would complete the devil look nicely.

"Hey, where's the fire?" George asked, jogging up behind Beth in his ridiculous angel getup. "Oh, I know," he stage-whispered, before Beth could reply. "Right . . . HERE!" He wrapped his arms tight around her midsection, pressing her to him and kissing her neck.

"George," Beth hissed, not finding one iota of humor in the situation. She felt like everyone was staring at them — at her — but, of course, since it was a Halloween party and people were in all varieties of King Kong masks and slutty schoolteacher costumes and groping each other, no one really paid attention.

As she and George worked their way into the party — George keeping a hand on Beth's waist the whole time — Beth tried to relax, tried to let go of her annoyance, but it was nearly impossible. The party was a mix of kids from Martin and other teenage Cape Cod vacationers. Party decorations were at a minimum. After all, who wanted to lug that stuff all the way across the state to the beach? Instead, everyone's attention was on one another's costumes, and they definitely made up for the lack of atmosphere. The party was all about circling and complimenting everyone's ideas, while silently jockeying for votes when Best Costume awards were handed out at the end of the night. Beth mingled her way through the crowd, heaping praise upon all the original ideas. If only her costume hadn't come out of a plastic package, maybe she would be in the running for this year's prize. But no one was going to vote her costume anything but perhaps Least Original Hussy. She caught several people glancing at her in surprise. And some guys ogled her, which made George grip her hand even tighter.

So she tried to focus on having some long overdue social fun. She chatted up friends she hadn't seen in a while, and tried to laugh it off when George kept sneaking up behind her and kissing her neck.

It was when she literally couldn't hear the conversation

she was having — thanks to George's tongue in her ear — that Beth decided that actually, she wasn't having that much fun and she was sick of pretending otherwise.

"Okay," she said, grinning to show that she wasn't mad, because there was a definite edge in her voice. And she *was* mad, she just didn't want the entire party to witness it. She was already getting way too much attention. She pulled George away from the conversation and glared at him. "You have to stop."

George frowned at her.

"Stop what?" he actually asked. "You don't like me kissing you anymore? Would you rather talk to that loser Pete Sanderson than to me?"

Beth stared at George and then back at Pete, who was the guy she'd been talking to when George had licked her ear.

"Pete Sanderson?" she echoed. "What are you talking about?"

"You just seemed really interested in talking to that guy all of a sudden," George said mutinously.

"He was telling me that he's on the swim team at his school," Beth said. "Also, are you suggesting I like him or something? He has a girlfriend. Who's standing right next to him."

"I don't know," George sort of mumbled. "You said you don't like your costume, but you seem to like people looking at you wearing it. Other guys."

Beth shook her head at him.

"You're crazy," she told him. "And not in a funny way. Why don't you go get us something to drink, okay?"

George stood there for a moment, like he was about to argue but thought better of it.

Beth felt relieved when he just nodded without another word, and headed toward the kitchen for drinks.

About an hour later, however, Beth's attempt at good humor was completely gone. Not that it had ever really been there to begin with. George would not leave her alone. If he wasn't caressing her skin, he was making suggestive comments into her ears. He was all over her, and it was so annoying Beth was trying to pretend he wasn't there.

Which was already hard enough, given the fact that George really was impossible to ignore.

Until he leaned over and told her he was getting their coats.

Beth blinked at him.

"What are you talking about? The party just started. We've only been here, like, an hour."

"I can't take it," George said. "You look way too hot."

"Meaning what?" Beth shook her head at him. She refused to believe she was hearing this. "You want me to change into something else?"

"Not at all," George said. He leaned into Beth until she was pressed against the wall.

It was a good thing they hadn't actually been talking to anyone else, Beth thought sourly, because hello, now they were hooking up? Just . . . right there?

"George!" she shoved at his shoulder. He ignored her and nuzzled her neck.

"I think we should go back to the hotel and make use of that king-sized bed," George whispered. "I can't wait to get you out of this thing."

And that was when Beth lost it.

"Get off me!" she snapped at him, not loud enough to cause a scene or anything, but definitely loud enough to get George's attention.

The worst part was, he honestly looked confused.

"What's the matter?" he asked.

"Are you kidding?" she demanded. "You've been all over me tonight, and here's a newsflash — it's not sexy. At all. I want to go home."

"That's what I just suggested —"

"Not the hotel, George," Beth snapped at him. "I can't believe you. This was supposed to be a romantic weekend. And you decide that means I should dress up like some ho. Then you paw at me all night, and now you think I want to go have sex with you? Who *are* you? What *happened* to you?"

Without meaning to, Beth felt tears well up in her eyes, and she started to cry. She could feel the tears trickle down her cheeks and was horrified, but that just made it worse.

"Bethy —"

But she was too upset. Where had her boyfriend gone? She didn't think she could bear it. And here she was, half-naked and crying at some party. She couldn't wait to get away from him.

"I want to go home to Martin," she told him through her tears. "Right now."

To: Kelsi.Tuttle@smith.edu
From: JTuttle@Eltonprep.edu
My dear Kels,
I'm sorry to hear that things are not at their best with Tim. He sounded like such the right guy for you last summer. But, at the risk of sounding like a cheesy eighties ballad, you need to go with what your heart is telling you. Or something like that.

Of course, I'm one to talk. My heart's all mixed up, and I don't even have a real boyfriend, unlike you and the other cousins. You remember that infuriating guy Dex, right? Well, he infuriated me so much I ended up making him out with him.

I know, I know. You told me so. But that STILL doesn't mean I like him! So there.

It was Friday, which meant we had our AP American History class, and he and I totally got into a political debate smack-down — I definitely think I won — and then when our teacher said my comments were "incisive," Dex looked at me with pure hatred in his eyes. So I gave him that look right back.

That night, we had an Oktoberfest (my school is too "progressive" for Halloween) dance in the main building. I got all decked out in my black strapless dress (you know, the one Ella made me buy) and went with my roommate.

Everyone was having a good time! I haven't danced like that since we all went nuts that time at Ahoy in Maine (I know you remember). After the dancing, I was really hot, so I got a soda and went outside for a few minutes, because it felt good to be out in the cold. There were the usual couples making out, and smokers just hoping none of the teachers saw them, and I was having this gorgeous, serene moment when suddenly Dex was right there. He walked outside like he had been following me or something and stood right in front of me.

Then he said: "Why do you hate me?" Just like that.

And I said, "I don't know what you're talking about."
Because hi, what was I supposed to say?

"You do." He was all arrogant about it, too.

"Well, I feel like *you* hated me first," I replied, all
maturelike.

"Maybe I did," he shot back.

And then the next thing I knew, we were kissing . . .
like REALLY kissing. And, Kels, it felt . . . nice. More
than nice. But then I got freaked out and told him I had
to go, and ran away, and have been trying to think of
ways to avoid him ever since.

I should let you go because I know you're expecting Ella any second, but I just wanted to share. . . .

Have fun with Ella; it will be good to get some sister time.

Love,

Jamie

To: JTuttle@Eltonprep.edu
From: Kelsi.Tuttle@smith.edu

Jamie,

Yes, Ella is literally due to arrive any second, but I
have four very mature words to pass along first:

I TOLD YOU SO!!

James, I saw this epic romance brewing from a mile away. You guys are totally going to get it on, get married, and then have lots of smart, competitive babies.

(Don't kill me.)

See you at Thanksgiving,

K

Kelsi wasn't sure she'd missed her sister while away at college. But when Ella came up for the long Veteran's Day weekend in November, Kelsi realized that she had. A lot.

After sending her e-mail to Jamie, she got to the Northampton bus depot early with a bouquet of flowers, and waited for Ella to arrive. Predictably, Ella missed the 4:00 P.M., leaving Kelsi with nothing to do but hang in the Greyhound station, buy vending-machine food with the change in the bottom of her purse, and read the magazines discarded by passing travelers.

But when Ella arrived on the 6:45 P.M., it was like no time had passed at all. Ella had barely stepped off the bus before Kelsi toppled her with a big hug. And while Ella seemed momentarily embarrassed by this very public display of affection (and the fact that her tank top was way too flimsy to survive such an aggressive bear hug) she didn't fight it because it clearly felt just as good for her to see her sister.

Ella's late arrival had put quite a crimp in Kelsi's pre-planned tour guide agenda, which she snarkily told her sister on their way back to campus. Kelsi knew the Museum of Art was already closed, but if they hustled, she could make up for it. So, Kelsi dragged her sister across the campus, touring the libraries, tracing Kelsi's daily paths to class, the boathouses on Paradise Pond, and the famous botanical gardens. The collegiate feel of Smith obviously impressed Ella. It was easy to get swept away in the academic-ness of it all. The glass Campus Center, lit up against the darkening sky, was almost breathtaking. Especially without any boys to distract you.

Unfortunately, Ella was far less impressed by the Smith dorms.

"This is, like, worse than prison," she said, taking in the small room.

Kelsi shrugged her shoulders. "It's cozy!" she said, though it didn't help matters that Taryn had left her half of the room in complete shambles. Kelsi had done her best to throw Taryn's clothes under her bed to make space for Ella's AeroBed. It was a challenge, and the mattress rocked on the lumpy pile underneath it.

"I mean, do you have any privacy?"

"Not really. I'm just lucky that Taryn and I get along so well. Plus, she goes out a lot. You know. With different guys. So I'm here by myself a lot of nights. It's perfect for studying."

"Um, what about Tim?" Ella asked. "Isn't *he* over all the time?"

"I guess so," Kelsi mumbled, even though she hadn't had him over since the Halloween disaster. It was weird, but for some reason, Kelsi didn't feel like she could open up to Ella about Tim. She felt close to her sister, who *was* an expert on love, but Kelsi was afraid that Ella would judge her.

Kelsi quickly suggested dinner, and the girls headed down to partake of the best of Smith cafeteria dining.

"This is gross," Ella said, poking at an unidentified fried substance baking under an orange heat lamp.

"Yeah," said Kelsi, grabbing Ella by the arm and pulling her toward the leafy greens of the salad bar. "This is going to be your best bet."

"No wonder I didn't see your Freshman Fifteen," Ella teased, rubbing her hand along Kelsi's middle.

The girls ate and laughed, and Kelsi deflected any Tim questions, and then they returned to Kelsi's dorm.

Kelsi flopped on the bed. She was exhausted. But apparently, organic spinach had done Ella some good. She seemed to have caught her second wind and was ogling a pair of Taryn's jeans that were dangling out of her dresser.

"So are we going out or what?" Ella asked, shaking back

her blonde ringlets. "I need to go out and have some wild times so I can have stories for Ryan when I get back home."

"Oh, right — I totally meant to ask you," Kelsi said, turning to her sister. "What's going on with this Ryan guy? How are things?" Kelsi was secretly mourning that her sister had parted ways with sweet, attentive Jeremy, but she knew better than to bring that up with prickly Ella.

"Good, but of course his main goal in life is to try to get into my pants," Ella replied in her usual blunt manner, and then laughed. "My whole plan is to keep him waiting, to hold out, until I know he's serious about me. I mean, that's the only way to test a guy, right? They'll sleep with just about anyone otherwise." She nodded wisely and Kelsi felt her heart sink as she thought of Tim.

There was a knock on the door, and Kelsi wondered if Tim had decided to show up after all. He'd gone on a road trip with a frat buddy for the long weekend.

She hurried over, opened the door, and felt her heart leap.

Bennett was standing there.

On impulse, she slipped into the hallway and shut the door on Ella's curious stare.

"Um, hi," she stammered. She wished her unpainted toes weren't poking out from beneath the frayed cuffs of her jeans. Bennett, of course, looked effortlessly hip in his dark coat, faded cords, and scarf.

119

"Hi," he said and smiled.

"Taryn's not here," Kelsi said. "I thought you guys were going to see your grandparents."

"Yeah. We leave tomorrow," Bennett said, studying her.

"Oh." Kelsi felt that zing of connection again, and she didn't know quite what to do about it, so she looked down, and wished again that she wasn't barefoot. The dorms at Smith were old and she could feel the November chill through the soles of her feet, even inside.

"I came to give you this," Bennett said.

When Kelsi looked up, he was handing her a CD. On the cover was a sketch in pencil with a dash of color. It took Kelsi a minute to realize it was a drawing of her.

She stared at it, too shocked to say anything.

"After we hung out that night I kept thinking about how alike our taste in stuff was," Bennett said, his eyes intent on hers. "So I decided to risk it and make the inevitable mixed CD. You'll either hate it and think I'm lame, or love it and dig some awesome bands."

"I don't know what to say," Kelsi said, which was true. She blinked as if that might clear her head. She felt dizzy, and worried there was too much color in her face suddenly.

"Well," Bennett said, and there was a laugh — not a mocking laugh, more like a fond laugh — in his voice. "You *could* say, 'Hey, Bennett, if you're not too busy, would you want to come in and chill a little? Especially because you haven't ever seen your own sister's room?' "

"You haven't?" Kelsi asked, glancing up in surprise.

"Nope," Bennett said, shaking his head as his eyes sparkled. "Sad, huh? Taryn and I are both so busy being busy we barely have time for sibling-support visits."

"Speaking of which," Kelsi said, pushing open her door to let Bennett in. "My sister Ella's visiting for the weekend."

The minute the words were out of her mouth, and the minute she and Bennett walked in to see Ella draped across the bed in her thigh-hugging jeans and pink tube top, her lips pouty with gloss, Kelsi regretted her decision. What was she thinking, letting a perfectly nice guy into her sister's path of destruction?

And then she reminded herself that she shouldn't care if Bennett fell for Ella, as most boys seemed to. After all, it wasn't like she was interested in Bennett.

Right?

But Bennett only gave the preening Ella a friendly smile, shook her hand as Kelsi haltingly introduced them, and set to fiddling with Kelsi's CD player, putting in the mix and hitting PLAY. As the music filled the room, Kelsi plopped down beside Ella, who was watching Bennett with curiosity — but not necessarily I-want-to-make-out interest. And Bennett sat on Taryn's bed, across from the girls.

"So. My sister's room. And Kelsi's room," he mused aloud, looking at the brightly colored walls. "Not bad." Then his eyes fell on Kelsi, and he smiled. "Very pleasant, in fact."

"Thanks," Kelsi murmured, wishing she wasn't blushing, while she felt Ella's eyes on her.

"So, you girls off for a night on the town?" Bennett asked.

"We sure are," Ella trilled, standing and taking in her reflection in the closet mirror. "Hopefully we won't have to fend off too many suitors. Guys love to play the whole sister card, pretending to want to hear all about how close we are as sisters, all the while just wanting to take us both home. Slimeballs."

Kelsi audibly gulped. Ella was just being Ella, but to an outsider, she could be really shocking.

"Um, speaking as a straight male, can I interject?" Bennett asked, raising his hand, with that same bemused, intelligent smile on his face.

"Sure," Ella said coolly, rolling her eyes.

"For the record," Bennett said, clearing his throat and readjusting his glasses in a totally adorable way. "Not *all* guys want to get to know girls only to sleep with them. That's not the end goal for everyone. Sure, I'd imagine it's an awesome bonus, but when I'm interested in a girl, I'm interested in, well, *her*. Her imagination, her laugh . . ." He trailed off, and Kelsi could have sworn he was looking at her.

And then it hit her, what Bennett had said: *I'd imagine it's an awesome bonus.* Meaning . . . what?

"Wait," Ella said, clearly on the same wavelength as Kelsi. She whirled around to Bennett. "Are you saying you're . . . a virgin?"

Kelsi tensed up at the word, but Bennett, looking chill, only shrugged. "Uh-huh. Not that I haven't wanted to — duh — but I guess I'm an idealist. I want it to be . . . right. And so far there just hasn't been, well, the right opportunity. Or the right girl." He was looking down as he spoke, but Kelsi could feel a deep connection to him. Her heart was pounding.

"I know what you mean." The words were out before she could stop them. "I'm — I'm one, too. I mean, I haven't ever, you know, done it with a boy. And even though I have a boyfriend, I . . ."

"Just don't feel ready," Bennett offered, his eyes understanding. "That's totally cool."

Kelsi nodded, feeling her throat close with emotion. So there *were* guys out there who understood. Guys who were in the same place as her, and who wouldn't feel the need to prove otherwise in front of their buddies. She wanted to leap up and fling her arms around Bennett, but held back.

"Anyway, I should go," Bennett said, getting to his feet. "Tell Taryn to call me, 'kay? Our mom's harassing me about Thanksgiving plans." Then, with a lingering smile, he was gone.

"So," Ella said, turning to Kelsi the minute the door closed. "Call me crazy, but if that guy plans to lose his virginity any time soon, I think I know who his prime candidate would be."

"Shut up," Kelsi said, jumping up and heading for her closet. But inexplicably, Ella's words made her heart jump and she felt herself smiling.

Ella, meanwhile, stared out into the courtyard through the small window. "He kind of reminded me of Jeremy," she added, looking melancholy. But then she gave her head a little shake, as if brushing the thought away. "Let's go party."

It was the final swim meet of the year, and Beth was ready.

The fact was, she loved to compete. The thrill of pitting your mind and body against the clock and your competitors — she loved it. She loved the rush of adrenaline when the starting gun went off and the clench of her toes against the racing block right before she dove in.

It was exhilarating.

It was also a great way to avoid thinking about the troubles in her own life. After the Halloween fiasco, things between her and George had been stilted and awkward. But Beth had been so busy practicing for the big meet, she'd managed to somehow avoid George — and avoid talking about what had happened. But it nagged away at her — in the shower, doing homework, IMing with Jamie — all the time.

But sitting in the locker room just moments after Coach Katy had finished her *go kick some butt* speech, Beth felt her stress begin to melt away and turn into adrenaline. She tucked her hair into her swim cap and grabbed her goggles and her towel. Then she took a deep breath.

"This is going to be fun," Katy said, falling into step beside Beth. "The other coach is this totally sexist old guy, and we're going to hand him his ass."

"Hell yeah, we are," Beth replied.

"Excellent," Katy said, and grinned at Beth as they stepped from the chilly corridor into the wet, humid heat of the pool room.

There was already a crowd, and pennants waving merrily at the ends of the lanes. Beth scanned the bleachers, and spotted George next to her parents. Her stomach clenched just a little. He gave her two big thumbs-up, and cheered. Despite any recent issues, she was so glad to have him there.

Beth grinned quickly in his direction, and then she focused on the water.

Don't think, she told herself. *Just do.*

Beth loved to swim. To race. She loved the ritual of the words.

Swimmers, take your mark.

Beth climbed onto her racing block.

Get set.

Poised and still for that breath, anything was possible, and Beth imagined herself reaching out so far she touched the other end of the pool in one long, elegant dive —

And then the gun.

Beth launched herself into the air. The flex of muscle and the sweet slice into the water. Then the pull against her hands, her side, her face. She sensed the right moment to glide forward and flip, then pushed off again with another huge push. More reaching. More pulling. Until she smacked the wall with her hand, and won her race.

By a long shot.

Beth climbed from the pool, beaming at the shouted congratulations and wet hugs from her teammates. Lance gave her an approving pat on the shoulder. And Katy looked at her with that measuring look she had, and then smiled.

"Good job," was all she said, but Beth knew that, from Katy, those words truly meant something.

The rest of the meet went by like clockwork. Starting guns, splashes, cries of Martin victory again and again. With each race, the crowd became more and more vocal, their cheers and fight songs reverberating off every wall. It was so loud that during the very last heat, the swimmers almost missed the pop of the starting gun. Almost.

Martin won, blowing the other team out of the proverbial water. Beth and the rest of her team leaped into the pool with wild victory cries. It had been such a long, hard season, but to Beth, so unbelievably worth it.

After she had changed, Beth made her way over to the stands, and found George.

"You were amazing!" he cried. "Congratulations!"

"Thanks," she said, and smiled at him, willing everything to stop being so weird between them.

Beth kissed and hugged her parents, who then busied themselves arguing about car keys.

"We should go out for a celebratory dinner," George announced. "Steak! Lobster! Steak and lobster!"

Beth smiled again, and looked away.

"That's really sweet of you," she said. She wished things didn't feel so stilted. Even the words coming out of her mouth. "But the team is going to hang out. There's a party."

"Oh."

She could have invited him. A few months ago, she wouldn't have thought twice. Beth wondered what was wrong with her, and blinked, then opened her mouth to issue the invite.

"Well, that's okay," George said. "It doesn't matter, right? The point is, now that swimming is over for the season, we can spend all our time together again." His eyes lit up. "I mean, sure, things haven't been ideal, and I'd like to officially apologize for being a bonehead as of late. But I think everything is going to go back to normal now." His relief was palpable.

Beth looked back across the stands at her teammates, then back at George.

"You think swimming was the problem?" she asked softly. How could he think such a thing, when swimming had been like a refuge for her over the past months? Didn't he know that?

"Well, yeah," George said with his trademark grin, but Beth could tell it was mostly bravado. "What else could it be?"

He was clearly as nervous as she was to find out. And Beth tried to hold on to the idea that maybe things between George and her would go back to normal, staring tomorrow. There'd be no more practice, no more distractions, no place for her to hide. But instead of feeling relief, all she felt was the water dripping off her fingers.

"I'll call you later when I get home. Maybe, if it's not too late, we can go catch a movie or something."

"Okay, Bethy," George said. He took her hand in his, gave it a little squeeze, and let it go just as quickly.

There were so many reasons to like Ryan, Ella thought with a happy sigh, reclining in the passenger seat of his shiny red car. He was so different from Jeremy.

Ella liked that Ryan noticed, even while he was driving, that her long legs were stretched out in front of her. He grinned, and then reached over to give her thigh a quick squeeze. Ella liked sitting in the fast little red car and having the people in all the other cars stare at them in wonder.

Not that they needed the car to get attention. That was just a bonus. There had been all kinds of staring going on in the movie theater, too. Ella had pretended not to notice the way a trio of hot boys had been eyeing her. And she'd loved the way Ryan seemed to attract the attention of every female in the place. Together, they practically glowed.

All in all, it was the perfect Friday night, Ella thought. And it was about to get even better.

"Where to?" Ryan asked when they arrived at the crucial intersection. A right turn would lead to Ella's house and the end of the evening, because Ella's mom didn't allow boys in the house. Left would take them to Ryan's, where, he'd made sure to mention, his parents had left him on his own all weekend while they visited old friends up in Waterbury.

Ella, naturally, had decided where the evening would end hours before Ryan had even picked her up.

"Oh," she said, biting her glossy bottom lip as if she couldn't decide. "My house, I guess."

"Really?" Ryan looked at her.

Ella pretended to consider. Then she pretended to waver when Ryan leaned over and kissed her lips slowly, sensuously, his hands in her hair.

"My house," she murmured again regretfully, when the car behind them honked impatiently.

"I don't want to take you home," Ryan said, but he turned right anyway. "I've been looking forward to this all week."

Which was all the more reason to make him wait for it, Ella thought. The physical came almost too easy to them.

Amazingly, they hadn't had sex yet. Not even once. It was hard as hell, but Ella knew it was the smart thing to do.

"I know," she said breathlessly, twisting in the seat so she could look at him.

"What about tomorrow?"

"Tomorrow should work," Ella said carefully. "I hope so."

"Me, too," he murmured, squeezing her thigh again.

When he pulled into the driveway, he turned off the car. Then he reached over to haul Ella into his arms for a hot, almost frustrated kiss.

She knew she totally had him.

So she relaxed into it, and kissed him back, their tongues meeting, their hands everywhere. It was almost perfect.

But the fact was, Ella wanted the *more* that Jeremy had taught her could exist in relationships. She wanted the emotional connection Kelsi always talked about. She wanted it *in addition* to lots of fun, incredible sex, but she still wanted it.

But then again, what good was the *more* if it was hundreds of miles away? Jeremy was a good guy — no, a great guy. That wasn't in question. She'd always think the best of him, maybe even see him as the one that got away. The reason for their breakup was purely a location issue. And Ryan was here, now. Simple as that.

And she didn't see any reason whatsoever that Ryan

shouldn't give her exactly what she wanted. After all, they were totally in sync with each other. Right?

She stopped him when his hand was getting a little too far up her skirt, and wriggled out of his hold, laughing.

"Tomorrow," she whispered, like she was making a promise.

"Yeah." He could barely speak.

"Oh," she said, pretending to be casual. "By the way . . . what does your family do for Thanksgiving?"

Ryan stretched, and ran his fingers through his hair. "Not much. It's pretty low-key. My relatives are all in South Dakota, and we don't go out there or anything."

"Oh yeah?" Ella considered. "Well, my cousins are coming here this year. I thought I'd, you know, show you off."

She expected him to grin and maybe preen a little bit. Instead, he shifted in his seat.

"Like, to your family?" He looked at her. "Why?"

"Because you're my boyfriend and you're hot," Ella said. *Duh.* And because she liked him and wanted to move things to a new level — which she knew better than to say.

"*You're* the one who's hot," Ryan told her, leaning in to her neck and starting to nibble on it. Ella pulled away.

"It's a big deal that I'm even allowed to invite you," she told him. "The only person who's ever brought a guy around before is my cousin Beth, and only because her boyfriend is like a member of the family."

"Uh-huh." He was paying far more attention to her breasts than he was to what she was saying.

Once again, she pulled away.

"So, do you want to come or not?" she asked with the slightest edge in her tone.

Ryan sighed, and sat back. He actually rolled his eyes. "Fine," he said. "Now can we stop talking?"

"Fine," Ella snapped at him, annoyed that he was agreeing solely to shut her up. Did he think she couldn't tell? But she smiled at him to take the sting out of her voice, and then climbed out of the car.

As she sauntered ever-so-slowly to the front door, knowing he was watching the way her hips swung back and forth, she congratulated herself.

Who cared why he'd agreed? He'd agreed. He would come to Thanksgiving dinner.

He would bond with her family, which would inevitably bring him closer to Ella.

They were perfect for each other, she reminded herself. The fact that Ryan was so much like her just meant she knew how to make sure he saw the light. She knew how to make him do whatever she wanted. No doubt about it.

The days were grim, cold, and almost sunless, which would have upset Kelsi if she had time to care.

Which she wished she did. Instead, she had midterms.

"Oh, my God," Taryn moaned from her bed, where she'd spread out all of her books and notebooks so she wouldn't be tempted to sleep. "I can't believe how much I hate *the entire world* right now."

"I finished my last two exams today," Kelsi replied in the same miserable tone from her place at her desk, where she'd been sitting and staring at a blank Word document for hours. "Which I would be happy about, if it weren't for the huge English paper I haven't started yet. You know — the one due tomorrow?"

Taryn made a *pfft* noise and waved her hand dismissively. "English is easy. You can make shit up."

"My theory exactly," Kelsi agreed.

"Unlike history, which, um, what the hell was I thinking?" Taryn rubbed at her eyes. "I have to compile research before I can even *begin* my paper, also due tomorrow."

"I'm flunking out," Kelsi said with a sigh. "I knew this would happen."

"Please, you've been studying so hard. I mean, when's the last time you even saw Tim? Like weeks ago?"

Kelsi's stomach dropped. It had been a while since they decided to meet for a study date. The coffee shop they chose had a strict No Talking During Finals Week policy, which Tim and Kelsi *seemed* all too happy to obey. They flipped pages and sipped java in stark silence, pausing every so often for a smile. But they didn't need a textbook to tell them that things were different. They just were.

"I've been busy," Kelsi stammered. "And Tim! You know, with all his frat stuff, he's really fallen behind in his classes. We're just, uh, taking an extended break for studying. Just to make sure we don't end up cleaning windows for a living."

Taryn shot Kelsi a wry smile.

The CD ended with a Bloc Party song and Kelsi hit play again, smiling when the music started. She'd been listening to the CD on repeat ever since Bennett had given it to her.

"So . . ." Taryn said.

Kelsi turned, and saw Taryn looking across the room at her with a curious expression on her face.

"What?" she asked.

"My brother wanted to make sure I told you he said hi," Taryn said, studying Kelsi's face, her eyebrows raised. "He made, like, a significant deal out of it."

"Oh," Kelsi said, keeping her face carefully blank. "That's nice."

"Yeah," Taryn said. "Because that's my brother. Randomly, insistently, *aggressively* nice."

Kelsi shrugged, and hoped the heat she felt on her face was because of the clanking radiator in the room and not her own tendency to blush.

"How many times have we listened to this CD?" Taryn asked. "One hundred and fifty-seven? Or maybe we're in the two hundreds by now, I'm not sure."

Again, Kelsi just shrugged, and this time she was certain even her ears were crimson with embarrassment.

Tim, she told herself firmly. *Think of Tim.* But it didn't work.

Since Halloween, it was as if Kelsi's eyes had been opened in a certain way, and she just couldn't close them again. It wasn't that she was mad at Tim exactly — she just felt less consumed by him. More removed from him. It didn't help that even though he never asked directly if she was ready, every time they fooled around, it was like she could *feel* him waiting. Like if she said one word, he would jump on it. On her.

It made her feel wary. And kind of sad. Like Tim was a different guy than that funny, irreverent one who'd won her heart by being such a wiseass last summer.

A sudden wave of panic got Kelsi into gear. She looked back at her laptop and began typing like mad about Chaucer and Shakespeare. She worked feverishly until a knock on the door broke her concentration.

It was Tim.

"I know you're busy," he said, looking around at the midterm madness that had overtaken the room. The place was a mess of notes, books cracked open, forgotten mugs, and bowls of dried-up ramen. He cleared his throat. "I just had to see you."

"Break time!" Taryn cried, standing up. "I'm going to get some coffee and snacks." Just like that, she cleared out.

Kelsi sort of wished she could, too.

"I've hardly seen you over the past couple of weeks," Tim said, walking over to her desk chair and putting his hands on her shoulders.

"I have midterms," Kelsi said, twisting toward him so he couldn't keep his hands there.

"We all have midterms," Tim replied at once. "You're avoiding me." His face looked hard.

Kelsi sighed. But she didn't deny it. "You haven't exactly been banging down my door, either, Tim. Our relationship is a two-way street."

"Right. I know." He crammed his hands into the pockets of his faded jeans. "I guess I've been scared."

Scared. Kelsi pondered the word. Was Tim scared that she didn't love him anymore? Or was he just scared that she'd never give it up? "I know college changes people, Tim. And we've both become so different over the last few months. But there's a part of me that hasn't changed. And I have to be true to myself."

Tim walked a few paces back. Kelsi watched him move. He was so athletic. He had that way of walking, of rocking back on his heels.

"I love you, Kelsi." Tim's eyes searched her face. "I've tried to be supportive. You know that. But, yeah — it's been hard."

Bennett's CD played in the background, and Kelsi suddenly thought about the jerk who'd dumped her in high school because she hadn't wanted to sleep with him. And the even bigger jerk in Pebble Beach who'd done the same.

Tim respected the fact that she wanted to wait until she was ready, but he assumed it would be a finite waiting period. Whenever Kelsi told him she wasn't ready, the "yet" was always implied.

Maybe Bennett was right. She was an idealist. But this was who she was right now. And she didn't want to be with someone who was waiting for her to change.

Kelsi didn't want to judge Tim too harshly, because she *did* love him. But she wondered if the reasons she'd loved him only made sense in the mess of last summer, when she was reeling from her huge fight with Ella, and Tim had seemed like such a rock. Maybe they weren't the people they'd seemed to be in all that sunshine and sea air. Maybe here, in their real lives, they were strangers after all.

"I don't think what's going on here is about my virginity," Kelsi said slowly. "Not really."

"What do you mean?" Tim looked confused.

"I don't like frat parties," Kelsi said, holding his gaze. "I don't think drinking beer is a fun sport, and I don't have any interest in football. You do."

"Here we go again with the dumb jock, frat-guy bull," Tim said, temper kicking into his voice.

Kelsi raised her hands in the air. "I'm not saying that," she said. "But maybe we don't have anything in common except the fact we love each other. And I'm . . . not sure that's enough."

Tim stared at her for a long moment.

"Are you breaking up with me?" he asked quietly, holding her gaze.

Kelsi could hear the melancholy chords of one of the songs, and she felt a tremendous sadness move through her.

"Yes," she said, and was surprised that her voice sounded so clear. So sure.

A few days later, after all the crying and talking, Kelsi was helping Taryn carry out armfuls of dirty laundry to stuff inside Bennett's hatchback. She felt much calmer.

"Can you believe that when you come back from Thanksgiving, all my clothes will be clean?" Taryn bounced up and down like a kid on Christmas morning.

Kelsi turned her head to the side to avoid a dangling sock potentially touching her mouth. "I honestly can't. I hope your mom's washing machine can take the workload."

Bennett was leaning against the bumper, but he straightened up when he saw Kelsi approaching. "Here," he said, racing over. "No one should have to touch my sister's dirty clothes other than her brother." He chuckled. "Wait, that sounded kind of weird."

Kelsi laughed, feeling her palms get sweaty.

"Alllllll-righty," Taryn said, having karate-kicked the last knot of sheets into the packed backseat. "That's that! I just have to run and grab my duffle bag. Kelsi, be a dear and keep my poor lonely brother company while I'm gone."

Kelsi's cheeks flamed red as Taryn raced back to the dorm. Luckily, the wind had picked up and blew her brown hair across her face.

Bennett hopped onto the hood of his car and patted for Kelsi to join him. "So, my sister said you liked the CD?" he said, picking off a sticker from the toe of his Converse.

"Oh yeah!" Kelsi said, leaning next to him. "I loved it. That one Pedro the Lion song might just be my favorite."

Bennet's face lit up. "You know, Pedro the Lion is playing a show at my school after Thanksgiving. Maybe, if you were interested I could try to score us some tickets. It would give us something fun to look forward to."

Kelsi smiled. "Maybe," she replied.

She knew it would be a long time before she healed from her breakup with Tim. She knew she'd need time to be by herself, to get to know herself again. But there was always the future. And she liked the idea that there were fun things like concerts, and new friendships, and surprises worth waiting for.

On Thanksgiving morning, Beth came back from her early run cold, panting, and not exactly thrilled to find George stretched out on her parents' sofa in the family room. He was dozing in front of the television.

"Don't sleep," she warned him. "We have to hit the road as soon as I shower."

George muttered something and waved a hand at her, so Beth left him there and raced up the stairs toward her bathroom.

She showered quickly, and sighed when she emerged from the bathroom to find George still stretched out — but this time, across her bed.

"I need a cuddle," George said, grinning at her. "The sun's not even up yet."

143

"Come on," she said. "We have to get going. This is why we should have left last night with my parents."

"I liked last year's Thanksgiving better," George said around a yawn. "Remember?"

"Of course I remember," Beth said. She pulled on a pair of jeans and her swim team sweatshirt, and packed a few changes of clothes into her duffle bag.

"Your mom cooked all morning, and we just lounged and made out and pretended we liked each other," George said. He grinned when Beth threw a look at him.

"Come here," he said, opening his arms. "Just for, like, five seconds."

Beth could see exactly where that would lead. She shook her head.

"Later," she said. "Right now, we have to get on the road."

George sat up slowly, and there was a tightness around his mouth.

"Do I, like, physically repulse you?" he asked.

Beth felt her eyes widen as she stared back at him. She shook her head. "What are you talking about?"

"You barely even look at me anymore!" He was half shouting. "You pull away. I thought we'd spend more time together when your swimming thing ended but you've spent the past week going out of your way to get rid of me."

"I've spent the past week catching up on stuff," Beth

retorted. "Like *sleep*. Maybe you missed the fact that I've been exhausted this whole term. Maybe you were too busy dressing me up like your personal slut for Halloween!"

George gaped at her. "I apologized for that about seventy times."

"Yeah, well, the boyfriend I thought I had would never have done it in the first place," Beth snapped at him. She looked at her watch. "Let's not do this now. We have to start driving."

But George ignored her.

"What's going on?" George demanded. "You've been acting weird for weeks now. You never touch me, you're always tired —"

"Maybe I'm not exactly thrilled that every time we even hug, it immediately leads to groping," Beth said, crossing her arms over her chest.

"That is such bullshit —"

"Like at the Halloween party?" Beth shook her head at him. "When you actually interrupted conversations by pawing at me?"

George looked down.

"I can't believe this is what you think of me," he said. "Like I'm some sex-crazed asshole."

Beth ran her fingers through her still-damp hair, frustrated.

"I don't know what to say," she said.

It was quiet then. Outside her bedroom window, weak morning light began to creep across the sky. The trees were bare and the ground was frozen over.

"I've been trying to convince myself otherwise," George said slowly. He frowned, and his eyes darkened. He searched Beth's face. "But all of this feels kind of familiar. Doesn't it." It wasn't a question.

"Not to me," Beth said, having no idea where Mr. Random was going. "It just feels *bad*."

"Well, I'm the one who would know," George said, and his voice was bitter.

He paused for a moment, and Beth felt something icy shiver down her spine. Like she knew in the breathless moment before he spoke what he was going to say.

"You're cheating on me again, aren't you?" George accused, getting up from the bed and facing her across it. "Is it that Adam guy again? The lifeguard? Let me guess, he's a big swimmer, right?" George's eyes were dark and angry, the way Beth remembered all too well.

Except this time, she hadn't done anything to deserve his wrath. This time, instead of feeling a wave of guilt and self-loathing, Beth looked right back at him and felt something like rage sweep through her.

"*What* did you just say?" Beth demanded.

"You heard me," George said quietly.

"I haven't even *thought* about Adam since we were in Pebble Beach," Beth spat at him.

"Then who is it?" George demanded. "I know it has to be some guy on the swim team, right? Because that's the only thing you have time for anymore. So, who are you sleeping with? Is it that jock coach guy? You like the jocks, don't you?"

"This is like a bad dream," Beth whispered. "I can't believe you would accuse me of cheating on you."

"Because you've never done something like that." George's tone was dripping with sarcasm.

"Screw this," Beth muttered. She grabbed her bag off the floor, swung it over her shoulder, and headed downstairs. She could hear George following her, but she didn't turn around. She just slammed her way outside and threw her bag into the backseat of her mother's car, which she was taking on the road trip to Connecticut.

The sun was barely up, and it was so cold outside it made Beth's hair freeze against her head.

"You're just walking away from me?" George asked. "Very mature, Bethy."

"I thought we'd dealt with this!" Beth threw back at him, with such force she was surprised it didn't crack the ice on the branches of the leafless trees. "What was the point of the last few months if you still don't trust me?"

"How am I supposed to trust you?" George exploded, his voice harsh in the hushed morning air. "You lie to me, you cheat on me, you pretend everything's okay but now it's like you'd rather be anywhere else than with me! What the hell, Beth?"

"I don't understand what happened," she burst out. "It's like the only thing you think about is sex. I can't even change my shirt without you wanting me to have sex with you. And when I'm not in the mood, it means that I'm cheating on you."

"It's actually *normal* to want to have sex with your boyfriend, Beth," George snapped at her. She knew the *normal* part was supposed to sting, and it did, but she shook it off.

"You don't talk about anything but sex." Beth started using her fingers to list her points. "You don't suggest we do anything except have sex. You don't *want* to do anything except have sex. When you complain that we don't hang out enough, I think you mean you want to spend time together, but no, you mean sex."

"Having sex is the closest two people can be!" George argued.

"It doesn't feel that way to me," Beth said quietly. "Not anymore."

George stared at her for a long moment, so long that Beth began to feel the November cold seep under her jacket. Then he shook his head.

"You had sex with me because you felt guilty," he said in the same anguished sort of tone. "That night in Maine. I've always known it. If anyone ruined what was special about us, it was you."

"Is *that* what this is?" Beth felt helpless and sick. She rubbed her hands up and down her arms as if that might warm her. "I'm the enemy here?"

And then, standing there in her parents' driveway, not far from the tree where they would hang the hammock when the weather was better — the hammock she and George had kissed in months before, before the summer even started — Beth considered the impossible.

She tried to imagine her life without George.

When she'd tried to do it before, she couldn't. Back in the summer, when things had gotten crazy, the bottom line was that she didn't know how to live without George in her life.

But whatever that was — that certainty — she didn't have it any longer. It was like she'd read about those feelings in a book once upon a time. Like she'd heard about it all happening to someone else.

She didn't want to live like this. She didn't want to feel like the cruel one. She wanted to swim without worrying what might happen when she came back out of the water.

"George . . ." She could barely say his name. She was so upset, and yet, somehow, knew that this was exactly what she had to do. That it was overdue.

He just watched her, like he couldn't understand how they'd gotten to this place.

Beth didn't know, either.

"I think this is it," she whispered.

"How is that possible?" he asked, barely above a whisper himself.

But he didn't disagree.

"I don't know," Beth said.

"I just can't trust you," he said. "And I keep trying to hold on, and it isn't working."

"I think we need to end things," Beth said, more because she had to say it than because it needed to be said. She felt numb. Oddly light-headed.

"I think you're right," George said.

They looked at each other as the winter wind kicked in and rustled in the bare branches above them. In a way, although Beth hadn't even considered this when she'd rolled out of bed earlier, she knew that this had been coming for a long time. Maybe even since the summer, when she'd tried to fix something that had stayed broken.

"I'm sorry," she told him.

"I know," he said. "I am, too."

Beth held his gaze for a moment, and then she climbed in the car, turned up the heater to high, and drove away.

They didn't say good-bye.

19

"So tell me," Ryan said, his eyes glowing suggestively. He leaned in closer. "What do you like best about Thanksgiving? Because I'm a big fan of dessert."

He made it sound naughty and appealing all at once. Most of the family – like Uncle Carr, Jessi, Jordan, and Drew – were outside tossing around the Nerf. Sneaking off to a quiet nook of the house with Ryan and chilling in the kitchen would have been perfectly fine with Ella, except for one small detail.

He wasn't talking to her.

He was leaning on the counter, talking to Jamie.

Granted, Jamie was cute. She was a Tuttle and was, by definition, cute. Today she had even backed away from her usual freaky bohemian thing, and was wearing black boots and a very low-key and yet flattering black dress from H&M, which made her green eyes seem to glow from beneath her curly dark hair.

Not that it mattered how cute she looked, Ella thought from her seat at the kitchen table. It didn't matter if Jamie looked like Keira Knightley — you would think that Ryan would know better than to hit on *Ella's freaking cousin* when Ella was *right there*.

Hello!

Jamie shot a mystified look at Ella.

"Um," she said. "I like the green-bean casserole, actually."

"No way!" Kelsi chimed in from the stovetop, where she was stirring flour into the rich-smelling gravy. Her voice was happy and light, as if her sister's boyfriend wasn't acting like a jerk right there in front of everyone on Thanksgiving afternoon. Ella knew it was for her benefit. "It's all about the stuffing!"

Ella shot her sister a look, mentally thanking her, but Ryan didn't seem to notice. He was concentrating fully on Jamie.

Ella knew exactly what that concentration meant. Not only had she once been the recipient of it, she'd given it out herself.

Ella watched Ryan reach across the counter and draw a little pattern on the Formica in front of Jamie.

"I can't wait to taste it," he murmured.

Jamie actually blushed. That was how dirty he'd made it sound.

"Um," Jamie said. She widened her eyes slightly in Ella's direction. Ella smiled as if everything was fine, but she didn't move from her place at the table. She was almost afraid to move. If she did, she wasn't sure what she would do.

"So whatever happened with that guy Dex, Jamie?" Kelsi asked in that same overly bright tone.

"Oh," Jamie said nervously, her eyes flicking from Ryan to Ella and then back again. "We're sort of seeing each other now. Actually, things are well, they're going really well."

"Define 'well,'" Ryan said in his sexiest voice. And that did it. Ella had had enough. She opened her mouth to rip him a new one, but Ryan straightened up and turned away from Jamie.

Not to apologize for whatever blow to the head he must have suffered that had made him forget which Tuttle he was with. But to take his vibrating cell phone out of his pocket, grin, and disappear into the hallway to answer it.

Ella actually gaped after him.

And then had to deal with the humiliation of turning back to find her sister and her cousin staring at her.

"Ella," Jamie began, frowning.

"I don't know why he's acting like this," Ella said, before Jamie could say anything further.

"You don't have to put up with that," Kelsi said from the stove. "You deserve better."

There was something about the matter-of-fact way Kelsi said it that made moisture prick at Ella's eyes. It made her think of Jeremy.

"When did Beth say she was getting here?" Ella asked, swallowing and dodging the emotion.

"Soon, I hope," Kelsi said, squinting at the clock. "She said she got on the road late."

Ella nodded and then decided Ryan had spent far too long out of sight. As he was supposed to be hanging on to *her* every word, this was unacceptable. He obviously needed a reminder.

She found him out in the front hall, sending a text message, while in the living room the adults chattered and the younger cousins could be heard laughing over the sound of the television from the den. They must have come back in; it had gotten freezing outside.

"Hey, baby," he said when he looked up. He finished the text and dropped the phone in his pocket.

"Who are you texting?" Ella asked.

"That gravy smells awesome," Ryan said instead of answering. He closed the distance between them and ran his hands down Ella's arms. "I like your sister and your cousin. But I wish we were alone."

"Are you deliberately not answering my question?" Ella asked, looking up at him.

"What?" He tried that smile on her. "I'm talking about maybe sneaking away for a little while. Just you and me."

Ella gazed up at him, and that sly smirk of his. His eyes were clear and bright and she knew every move he was making. If she wanted to, she could probably figure out who he was texting, too.

But the truth was, she didn't care.

He was acting like a tool. And Ella was kind of embarrassed that the first time she'd brought a guy home for Thanksgiving, it was this one.

"This is a mistake," she said. The crazy part was, she wasn't even mad. She just absolutely knew that she wasn't the same person anymore.

"I'm not so good with family stuff," Ryan said with a rueful grin. "But I make up for it in other ways."

Ella shook her head at him. "I can read every single move you're making, you know." It used to be fun to play off of each other. But Ella was getting very tired of all Ryan's hackneyed lines, his stale come-ons, his lifeless flirty banter. He just sounded . . . gross. And, in a sudden swoop, Ella felt incredibly grateful that she *hadn't* gone all the way with Ryan. They'd come close, so close, just last week, but at the last minute, she'd pulled back. Put on the brakes. As if she'd *known*.

"I know you can," Ryan said. "That's what makes you so much fun."

The thought made Ella shiver. She *wasn't* like Ryan, at least not since last summer. That was the old Ella. This Ella was so much different.

"Maybe that's what made me so much fun," she said. "But I'm not there anymore."

Ella felt her confidence rushing back. She felt like she did that morning of the assembly, when all the other girls were primping in the mirror. She was beyond this moment. Jeremy or not, she was better than this.

The common wavelength between Ryan and Ella had shifted. He searched her eyes as though he was looking for something he could recognize, trying to pin a flirty subtext to her words. "Wait," he said, amazed. "Are you mad?"

"I'm not mad," she said. "I'm just over — you."

"Over me?" he shook his head. "Impossible. We're practically the same person."

Ella felt so far removed from him it was as if they'd never been together at all.

"Not anymore," she told him. Then she cocked her hip, set her jaw, and pointed to the door.

"Is there a medical reason you have to sit in that chair

and watch?" Kelsi asked Ella some time later. "Because you could help me, you know. We told Mom she should relax and we'd do all this. You were there, remember?"

"By *we* I pretty much meant *you*," Ella drawled, twirling a lock of blonde hair around one finger. She was glad Kelsi was home. She'd missed her.

But that didn't mean she was going to subject herself to domestic labor out of some misplaced sense of sisterly devotion. Especially when she was feeling so depressed about Mr. Sketch-Man. *God.*

"Don't make me force you, Ella," Kelsi warned her.

"I don't cook," she reminded her sister. "I don't really do kitchens, either, but in the spirit of Thanksgiving, I decided to keep you company today."

"You're always giving, El," Kelsi replied, rolling her eyes. But she was grinning. "That's what I love about you."

"You love *everything* about me," Ella retorted with a sniff. "And who can blame you?" But there was a part of Ella that didn't believe it. A crack in her armor.

"Get up and chop onions," Kelsi ordered her.

And then Ella was saved, literally, by the bell.

The doorbell, to be precise.

"I'll get it!" she said, shuffling her feet. A tiny part of her wondered if it was Ryan, begging for forgiveness. Then she pushed that thought aside. Assuming it was Beth who had finally arrived, Ella hurled open the door, letting in the cold

November wind and the rain that had started earlier that morning, and was starting to look like snow.

Then she froze in place, staring, because the person at the door was Jeremy.

"Hi," he said. His dark eyes were warm, as if he hadn't broken her heart at all. Which she wasn't even sure he had until just that moment, when she could really look at him. Ella loved the way his shaggy hair almost fell into his eyes, and the shy, crooked smile he aimed at her.

She thought maybe she was dreaming.

But then Jeremy thrust a quilted bag at her. Whatever was inside it was heavy and warm and smelled like butter. Ella was pretty sure that she would not dream about green-bean casseroles. She stared down at it, and then back up at Jeremy.

"I love you," he said softly, his eyes never leaving her. "I'm an idiot. And I'll do whatever it takes to make you love me again."

Ella swallowed hard. Seeing Jeremy again made every-thing click suddenly into place. When Jeremy wasn't there with her, she simply didn't have the skills to deal with her emotions. With her missing him. She didn't know what to do with the longing.

Or that fear that takes over when you feel yourself changing.

"It's okay," Jeremy whispered.

"How can it be okay?" she asked. "You dumped me. I dated someone else, but then I dumped him. Nobody dumps me."

He stepped inside at that moment, and closed the door behind him. "We'll talk about it. We'll work it out. Just trust me," Jeremy said, like he could read her mind. He leaned forward to rest his forehead against hers. His dark eyes were so close. "Can you do that?"

"I can try," she said. She pulled back to look at him. "I want to try."

"Okay, then," Jeremy said, and he smiled as if they'd never spent a moment apart. "And I'm going to trust you, too."

"Okay," Ella echoed. And she didn't feel wild or free or any of those things.

She felt like herself. At last.

She felt like she was home.

20

Hours later, stuffed and dazed from too much food, Beth staggered into the den, where Jamie was already stretched out on the couch, looking about to burst. The family company had been wonderful, with everyone passing warm plates and clinking wine glasses and laughing over Thanksgivings past. But now, as the turkey-comas were setting in, and the grown-ups drowsed over coffee, the girls were happy to just be with one another.

"I'm so glad you made it here in time for that turkey," Jamie said, smiling up at Beth as Beth dropped onto the sofa next to her. "Otherwise I might have had to eat even more of it."

"You could have had a veggie burger," Kelsi said, coming into the room. "No one forced you to eat all that turkey."

Jamie and Beth rolled their eyes at each other. Kelsi went over to the stereo and stuck a CD into the player. She pressed a button, and a mellow alternative ballad began to play. Beth watched Kelsi smile almost to herself as she sat down on the loveseat.

The three girls sat there, enjoying the stillness and the music, until Ella sauntered in a few moments later, a smile across her face.

"It was nice seeing Jeremy again," Beth said. She'd been so surprised when she finally arrived, out of breath and wound up, to find Jeremy sitting at the dining room table. She'd been expecting the new guy. Jeremy had been his usual shy-funny self before taking off to make it home.

"I know I don't need to say it, but he's so right for you, El. Unlike Ryan," Kelsi said.

"Who was totally hitting on me," Jamie told Beth in a low voice.

"I told you guys last summer that I wanted a real boyfriend," Ella said, as if she hadn't heard any of their murmurs. "I guess it just took a little while to figure out how to be a real girlfriend." She wandered over and settled next to Beth on the couch. "Like you, Bethy."

Beth hadn't told anyone that she and George had broken up. She'd claimed he had to work, and left it at that. For one thing, she knew that as soon as she said it out loud, it would be true. She wasn't ready to really accept that yet. And more so, her cousins loved George. They would be so sad, and Beth didn't want to do that to them on Thanksgiving. They didn't get to see one another enough during the year and she hated to ruin what little time together they had.

So she just smiled at Ella and scooted over to make room for her.

"Are you sad about Tim?" Jamie asked Kelsi. "I feel weird that I never met him."

"We just . . . grew apart," Kelsi said. "I don't think it was anyone's fault, you know? Things just happen."

The four girls sat there for a moment, reveling in being together. Then Ella got back on her feet.

"I thought we were watching a movie," she complained. "Not listening to this emo crap."

"I like this emo crap," Kelsi retorted.

"If we're watching a movie, I think we need pie," Jamie chimed in. "And there better be vanilla ice cream this year, that's all I'm saying."

"Vanilla is boring," Ella said haughtily, and then let out her snort of a laugh when Jamie threw a pillow at her. "Duh. Of course we have your ice cream, Jamie."

Beth sank back against the couch, and basked in it all.

Kelsi talked about *growing apart* as if it were inevitable. No blame. No fault. Just what happened, like autumn after summer.

Maybe that was true. Maybe that was why, underneath her sadness, Beth knew she'd be okay.

Beth kind of felt the way she did just before she dove into the pool. Everything in her body felt tense and ready to fly, knowing that the water waited below. Her unknown life without George stretched before her like the lanes in the pool, calm and smooth, waiting.

Outside, the first few snowflakes of the season began to fall against the windows, but inside in the den it was warm and cozy. She had her cousins all around her and more food than any of them were likely to finish.

The future waited, with George, without George — who knew?

All she had to do was jump.

Read all the books in the sizzling
SUMMER BOYS series

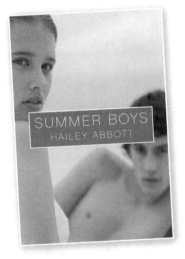

And don't miss:

It's the Tuttle girls' last summer
at Pebble Beach. In between
sunning, surfing, and kissing boys,
will they be able to make the
most important decisions
about their futures?

Spring Break in South Beach.
Could it get any hotter?

Turn the page for a sneak peek at
SOUTH BEACH,
the *New York Times* bestselling novel
by Aimee Friedman

"Hello?" she asked cautiously.

"Holly!" A girl's voice bubbled over the line, warm and fizzy. "It's me. Alexa!"

Holly's stomach tightened. Alexa St. Laurent? How random was *that*? She and Alexa hadn't spoken in years. Holly had deleted Alexa's number from her phone in the ninth grade, marking the final break from her former best friend.

"Holly? Are you there?" Alexa asked, after Holly had been silent for several long seconds.

Holly chewed on a thumbnail, now officially nervous. "Yeah. I'm here. Hi." What could she say? Why was Alexa even calling her?

"It's kind of weird to hear your voice." Alexa paused. "It's been forever, huh?"

"Tell me about it," Holly managed. Her tongue felt clumsy in her mouth. Was Alexa delusional or something? Did she think they were still friends?

"What have you been up to?" Alexa went on. "Still running track?"

"Yup." Holly thought about telling Alexa that she'd just been named co-captain, but she resisted. Would Alexa even care about something that didn't involve male models or designer labels?

"I always admired that about you," Alexa said. "I'm so lazy. Trying on Mavi jeans is my only form of aerobic workout."

Holly gave a hesitant chuckle. She was thrown by Alexa's sudden friendliness, but she also couldn't help feeling flattered by her words. Alexa had always been disarmingly charming.

"Well, you don't need to worry," Holly replied bashfully. "You're skinny, anyway."

Whenever Holly thought of Alexa, she first pictured the Alexa she'd known best — the short, slender, flaxen-haired girl in plaid skirts and knee socks, who spoke with a hint of a French accent and could make Holly burst into hysterical laughter just by crossing her enormous blue eyes. Then,

Holly had to remind herself to replace the picture with the way Alexa looked now — tall and gorgeous, decked out in fur-trimmed tweed blazers and spike-heeled Jimmy Choos, striding through the Oakridge halls with her ever-present Starbucks latte and a boy at her side. Holly couldn't imagine the present-day Alexa ever crossing her eyes. Or trying to make Holly laugh at all.

"Thanks," Alexa said. "But lying around the house and stuffing my face with chips every day next week isn't going to help much."

Next week? Holly thought, confused. "Don't you have plans for spring break?" she blurted, regretting her words an instant later. Of course, Alexa had plans for spring break. She was probably flying to Aruba or something. What a dumb thing to even ask.

"I did, but they fell through," Alexa replied with a sigh. "What about you?" she volleyed back casually.

"Um, not really," Holly said. A deep blush warmed her cheeks. Couldn't she have lied or something? Leave it to Alexa to make her feel like the biggest dork alive.

"I wasn't sure if you'd be busy or not," Alexa said. "But I had the craziest idea. . . ."

Wait a minute, Holly thought, suddenly wary. Where was Alexa steering their little chat?

"I was sitting in my room, thinking about how I used to

go to the Catskills with you and your family. Those long car rides . . ." There was a note of wistfulness to Alexa's voice that Holly hardly recognized.

"I remember," Holly replied. She thought back to sharing a bunk bed with Alexa in the cabin upstate — trading ghost stories while the tree branches tapped against their window, frightening them in a delicious way. Back then, Alexa had practically been like Holly's sister. "That was a long time ago," Holly added quietly. She wasn't sure what purpose this trip down memory lane was serving.

"I know," Alexa said. "That's why I was wondering . . . wouldn't it be cool to go somewhere together this year? You and me. Like old times. But without parents, of course. Just this total whirlwind getaway." Alexa paused. "What do you think?"

Holly was speechless, but her mind was racing. *So I'm your sloppy seconds,* she longed to retort. *Do I seem like that much of a sucker?* Holly twisted the ring around her middle finger, silently stewing. It was so obvious. Alexa had called Holly, dripping kindness, only because all her other plans hadn't worked out. Did Alexa honestly think that after what had happened between them — and all their years of not being friends — Holly was going to get all giddy at the thought of their spending spring break together? Holly took a deep breath, searching for a way to articulate her bubbling emotions. She'd never been very good at confrontations.

"I — I don't think I'm up for that," Holly spoke at last, her face burning. "I mean . . . we haven't talked in so long. What made you even think to ask me?" God, this was awkward.

Alexa sighed dramatically. "Oh, there was this boy drama, and then all my stupid friends left me adrift, and to be honest . . ." Alexa gave her small, tinkly laugh. "I'm kind of sick of them, anyway. At this point I would *completely* prefer to go away with you. If you'd want to." Suddenly, Alexa sounded just the slightest bit vulnerable, and Holly could feel herself starting to soften. "Don't you remember how much fun we used to have?" Alexa went on. "Like the time we played Truth or Dare, and I dared you to crank-call my cousin Pierre in Paris and pretend to be me?" Alexa asked with another laugh.

Holly smiled, despite herself. "How could I forget?" she asked. "My parents saw the phone bill afterward and grounded me for a month." Holly remembered how she'd mimicked Alexa's voice into the phone, dropping in random French words that Alexa whispered to her, thoroughly fooling Pierre. Afterward, she and Alexa had fallen into a heap of laughter on Holly's bedroom floor. Alexa had often gotten Holly into scrapes that were wildly fun in the moment, but ultimately ended in some sort of parental trouble.

"But it was worth it," Alexa mused aloud. "We had a good time."

"That we did," Holly had to admit. She'd always had trouble staying mad at Alexa — her boldness and energy could be irresistible. Holly glanced down at the beach umbrella she'd drawn in her notebook. She had been dreaming of an escape, hadn't she? But there was still the teensy problem of her parents. Maybe Alexa would at least have some ideas for how Holly could get away.

"So your parents probably haven't changed much, huh?" Alexa asked, as if she'd read Holly's mind. Her voice was full of understanding.

Holly bit her lip. Alexa knew about Holly's issues with her parents better than almost anyone, because she'd been there at the start. In the fourth grade, Holly's parents decided that Holly shouldn't go to sleepover parties. Alexa got to attend them all, and would always have some life-changing experience, like getting her ears pierced or seeing an R-rated movie. She'd fill Holly in on all the details the next day. It had been painful, but also sort of pleasant, to live life vicariously through Alexa.

"Yeah. Mom and Dad are pretty much the same," Holly replied with a sigh of resignation.

"So that's why you're home for the break?" Alexa pressed on gently.

"Basically," Holly confessed. "I can't even think of a place they'd let me go." She dropped her voice, glancing over her shoulder in case her mom walked in again.

"So let's brainstorm," Alexa suggested. "There's got to be somewhere!"

"The Galleria?" Holly asked with a snort.

"Stop it, Holly." Alexa laughed. "You can't spend spring break shopping in Oakridge like some old lady."

Old lady. Holly's heart leaped. How had it not occurred to her before? She'd totally forgotten about her grandmother, who lived near the ocean in Miami Beach. Holly's parents wouldn't hesitate to let her stay at Grandma Ida's over break. And Miami was gorgeous and sunny, and . . . Holly's pulse quickened as she remembered her last visit to Miami Beach, three years ago. It had been magical. That night on the beach, under the full moon . . .

Suddenly restless, Holly stood up. "There is one place," she said, as she began to pace the length of the kitchen. "My grandmother. She has an apartment in Florida. Josh and I visited her the summer I was thirteen." Alexa hadn't known about that trip, Holly realized, because by then, they'd stopped being friends.

"Your grandmother?" Alexa asked incredulously. Holly could practically read Alexa's thoughts: *That's the lamest plan in the history of spring break.*

"No, but listen," Holly went on, trying to maintain some dignity. "She's really cool. I mean, for a grandmother. And her neighborhood's nice. There are all these beaches, and you can take the bus down to South Beach. . . ." *What am I doing?* Holly asked herself. Was she trying to convince Alexa that they should go away together?

"South Beach?" Alexa cut in. Now, there was tremor of excitement in her voice. "South Beach is supposed to be this amazing up-and-coming spring break spot. And I think it got written up in Elle as one of the world's sexiest getaways!" Holly heard Alexa rustling about in her room, most likely going through her giant stack of fashion magazines.

"Here it is," Alexa said after a minute, then read aloud: "'South Beach, Florida. The land of rhythm, rumba, and rum margaritas!'"

"Does it really say that?" Holly asked, laughing.

"Let me finish," Alexa said. "'South Beach is a glamorous, glitzy town with an unmistakable Latin flavor. SoBe, as it's commonly called, overflows with sandy beaches for sun-worshiping, and spicy clubs for dancing the night away.'" Alexa giggled with delight. "And there's this photo of the ritzy Rose Bar, in the Delano hotel. Holly, it sounds perfect! Let's do it."

Holly was overwhelmed. South Beach did sound appealing . . . and very grown-up. Not Disneyland at all. Holly was still unsure about Alexa, but going to Florida with her would definitely be an improvement over staying home with her entire family.

At that instant, both Holly's parents entered the kitchen:

Her dad walked through the back door with Mia, and her mom came in from the den and opened the refrigerator.

"Holly, would you start breading the chicken cutlets?" her mother asked, pulling out a carton of eggs as Mia barked loudly.

"Uh, hang on," Holly whispered to Alexa, flustered by all the commotion. She turned to her mom and said, "I'll be back in a second. I'm — I'm having an important conversation." Holding the phone to her ear, Holly hurried out of the kitchen and upstairs to her room. She was surprised by herself. When her mom asked her to get off the phone, she usually did it immediately.

In her bedroom, Holly shut and locked the door, then plopped down on her plaid bedspread. "Okay," she said to Alexa. "I'm back."

"Great," Alexa said. Holly could hear the clickety-clack of her fingers on a keyboard. "I'm on Orbitz right now. I can look up flights for Miami and —"

"Wait," Holly interrupted. This was moving way too fast for her. "I need to think about it a little. And ask my grandmother if we can stay with her. And ask my parents if I can even go." She dreaded the mere thought of that.

"Okay," Alexa said. "You think, and take care of all the yucky permission stuff. Meanwhile, I'm going to find us cheap flights. Call me back!" Then she clicked off.

Holly remembered her childhood nickname for Alexa:

"Little Miss Bossy." She wondered how that aspect of Alexa's personality might play out on their trip — if they did end up going.

Holly snapped her phone shut and stretched across her twin bed, hugging a stuffed panda to her chest. She looked at the framed photo that hung above the bed, of her, Meghan, and Jess. Sweaty and triumphant after a track meet, they stood with their arms around one another's shoulders. Holly's friends would probably freak if she told them she was going away with Alexa. They thought of Alexa and her impeccably dressed crowd as total snobs.

But now that the kernel of Miami Beach was in Holly's head, she could feel it expanding and growing, taking the shape of reality. She wanted to go, she realized. With or without Alexa. But, because Holly's parents didn't let her fly anywhere alone, Alexa's being there was a necessity.

If Holly was being completely honest with herself, her desire to go to Miami had something to do with a boy. The boy she'd met down there, three years ago. Holly felt a flush climbing her neck into her face. She hadn't thought about Diego in a while. But talking about Florida had triggered all the old memories. They rushed back now, as vivid as ever.

Diego Felipe Mendieta. He'd been fourteen at the time, but tall for his age. His skin was the color of cocoa butter, his eyes were black as olives, and his hair was dark and glossy.

Whenever he smiled, the two deepest, most adorable dimples appeared in his cheeks. Diego lived in her grandmother's apartment building and he'd introduced himself in the lobby one day, which had absolutely floored Holly. Boys like Diego never talked to her. But the two of them had ended up spending the whole week together — surfing on Haulover Beach, bike-riding north to Sunny Isles, eating triple-scoop ice-cream cones on the boardwalk. Then, on Holly's last night, Diego had given Holly her first — and, so far, only — kiss.

Holly closed her eyes, summoning that one yummy memory. It had been around ten o'clock, a muggy, sticky Miami night. She and Diego had gotten chocolate chip ice-cream cones, and decided to bring them down to the beach. The full moon had cast its pale reflection on the surface of the ocean. Holly remembered the feel of the cold ice cream on her tongue and the foamy water on her bare toes. She and Diego had fallen silent, gazing up in wonder at the moon, and Holly had felt an odd shift between them — a kind of electric spark. She'd never felt that happen with a boy before. And she'd suddenly become aware of Diego's arm so close to hers. She'd resisted the urge to touch him — to rest her hand on the sleeve of his T-shirt — but then Diego had touched her. He leaned over, brought his fingers to her lips, and lightly wiped the corner of Holly's mouth.

"Ice cream," he explained with a half smile. Holly

wanted to die of mortification, but before she could, Diego kissed her. Really kissed her. The fullness of his lips and the salty-sweet taste of his mouth, and his warm hand on her waist made Holly's knees wobble. She almost dropped her cone in the sand. Kissing was so much better than Holly had ever imagined — soft and warm and easy. She'd wanted the kiss to last forever, but Diego had gently ended it, smiled at Holly, and turned back to the ocean. Still, when they'd gone back up to the boardwalk, their fingers had brushed together as if they were about to hold hands. And when they parted ways in the elevator, Diego had given her another kiss, this time on the cheek, and promised to stay in touch.

And they had, Holly remembered as she lay on her bed. They'd e-mailed and IMed for the rest of the summer and into the school year, trading reminisces about their week in Miami. Holly remembered how her heart would bang against her ribs whenever she saw his name pop up on her screen. But, as the year went on, their correspondence had petered out. After some time, Diego faded in Holly's mind, remaining a blissful, if distant, memory.

Holly opened her eyes and swung her legs off the bed. She looked at herself in the round mirror above her desk. Her green-gray eyes were very bright and her freckled cheeks dark pink. Holly had sometimes teased herself with the thought that she'd go back to Miami Beach one day and have a romantic reunion with Diego. But she'd gotten so busy with schoolwork and track, and sports camp in the summer, that there hadn't been another chance to visit Grandma Ida.

Until now.

Sure, things were weird with Alexa. The setup was far from ideal. But Holly knew she'd be insane to throw away this opportunity to reconnect with her old crush. Maybe it was fated that she see Diego again. There was a very good chance she'd run into him in Grandma Ida's building. Diego would be seventeen now, probably even hotter, and most likely an even better kisser. The answer was staring Holly right in the face. She grinned at her reflection. She was going to Miami.

"Holly Rebecca!" Her mother's voice thundered from the kitchen. "Are you still on the phone?"

"Are you upstairs?" her dad chimed in.

Holly took a deep breath. Right. She still had to clear the hurdle of her parents. They'd probably be okay with the Grandma Ida plan, but the Alexa element was a wild card. Holly's mom had never been a fan of Alexa's; she had been ecstatic when the girls' friendship faded. Alexa was a good student at Oakridge High, and never got into any trouble, but, as assistant principal, Holly's mom had personally busted a few of Alexa's friends for smoking on school grounds. As far as Holly's mom was concerned, Alexa was still nothing but trouble. So Holly was somehow going to have to make her old friend seem otherwise.

Before Holly turned to go downstairs, she closed her eyes and rehearsed a brief speech in her mind: *Mom and Dad, I miss Grandma Ida so much! She must be lonely down in Florida. I thought, since I'll be on break next week, I could go see her. And I wouldn't be traveling alone. Alexa St. Laurent asked if she could come along, too. Just her, none of her friends. She's much more down-to-earth than she seems at school, and I think Grandma Ida would really like her. . . .*

Will that work? Holly wondered. Holly knew this sudden urge to see her grandmother might seem suspicious. But her parents would likely be so impressed with Holly showing, as her mother called it, "family commitment," that they wouldn't think twice.

Holly tightened her ponytail, straightened her shoulders, and strode out of the bedroom. She'd march into the kitchen, and sit her mom and dad down. She'd make this thing happen. She had to. Holly was fed up with watching her friends do exciting things while she sat at home, life passing her by. It was time to take her destiny into her own hands.

Be sure to check out more of Alexa and Holly's scandalous adventures in:

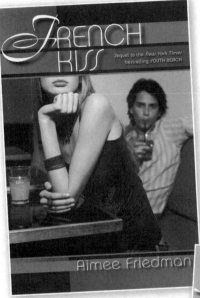

and